WOODWORKER'S SOURCE BOOK

2ND · EDITION

WOODWORKER'S SOURCE BOOK

2ND EDITION

CHARLES SELF

BETTERWAY BOOKS
CINCINNATI, OHIO

99 98 97 96 95   6 5 4 3 2 1

Library of Congress Cataloging-in-Publication Data

Self, Charles R.
     Woodworker's source book / by Charles Self. — 2nd ed.
         p.   cm.
     Includes index.
     ISBN 1-55870-391-8
     1. Woodwork — Equipment and supplies — Directories. 2. Woodwork — Directories. I. Title. II. Title: Wood worker's sourcebook.
TT186.S43   1995
684'.08'028 — dc20   94-49644
                                                        CIP

Edited by Adam Blake
Designed by Angela Lennert

About the Author

Charles Self is the author of numerous books and magazine articles ranging from woodworking and home and automobile repair to motorcycle racing and touring. His articles have appeared in publications such as *The Family Handyman*, *Popular Science*, *Popular Mechanics* and *The Homeowner*. He has also worked on projects for companies such as Time-Life, United Gilsonite Labs and Georgia-Pacific.

Other Books by the Author

Backyard Builder's Bible

Bathroom Remodeling

Bricklaying: A Do-It-Yourselfer's Guide

Brickworker's Bible

Building Your Own Home

Chainsaw Use & Repair

The Complete Book of Bathrooms

Creating Your Own Woodshop

Joinery: Methods of Fastening Wood

Kitchen Builder's Handbook

Making Birdhouses & Feeders

Making Pet Houses & Other Projects

Movable Storage Projects

101 Quick & Easy Woodworking Projects

Vacation Home Building

Wood Fences & Gates

Woodworking Tools & Hardware

Working With Plywood

Contents

HOW TO USE THIS BOOK

Use this table of contents to find what you are looking for by subject. All sources are also compiled alphabetically in the index at the back of the book. If you know the company name, look for it in the index.

INTRODUCTION 1

SECTION ONE
SHOPPING BY MAIL 3

SECTION TWO
CARVING

    Foam 10

    Knives 10

    Machines 10

    Tools 11

SECTION THREE
EDUCATION AND INFORMATION

    Associations 14

    Books and Magazines 16

    Catalogs 24

    Schools 28

SECTION FOUR
FINISHING

    Color Touch Up 34

    Equipment and Tools 34

    Outdoor Treatment 34

    Preservatives 35

    Spray Systems 35

    Stains and Finishes 36

    Stripping 40

    Surface Preparants 40

    Wood Patch 41

    Wood Treatments 41

SECTION FIVE
HAND TOOLS AND ACCESSORIES

    Branding Irons 44

    Brushes 44

    Calculators 44

    Chisels 44

    Clamps 45

    Files 46

    Japanese Woodworking Tools 47

    Knives 47

    Measuring Tools 48

    Moisture Meters 48

    Miter Equipment 50

    Planes 51

    Pliers 51

    Saws 51

    Striking Tools 52

    Surface Preparation 53

SECTION SIX
MATERIALS

    Basket 56

    Fabrics 56

    Glass 56

    Insulation 57

    Metal 57

SECTION SEVEN
PLANS AND KITS 59

SECTION EIGHT
POWER TOOLS AND ACCESSORIES

    Air Compressors 76

    Dryers/Kilns 76

    Generators 77

    Grinders 77

Hole Boring Machines 78
Jigs 78
Lathes 79
Multipurpose Tools 80
Nailers 81
Presses 82
Routers 82
Sanders 87
Sawmills and Chainsaws 89
Sliding Tables 90
Staplers 90
Stationary Power Tools and Accessories 90
Wood Carvers 96

SECTION NINE
SHOP SUPPLIES

Bags 98
Carts 98
Cleanup 99
Doors 100
Gloves and Aprons 100
Lamps and Lighting 100
Organizational Items 101
Safety, Health and Security . . . 102
Tool Carriers 104
Utilities 104
Vacuums 105
Workbenches 105

SECTION TEN
TOOL DISTRIBUTORS 107

SECTION ELEVEN
WOOD

Accents 124

Boxes, Bowls and Other Objects 124
Building Supplies 125
Chairs and Rockers 125
Cutouts 126
Drawers and Doors 126
Flooring 127
Legs 127
Millwork/Moulding 128
Miniatures 129
Shingles 129
Turnings 130
Types of Wood 130

SECTION TWELVE
WOODWORKING SUPPLIES AND SERVICES

Abrasives 140
Adhesives 141
Anchors/Fasteners 144
Bits and Blades 144
Cleaners 148
Coatings 148
Cutters 149
Framing 150
Guards 150
Hardware 150
Lifts 154
Rails 155
Repairs 155
Restoration 155
Sharpening Stones 156
Templates 157
Transfer Paper 157

INDEX 159

Introduction

Introduction

This second edition of *Woodworker's Source Book* is an up-to-date resource for woodworkers who need to find materials, supplies and other resources. One of its chief aims is to allow you to locate items you either know exist or feel might exist somewhere. We also aim to provide you a look at a slew of things, whether tools or tips, plans or paints, that you may not know exist. In part, this is a source book for hard-to-find and unique tools, but it is also meant for the person who doesn't have access to a truly good hardware store—and there are fewer and fewer truly good hardware stores as time goes on. We have an overabundance of home centers, many of which are short on supply and high on asking price. This book is meant to provide you with convenient, affordable access to the tools and materials you want or need.

I have had a great time going over catalogs, plans, product sheets, course catalogs and other materials. I hope you find listed herein useful, interesting and enjoyable material. Our goal has been to help you find information, products and supplies so that you can enjoy woodworking more. I also wanted to make this a browser's book—something you can enjoy looking through even when you're not searching immediately for a specific item.

Much effort has been put forth in getting current information (I've worn out my dialing finger and laser printer), but companies change addresses and go out of business often. So, never, ever send money without first checking that the information is still up-to-date. The variety of products available to the woodworker is exceptionally wide in order to suit the wide range of interests and abilities of woodworkers in general. One of our goals has been to reflect that variety in the book's contents. I believe we have met that aim, and I hope you will agree.

Shopping by Mail

Shopping by Mail

Trading, buying and selling are long-standing traditions of the human race, ones that will be maintained into the foreseeable future. Within these traditions, different characters do different things—bad reputations abound, and good reputations often don't get as much attention as they should. We need little protection from businessmen and -women with good intentions and repute, but there's always a need for reliable help in dealing with those who are less honorable.

I cannot vouch for every company listed in the book. In fact, because of the changing nature of business, I can't vouch even for the ones I've dealt with for years. What I can do is state that those I've dealt with have all been honest in filling orders and as speedy as an appropriately stocked warehouse allows. Even the largest woodworking mail-order houses do not compare in size with J.C. Penney or even today's sadly diminished Sears. L.L. Bean outstrips many at a time. Economics states that a certain number of each item needs to be on hand, but on occasion a seller has to get caught short. I've walked the aisles of McFeely's with owner Jim Ray and have seen that he keeps more than sufficient stock on hand, but a sudden spurt of orders for any one item can draw that down to zero. Sometimes, a bit of patience is essential to getting satisfaction.

Do Your Homework

The selection of tools and supplies for woodworkers widens appreciably when you shop by mail. A selection that large, however, requires research—and caution. Research acquaints you with the variety and quality of products available in our vast marketplace. Caution results in getting the best value for your money.

Mail-order shopping among the woodworking suppliers, whether from makers, retailers or plans services, is not totally risk free, but it is generally better than with other products. In recent years, I know of only one major case of outright intent to defraud from the outset by a tool mail-order company, now out of business. This fit the too-good-to-be-true criterion perfectly. Computer shoppers are far more often ripped off by mail-order suppliers who never intend to supply what is sold. This occurs, in part, because the prices are extremely volatile in the computer field, so ads for spectacular deals are not always rip-offs. Seemingly too-good-to-be-true advertisements in other fields—including woodworking—are a red flag for avoidance. If it's too good to be true, then it isn't true. Period.

Call the Better Business Bureau

Start by doing a little research on any mail-order company where your order is apt to amount to more then a few dollars. Check with their local Better Business Bureau (BBB) to see what their standing is. Most of us don't bother with the extra work when we're ordering only a few bucks worth of supplies, but major tool purchases definitely need at least minimal research to determine how long the company has been in business, whether it has received extensive complaints, and how it has resolved complaints. A small number of complaints against a company need not deter you from making a purchase from them, as long as: (1) they've been in business for some time; (2) the complaint number coincides with the BBB's consideration of a typical, or reasonable, human-error factor; and (3) the complaints that deserved resolution received it promptly and equitably. If complaints have not been quickly resolved, and there are large numbers of them going back more than ninety days, keep your money in your wallet or find another company offering the same products, even though the cost may be a few dollars higher.

Check for Hidden Fees

Before you place your order, check to see if the company charges a restocking fee. As a rule, warranties that state "satisfaction guaranteed" generally mean there is no restocking fee, but it doesn't hurt to be sure. Restocking fees run up to 15 or 20 percent of the cost of the item to return it to the seller's shelves. You have to decide whether or not such a chance is worthwhile.

Use Credit Cards

ADVANTAGES

Protection Against Fraud

Using charge cards when ordering gives you protection from fraud. I'm not a lover of plastic because of the obscene interest rates they all charge (including those who charge several percentage points lower than most) and the ludicrous annual fees. But credit cards do give you greater protection against fraud, because you can refuse payment if an article is not up to snuff, or is charged but not shipped. Paying with a credit card gives you much more leeway in backing out of a sour deal than does paying by check or money order. If ordered material doesn't show up, but a credit card charge does, you do not have to pay that charge. If ordered material is not what was described, you can return objects without major fiscal penalty, though you may end up paying shipping. Just make sure you get a return authorization if the retailer or distributor requires one.

Leverage in Disputes

In addition, you may refuse payment to the credit card company when there is a dispute with the retailer over costs, quality or nonsupply, and the credit card company cannot make adverse comments to credit bureaus until the situation is resolved. (Of course, if it's resolved in your favor, they still cannot make adverse comments.)

Speed of Delivery

Although charging it can sometimes add a small percentage to your order, this added cost may prove worthwhile because credit cards speed orders. A personal check isn't going to let you get next-day delivery on anything, no matter how badly you need it. In most cases, it takes several days after arrival for a personal check to clear. And a personal check cannot have payment stopped after clearing your account. As mentioned earlier, you can hang up a credit card account on disputed charges. That gets the credit card company into the act, which can help resolve situations fairly.

DISADVANTAGES

Interest Rates

Part of the reason I dislike high interest rates — beyond paying them myself and noting how long it can take to pay off an account using the monthly minimum payment, while you pay many, many times the cost of the item purchased in interest — is the fact the issuing banks nail merchants with a rate ranging from 2 percent to as much as 6 percent of the sale cost of an item.

Extra Charges

Keep an eye out for disclaimers such as "The above prices reflect a discount for cash." Pay by credit card, and they can stick you with a further percentage, which can get painful when buying an item like a large table saw. This percentage, whether noted or not, is paid no matter how fast you pay off your credit card. Beat the 9 to 26 percent interest blues, and they're still charging you 3 to 6 percent additional, whether or not it is listed as a surcharge.

Surcharges are illegal in several states (currently California, Florida, Kansas, New York, Connecticut, Maine, Massachusetts, Oklahoma and Texas) and are against the stated policies of the big-three credit card issuers. Still, I know I have paid surcharges to photographic suppliers in New York City many times, and will again. This extra 5 percent (and overblown shipping charges) appears modest when applied to sup-

plies that would cost me 20 percent or 25 percent more if bought locally.

To date, I have not seen surcharges listed in woodworking mail-order ads or catalogs. If you do, don't automatically dismiss the idea of ordering; you still may be ahead.

Shipping Charges

Shipping charges are another area of interest. While these charges apply no matter how you pay, they are worth mentioning here. Companies can bilk consumers out of thousands of dollars annually by inflating the costs of packing and shipping, and too many do. Again, this cost is often worth it.

Order COD

ADVANTAGES

Protection Against Fraud

If a credit card order isn't available, order COD. Cash on delivery means you are assured of at least getting the merchandise, or something similar to the merchandise, before you lay out any money.

If possible, pay COD charges by check, not cash or money order. This allows you to stop payment if the object you ordered is not as described. You can stop payment on the check and sort out the financial hassles by mail and phone later. Often the stop-payment charge will be less than your loss if the company you ordered from is trying to pull a fast one.

Although some shipping companies will not accept checks, most will. UPS drivers, for example, do not like to accept cash because it makes them more vulnerable to robbers.

DISADVANTAGES

Extra charges

COD is not cheap — and stopping payment on a check is another of those bank charges that pay banks about 973 percent profit — but they are better than losing the total cost of the item ordered.

Record Your Ordering Actions

After working through the catalog, brochure or other literature, write down exactly what you are ordering, including catalog number, description, catalog page number, price, shipping cost, and total price including any taxes. Make sure you note the date. If you're mailing the order, make a separate copy and file it in your files. If you're phoning in the order, note the name of the person you deal with, any order number that is supplied, and the promised delivery date, as well as any added costs.

Like too many consumers, I have until recently had a very bad habit on phone orders: I seldom wrote down anything but the item number and description; I paid no attention to price, name of order recipient or similar information. As a result, I recently received four of an item when I had ordered two and would have had to do a ridiculous amount of work to return the extra two, ultimately at my own expense for packing and shipping. Fortunately, the items make superb gifts, so they're in a closet for now. But I might well have found myself out $40, plus shipping, if I had no further use for the material, simply because of human error (my assumption is human error, because I've done business with this company a number of times, and found them scrupulously honest—and fair).

The company might well have accepted the return, and they might even have credited the shipping costs, but in the process of straightening it all out, I'd have lost a couple hours I don't have to spare. The time to correct the error would have been shortened to repacking the extras with a fast note if I had kept better order information.

If you have the attitude "don't write it down, they won't goof," revise it now.

Check Your Order

When your order arrives, check the outside of the package. If you're dealing with a trucking company, make your notes on the bill of lading before signing your name. Note size and location of any apparent damage, and sign as taking receipt with recourse if damage also proves to be internal. Most of the time, with modern packaging, it won't. Large tools are packed in heavy cardboard—and the heavier items have wooden supports in the cardboard. Smaller items are usually thoroughly surrounded with Styrofoam or a similar material. Protection in the packaging is excellent, but truly rough handling can damage things anyway. Check to be sure, and always leave yourself an out. Let both the shipping company and the selling company know immediately if you discover damage.

When you open the package, check the contents against your order list. If all is in good condition and matches the list, most of the time your chores are about over. Check for costs. If you've paid in full, by credit card or other means, that should be so noted. Next, fill out any warranty cards and return them to the indicated addresses, keeping a copy of the card and address to which it is sent (I've gotten some warranty cards that don't even have the name of the manufacturer on them; make note of the maker's name if that's the case).

After checking the above, I like to take two extra steps. I assemble all items that need assembly and take a test run with any tools before mailing the warranty cards. This is another lesson learned from experience. Years ago, I bought a new camera, unpacked it, tossed the packing material, and mailed in the warranty card. I then used the camera to shoot a roll of film, which I should have done before shipping off the card or destroying the packaging. The camera was defective, and I ended up having to trade it back to the dealer as used. I felt ripped off, and I was, so I never dealt with that dealer again. But I recognize that I invited the problems I had by discarding the packaging and prematurely mailing the warranty card to the maker. The dealer had to go through a longer process to get the camera either repaired or replaced, and there was no way it looked new when it got back there. A better dealer would have worked with me to replace the defective unit, but this one got snotty, and I got angry in return. I ended up with a much more costly camera, which I used happily for fifteen years; heartburn; and absolute delight when, three years later, the dealer went belly up—after never seeing another dollar of mine.

Handle Problems Immediately

BROKEN OR MISSING ITEMS

If you have problems matching your order list or you find broken items, your work begins. Note the problem with the camera dealer, and learn from my temper. The first rule is to keep your cool. Get all your paperwork in front of you. If necessary, write some notes on the problem. Then call the dealer.

From this point, you will deal at least partly in luck. Today, most mail-order dealers work on, or close to, the "Satisfaction Guaranteed" policy introduced a million years ago by Sears. People handling the phones are instructed that the customer is always right, even if the customer comes across as a drooling fumble-wit (they're instructed to hang up on abusive customers, so going hog-wild won't help you at all).

Find out the name of the representative on the phone and write it down. Explain the problem. Expect an appropriate reply or a transfer to a supervisor who can provide a substantive response. If such a response isn't forthcoming, move up a step within the company, if possible. If not, explain to the person with whom you are speaking that you will follow up with a letter to their local Better Business Bureau that includes their name, the company's name and address, and details of the problem.

If this doesn't get the results you want, follow up on your promise by writing a clear and logical letter detailing the problem and mailing it to the company's local BBB (ask your local BBB for its address). Mail a copy of your letter to the company as well.

FRAUD

If you feel you've been defrauded, the next step is to go to the postal authorities. Though very little mail order is done through the U.S. Postal Service today, much other company business is conducted that way—and a fairly large number of people still use the mail, rather than the telephone, to order. The threat of action is often enough to solve the problem—if you make a reasoned case, with clear details.

Keep Accurate Records

As mentioned above, it is important that you keep accurate records throughout the process of ordering by mail. This is especially true when dealing with prob-lems. Any time you take unilateral phone action to stop a check, make a complaint, or carry through a promise, you need to notify the company in writing that you have done so. A letter of this type is a much better record of the proceedings than a phone bill with a number and date on it, but make sure you save those phone bills, too, in case of a later dispute over contact dates.

If all this seems to make a sad, gray case for mail order, it shouldn't. For every poorly handled transaction, there are several hundred handled pleasantly and efficiently. But with the cost of some tools today, it pays to know your options just in case something goes wrong. Protecting yourself takes only a moment or two. It may never be needed, but, like most insurance, it is great for peace of mind.

Carving

Carving

FOAM

JIFFY FOAM, INC.
221 Third Street
Newport, RI 02830
(401) 846-7870
(800) 344-8997
(401) 847-9966

Jiffy Foam manufactures Balsa Foam, a paintable, carvable foam that works nicely for many carving demands and can even be cut with cookie cutters. It's great as a starter for wood-carvers. It can be sawed, carved and chiseled, will take impressions, sands well without gum-up, and takes oil-based paints. It glues readily with polyvinyl resin (white) glues. Generally available at hobby shops, Balsa Foam can also be located by calling Don Anderson at the above numbers (Jiffy Foam is *not* a retailer but will set up a small, trial order for a hobby or similar shop). Jiffy Foam sent me a couple of samples, and though I'm not a wood-carver, I was impressed with the strength and actual ease of carving it affords with a sharp tool. In addition, you get resistance with a dull tool, so press-in impressions work nicely. The material is a dun color and does not resemble Styrofoam at all—it's much finer grained.

KNIVES

NORTH BAY FORGE
Box S
Waldron, WA 98297

As all hand-forged tools, North Bay's products tend to be pricey compared to factory-made items. In many senses, that's a matter of choice when selecting tools, though a handmade tool has a greater beauty (and I don't think good machine-made tools are ugly at all, though cheaply made ones surely are) that is often worth the cost. With some makers, the beauty extends into the tool's handling—I can't comment on North Bay's tool handling, but the production is definitely by hand and in the old manner. North Bay Forge is located on Waldron Island, which has no phones (note the lack of phone number above) and which also lacks electricity! That doesn't mean no machines are used to produce North Bay Forge tools,

but it does mean greater attention must be paid to each operation. The catalog, featuring scorps, drawknives and carver's knives, is free.

CARVING MACHINES

FOREDOM ELECTRIC CO.
16 Stony Hill Road
Bethel, CT 06801
(203) 792-8622
(203) 790-9832 FAX

Foredom's product manager asks that you call for their free catalog (and dealer's name) on Foredom flexible-shaft tools, including the "SR" reversible motor and 35,000 and 45,000 rpm Micro Motors. There is also a complete accessories catalog that covers tungsten carbide bits, ruby carvers, carbide burrs, and all sorts of cutting, grinding and polishing accessories. Foredom is probably the oldest name in the flexible-shaft tool industry, having started in 1922, and may well make the widest line of such tools today—I got confused and quit counting after noting fifteen different power heads!

PROCORP, INC.
P.O. Box 5218
Grove City, FL 34295
(813) 698-0222

Procorp manufactures flexible-shaft, rotary power tools offering state-of-the-art equipment under the Mastercarver name. The system includes a ¼ horsepower, reversible 19,000 rpm motor, a 38½" flexible shaft, and a reciprocating handpiece with five cutting blades.

TERRCO, INC.
222 First Avenue NW
Watertown, SD 57201
(605) 882-3888
(605) 882-0778 FAX

Terrco produces a full line of machine carving and duplicating equipment, including Marlin Division sign-carving outfits. The Master Carver series starts with eight spindles but may be had in less complex outfits meant for start-ups, with intermediate duty served by the two-spindle unit. The Marlin Woodcarvers carve signs and will also produce flat panel carving in 3-D. Write or call for the twice-yearly brochure issues, which are free of charge. Terrco takes MasterCard and Visa.

TOOLS

WARREN TOOL COMPANY
2209-1 Rt. 9G
Rhinebeck, NY 12572
(914) 876-7817

Fred Clark offers a multiplicity of carving tools, with interchangeable blades for the many handles, as well as a variety of kits. Warren Tool also carries sharpening tools for most carving implements, books, sharpening accessories and related tools. For example, he carries the Nibsburner and American basswood cutouts of birds (chickadee, cardinal, robin, and, in miniature, the Canada goose, the canvasback and wood ducks). Fred's line of carving knives seems especially wide, and he offers a basic wood carving kit with a book, a handle, a small blade and a basswood cutout for less than $16. He does not carry power tools. The catalog is $1. Fred also offers his line for wholesale, so you may wish to check to see if you are eligible for his wholesale requirements. Fred does not take credit cards; use a check or money order for this company.

Education and Information

Education and Information

ASSOCIATIONS

AMERICAN ASSOCIATION OF WOODTURNERS (AAW)
667 Harriet Avenue
Shoreview, MN 55126
(612) 484-9094

The AAW offers symposia on wood turning and is an international nonprofit organization aimed at advancing this craft. In essence, the Association provides information, education and organization to those interested in lathe work, through a quarterly journal, *American Woodturner*, the membership directory and other benefits, including the symposia. General membership is $25 annually. You may also contact them for dates and places of events. The Association takes MasterCard and Visa.

AMERICAN FOREST & PAPER ASSOCIATION (AFPA)
1111 19th Street NW, Suite 800
Washington, DC 20036
(202) 463-2700
(202) 463-2791 FAX

The AFPA incorporates the American Wood Council and was formerly the National Forest Products Association. Their specific goal is the promotion of the use and acceptance of wood products, and toward this end, the Association offers a list of construction publications that may provide assistance in using wood in larger projects (small buildings, shops, barns, etc.). Write or call and ask for the free brochure on publications. The Association does not accept credit cards.

AMERICAN PLYWOOD ASSOCIATION (APA)
P.O. Box 11700
Tacoma, WA 98411-0700
(206) 565-6600 Ext. 189 for literature list

Founded in 1933 as the Douglas Fir Plywood Association, the APA now covers much more territory in setting standards for plywood and in providing plans for woodworkers, homeowners and others. Plywood in large amounts and numbers of types must be bought. The Association maintains five product-testing labs in key producing regions to keep up with the industry's and its consumers' needs. Ask about a listing of technical bulletins if you foresee any kind of technical problems when working with softwood plywood, oriented strand board, medium-density overlaid ply-

wood or other types. The APA is almost totally softwood-plywood oriented and really does have some terrific plans that are usually reasonably easy to construct. The Handy Plan catalog is $2; it lists and shows a wide variety of projects built primarily of plywood in one form or another. The APA also offers many low-cost booklets, brochures and tech sheets that are of great help when larger projects loom. The Association doesn't take credit cards but will bill for literature.

CALIFORNIA REDWOOD ASSOCIATION
405 Enfrente Drive, Suite 200
Novato, CA 94949
(415) 382-0662

For a wide range of literature on types and uses of redwood lumber, the California Redwood Association can't be beat. The emphasis is on outdoor use, as one might expect, though I've found redwood to be an interesting material for large and small indoor projects as well. (I built two redwood bookshelves some time ago: They continue to stand in my dining room, where their appearance often draws comments because redwood is seldom used for such projects. Most indoor redwood projects are architectural, such as wall paneling and molding.) The Association's literature list offers everything from a Design-A-Deck plans kit to nail-use information. Exterior and interior finishes are covered in large brochures, and there are pamphlets on the industry and its harvesting methods, as well as the environmental impact of using redwood. I'd suggest giving the Association a call, or dropping them a note, to request the literature list, at which time you can ask them about shipping costs that are added to literature prices on the list.

CEDAR SHAKE & SHINGLE BUREAU
515 116th Avenue NE, Suite 275
Bellevue, WA 98004
(206) 453-1323

I had to think for a few minutes before including this one. The Bureau represents makers of cedar shingles and shakes, which seem a bit more of a finished product than most woodworkers want. Still, they can provide information on producers, and they have all sorts of brochures on using cedar as roofing and siding and decorating with shakes. I've used the ridge type as covers for birdhouses and bird feeders for years, so someone else is apt to find another use for cedar shakes or shingles. The Bureau has been around since 1915 and can give you the lowdown on current costs for booklets and brochures when you call or write. At this moment, the twelve-page manual for exterior and interior walls goes for $1, as does the remodeling booklet and several other booklets. Some are half a buck.

GUILD OF AMERICAN LUTHIERS
8222 South Park Avenue
Tacoma, WA 98408-5226
(206) 472-7853

The Guild presents the foremost magazine on wood instruments, and there are exhibits and other events presented and listed. Timothy Olsen is founder-editor. As the Guild describes itself: "a nonprofit, tax-exempt educational organization, formed in 1972 to advance lutherie, the art and science of string instrument making and repair, through a free exchange of information." I don't have a great deal of interest in instrument making, but I must admit to fascination with some of the subjects covered in back issues of the quarterly magazine, including articles on cherry wood, working with koa, improving round-bottom planes, bending with rubber heat blankets, and much more. Members also get breaks on instrument plans and a good bit more for their annual $30.

HAND TOOLS INSTITUTE
25 North Broadway
Tarrytown, NY 10591

This very useful association provides some excellent guides to hand-tool use and safety, at low cost. There's a good deal of basic, intermediate and expert information in this material, making it well worth a woodworker's while. For example, the #203 guide to Hand Tools, at ninety pages, is $3 each, but the Striking Tool Safety Flyer is $3 per hundred, as is the Struck Tool Safety flyer. Hand Tool Reference Wall Charts are $1.25 each, as are Automotive Tool Reference Wall Charts; payment must accompany orders.

NATIONAL HARDWOOD LUMBER ASSOCIATION (NHLA)
P.O. Box 34518
Memphis, TN 38184
(901) 377-0518

This nonprofit, hardwood-lumber trade association represents the hardwood lumber industry. It maintains the grading rules for hardwoods and operates a vocational lumber graders school in Memphis. NHLA also runs continuing education workshops and is involved in public education and hardwood promotion. There is a price list of publications, with rule books for lumber grades, introductions to the grading of hardwood lumber, a membership directory, a forest-resources fact book, and a number of others, including coloring books for children. They also have several videotapes on lumber grading, forestry management, and hardwood in general, its preparation, and its use. NHLA has some fairly technical information that may be of help to serious woodworkers, hobbyist and pro. Write or call and ask for their brochure. The Association doesn't take credit cards.

SOUTHERN FOREST PRODUCTS ASSOCIATION (SFPA)
P.O. Box 52468
New Orleans, LA 70152

SFPA is a great source for technical information on wood and its uses, emphasizing Southern Pine, and provides a number of plans they call the YouCan-BuildIt series, a series that grows with time. Currently, the list includes a 12' × 12' gazebo, a planter box, a 10' × 12' deck, a 20' × 20' deck, a 14' × 16' flexible pattern trellis, a planter bench, a fence, a potting shed, a 6' × 6' playhouse, an 8' × 10' storage shed, a small deck, a two-level deck with a sunscreen, and a double-decker 12' × 24' railed deck. One of the nicest projects is the 4' × 8' playdeck/pool/sandbox. Plans are reasonable to low cost, and the plan list is #410, sold for thirty cents. Or you may ask for their catalog, which includes descriptions of literature, plans, and audiovisual material on softwood moisture-content requirements.

WESTERN WOOD PRODUCTS ASSOCIATION (WWPA)
522 Southwest Fifth Avenue
Portland, OR 97204-2122
(503) 224-3930
(503) 224-3934 FAX

Founded in 1964, WWPA presents technical information, grading information and standards for the species of wood their association emphasizes (Douglas fir, hem-fir, Engelmann spruce, Idaho white pine, lodgepole pine, sugar pine, Ponderosa pine, Western larch, Western cedars and incense cedar), plus a good series of large and small plans at low cost. I'm looking at a plan for kid-sized storage modules now, their #62: It is easy to build and uses standard lumber sizes. Plan #61 is a mobile workbench that looks no harder to build. Drop a note (or call, if you wish) asking for the current literature list or a catalog of plans. The list is too long to reproduce here, but it contains a good variety of plans that will almost certainly have one of interest to you. The Association takes MasterCard and Visa.

WOOD MOULDING & MILLWORK PRODUCERS ASSOCIATION

1730 Southwest Skyline Boulevard, Suite 128
Portland, OR 97221
(503) 292-9288

The Wood Moulding and Millwork Producers Association is the North American trade association that represents manufacturers of hardwood and softwood moulding and millwork products. The Association primarily serves its members, but part of that service includes literature that may be of value to some woodworkers. Their consumer literature on wood moulding includes a thirty-two-page booklet on working with lattice, a brochure on working with wood moldings, a how-to on making picture frames, and five hundred moulding projects. Drop them a note, or give a call for the literature brochure.

WOOD TURNING CENTER

P.O. Box 25706
Philadelphia, PA 19144
(215) 844-2188

The Wood Turning Center offers books and videos on lathe turning. It also stages exhibitions, workshops and symposia. Members get discounts on more than forty different titles; dues are $25 a year. Membership also brings the magazine *Turning Point* four times annually. The Center takes MasterCard and Visa.

WOODWORKERS ALLIANCE FOR RAINFOREST PROTECTION (WARP)

One Cottage Street
Easthampton, MA 01027

Dedicated to the preservation of rain forest areas, WARP presents ideas for conservation and preservation of wood, aiming at sustainable development of all forest resources. The WARP mission exists to protect forest ecosystems for the benefit of forest inhabitants, the woodworking community and future generations. Part of this includes exploring the methods of sustainable timber harvest, encouraging local control of forest resources, and educating the public in responsible timber use. The brochure they send out explains the problem and checks out the actions of WARP, which, as it turns out, was founded at the University of Massachusetts in 1990. Dues are $25 in the United States and $35 in Canada; members receive a quarterly WARP journal. I'd suggest checking out the

brochure, at least. I'll be sending my membership check in shortly.

WOODWORKING MACHINERY DISTRIBUTORS ASSOCIATION

251 West DeKalb Pike-109A
King of Prussia, PA 19406
(610) 265-6658
(610) 265-3419 FAX

The Association is made up of distributors, dealers and importers of woodworking machinery located throughout the United States and Canada. It serves its member companies by sponsoring sales and service tech seminars, assisting at major trade shows, and publishing management reports and surveys. In addition, it has insurance programs and discount telephone, car rental and some equipment purchase plans. The biennial Membership Directory/Buyers Guide is $35, and a year's subscription to *The Vital Link*, the Association news bulletin, is $25.

BOOKS AND MAGAZINES

AMERICAN ASSOCIATION FOR VOCATIONAL INSTRUCTIONAL MATERIALS

745-A Gaines School Road
Athens, GA 30605
(706) 543-7557

The American Association for Vocational Instructional Materials is a nonprofit developer, publisher and distributor of instructional videos, books, computer software, and other resources for vocational students. Primarily, their customers are schools. On request, they'll send a copy of their ninety-page catalog, which describes woodworking educational materials in the industrial education section. There are a lot of videos, the cheapest being a project video, complete with a twenty-two-page booklet. Shopsmith's series of woodworking videos is included in the list and is reasonably priced. Regardless of price, there are a fair number of videos and a couple of programs I'd love to own. Most come under the heading of "Maybe, some day," but you may find desires and wallet power that are both stronger than mine. The agriculture section includes some reasonably priced materials on fence building, and the construction trades sections contain a lot of material on larger projects with wood. Tip: Get the manuals and forget the software unless you plan to teach classes.

AMERICAN WOODWORKER

33 East Minor Street
Emmaus, PA 18098
(800) 666-3111 Customer communications
(610) 967-8362
(610) 967-8956 FAX

American Woodworker is a Rodale Press magazine, which comes out six times a year; projections have been made for a seventh issue each year. It is now more than seven years old and has changed from an oversized black-and-white magazine to a standard (8½″ × 11″) four-color format. *AW* offers tech tips, technique articles, many good project articles, finishing tips, a wood-fact column, and its own look at subjects every other woodworking magazine looks at. Fortunately, the angle at which *AW* looks at woodworking is just off-center enough to be interesting in its own right. The magazine is aimed at the woodworking enthusiast, with a range that will interest beginners and much that should interest professionals. Projects range from the elegant and moderately difficult and enjoyable for one level of woodworker to the simple and fun for the tyro. Tool tests are rational and accurate: In the past couple of years, the tests have become as exhaustive as those in any other magazine. The information presented, which is accessible and accurate, is almost never dry. Overall, you'll find *AW* to be a very likable and useful publication with its own personality. Six issues per year cost $23.70, and back issues are $4.50 each.

ARCH DAVIS DESIGN

P.O. Box 119
Morrill, ME 04952
(207) 342-4055

Arch forced me to work extra by sending me his book on making raised panels on a table saw (*The Raised Panel Book*, $9.95, plus $2 shipping) and a booklet on knowing wood moisture content ($2, postage and handling included). I found the description a bit light, as Arch covers most methods of making such panels and the doors in which they're normally included, for many different applications from cabinets to household doors. He includes several interesting projects as well. The booklet on wood moisture shows how to use a vernier caliper to determine moisture content. It's a bit complex and time-consuming compared to sticking a meter's probes into the wood, but it should be accurate. Arch Davis also sells plans for a lobster boat and a sailboat and is aiming to have three more plan packages ready shortly. Drop a note for his price list. The plans, from which he sent me a couple of sheets, are very nicely done, too. Arch takes MasterCard and Visa.

BETTER HOMES & GARDENS BOOK CLUBS

150 E. 52nd St.
New York, NY 10022
(212) 319-5380
(212) 715-8783 FAX

The Country Homes & Gardens & Crafts Club of Better Homes & Gardens offers titles dealing with crafts, cookbooks, women's interest books, country lifestyle, hunting, fishing, and men's how-to books.

BETTERWAY BOOKS

F&W Publications
1507 Dana Avenue
Cincinnati, OH 45207
(800) 289-0963
(513) 531-2690
(513) 531-1843 FAX

This book imprint covers a wide variety of topics and includes a rapidly growing line of how-to woodworking books (including the one you're holding). Titles like *How to Sharpen Every Blade in Your Woodshop*, *Make Your Own Jigs & Woodshop Furniture*, and *Building Fine Furniture From Solid Wood* give you a good idea of what they're all about. Call or write for a free catalog.

BOOK-OF-THE-MONTH-CLUB, INC.

Time & Life Building
1271 Avenue of the Americas
New York, NY 10020-2686
(212) 522-4200
(212) 522-1212 HomeStyle and Crafter's Choice
(212) 522-0303 FAX
Shipping:
Customer Service Center
Camp Hill, PA 17012
(717) 697-0311

Two of Book-of-the-Month's clubs that may offer titles helpful to woodworkers are the HomeStyle Books Club, which publishes *HomeStyle Books News*, and the Crafter's Choice Club, which publishes *Crafter's Choice Collections*.

DECORATIVE WOODCRAFTS

6060 Spine Road
P.O. Box 54696
Boulder, CO 80323-4696

This magazine is aimed at those of you who are interested in painting and otherwise decorating your woodworking projects. There are at least a dozen projects found in each issue; some issues contain removable, full-sized patterns for some of these projects. Bimonthly, it costs $19.97 per year.

DOVER PUBLICATIONS, INC.
31 East 2nd Street
Mineola, NY 11501
(516) 294-7000

Dover's catalog is free, and it lists many woodworking titles and related titles, from old to new. At one time, Dover published only reprints, but in recent years, they've gone to publishing more and more new material, while retaining the lead in publishing old crafts (and other) material. They have books on wood turning, for example, that go back centuries to provide plentiful examples of how it was done, with some help toward getting it done today if you apply some study and thought. Always an interesting book, the Dover catalog in recent years has turned more into a series of catalogs on different subjects, plus a full-line catalog. Ask for the full-line catalog or the crafts and hobbies catalog: The latter is about the only place you can get information on making marbleized boxes. Check out the 1910 edition of the Sears Home Builder's Catalog; check out photo studies of ornamental carpentry on nineteenth-century houses; get a look at *Popular Mechanics*' original Mission furniture plans book; check out plans for sixty-two projects by Gustav Stickley; get John Shea's measured Shaker furniture drawings and a host of similar items. Dover does not accept credit cards.

FINE TOOL JOURNAL
P.O. Box 4001
Pittsford, VT 05763
(802) 483-2111

Published quarterly, *Fine Tool Journal* is jammed with articles on evaluating modern hand tools, historical perspectives for the collector of tools and methods, how-to articles on tuning old and new tools, book reviews, and much else, including listings of antique, obsolete and modern tools for sale. One year (four issues) is $20 ($25 [American] in Canada).

FINE WOODWORKING
Taunton Press
63 South Main Street
P.O. Box 355
Newtown, CT 06470
(800) 888-8286 Orders
(203) 426-8171

Currently at $25 per year, *Fine Woodworking* is the exemplar of a magazine for top woodworkers of whatever skill level. Those at the beginner's level will not be able to reproduce many of the projects, of which there are fewer than in other magazines, but they will definitely learn something from each issue. After working through enough of the technique articles in *FW*, nearly anyone will be able to do almost anything. Many, many, many shop tips are included in each of the six issues per year, plus book and video reviews, a look at upcoming events, letters, tool tests, and so on. Some, too often much, of the material tends to the esoteric, such as an article a few years ago on tensioning a bandsaw blade by tone, something that probably works fine for a few but is dead useless to those of us who are tone deaf. You'll find lots of ads, lots of copy in this oversized magazine, which is offered at a reasonable price. Taunton takes American Express, Visa and MasterCard.

GLASS ART
P.O. Box 1507
Broomfield, CO 80038
(304) 465-4965

For the woodworker who wants to accent projects with glass, this is a good magazine with a lot of basics. It is $4 per issue, $24 for six issues per year.

GLASS PATTERNS QUARTERLY MAGAZINE
P.O. Box 69
8300 Hidden Valley Road
Westport, KY 40077
(502) 222-5631
(502) 222-4527 FAX

This magazine is for those among us who use, or want to use, glass as an accent material in our woodworking projects. Each panel produced for this project is shot in a wooden frame, which should also enhance ideas. The magazine comes out four times per year, as its title indicates, and it has a sixteen-page pullout section in each issue, full of patterns. The magazine costs $18 per year or $3.50 per single copy.

HOMEOWNERS' DO-IT-YOURSELF BOOK CLUB
P.O. Box 11474
Des Moines, IA 50336-1474
(800) 678-2713
(515) 284-3000
(212) 715-8783 FAX

This club specializes in nonfiction titles on home how-to, woodworking, house building, cabinetmaking, furniture making, tool usage and masonry techniques for do-it-yourselfers and craftsmen.

INFODEX SERVICES
10609 King Arthur's Court
Richmond, VA 23235-3840
(804) 320-4704

David Jordan offers his PC program, a large wood-working index, with a subscription service for up-dates. The program, INFOWARE, provides (at the time this book is written) a database covering more than 6,500 articles in two hundred ninety issues of eleven woodworking magazines. Touch the right key, and you can find any of the 1,358 projects and plans, or another article or tool test you wish. The eleven magazines include the best, from *American Wood-worker* to *Workbench*, with nine stops in between. The program comes on 5¼" or 3½" disks, needs 2.5 megabytes of hard-disk space and DOS 3.3 or higher. Approximately 1,500 articles are being added to the database each year. The service offers free informa-tion and prices. Subscription updates are mailed in January and June.

KNOTWHOLE PUBLISHING
5629 Main Street-Putney
Stratford, CT 06497
(203) 386-1270

The Guide to Published Woodworking Plans & Tech-niques, by Art Gumbus, is a well-done compendium of 13,900 articles from eight hundred issues of wood-working magazines. It contains data on twenty-one dif-ferent woodworking magazines, in several instances going back to the magazine's first issue. The book is available alone, for $25, and with a PC Search Info-base for $37. Divided into thirty-five major categories, the book contains information on ordering back is-sues from different publishers. The index was de-signed and has been tested by woodworkers. It is completely updated annually—that is a *huge* amount of work. The book is about 290 pages in a three-ring binder. *The Guide to Published Woodworking Plans & Techniques* is available from many woodworking mail-order houses, or it may be ordered directly. En-close a check or money order, as KnotWhole doesn't take credit cards.

LINDEN PUBLISHING, INC.
3845 North Blackstone
Fresno, CA 93726
(800) 345-4447
(209) 227-2901
(209) 227-3520 FAX

Linden is a publisher of crafts books, with a list of in-teresting and unusual reprints and new books, includ-ing *Circular Work In Carpentry and Joinery*, *The Cooper and His Trade*, *Contract Joinery*, *A Treatise on Lathes and Turning* (originally published in 1868), *The Conversion and Seasoning of Wood*, and *Making Wooden Clock Cases*. The catalog of more than three hundred titles, from Linden and other pub-lishers, is $1 for a two-year subscription. The com-pany takes MasterCard and Visa.

POPULAR WOODWORKING
F&W Publications, Inc.
1507 Dana Avenue
Cincinnati, OH 45207
(800) 627-3719
(513) 531-2690
(513) 531-1843 FAX

Popular Woodworking continues to be one of the better woodworking magazines. The change in owner-ship in 1994 and some recent issues lead me to con-clude it will remain so and improve even further. Im-provements are evident in all areas, including more and better pictures, illustrations and instructions. The content is well-balanced with project and technique articles geared for the advanced beginner, intermedi-ate and advanced hobbyist. They still feature the pop-ular Pull-Out Plans. Providing "over-the-shoulder" ad-vice from some of the world's master craftsmen, *PW* offers practical no-nonsense solutions to the everyday problems woodworkers confront. In addition to the projects and techniques, *PW* features regular columns on finishing, tool reviews, the business of woodwork-ing, book reviews and shop tips. Subscriptions cost $19.97 for one year (six issues) and $39.94 for two years (twelve issues).

PROFESSIONAL BOATBUILDER MAGAZINE
P.O. Box 78
Brooklin, ME 04616
(207) 359-4651

A part of the WoodenBoat complex, this magazine is aimed at the small professional boat builder. *Profes-sional Boatbuilder Magazine* is a controlled-circulation (currently 21,000) bimonthly that costs $35.95 a year for nonqualified subscribers and is free to those who are qualified. Some of the most sophisti-cated woodworking anyone will ever see goes into modern pleasure boats, though the magazine is not directly devoted to woodworking. Issues may cover light-curing resins (for fiberglass and composite ma-terials), shrink-wrapping boats, choosing batteries, and building replicas, or a project design for a fold-up table to save room: The current issue contains nothing directly on woodworking, but shows how to work with rotomolded polystyrene in building plastic kayaks (and other boat-related items), and how to work with woven and stitched (knitted) fabrics for laid-up fiberglass boatbuilding. Over time, there are some truly deep articles on marine finishes, adhesives and similar items, so the magazine is well worth a look when available. For those outside the business, it isn't going to come close to being worth the price, but it certainly is interesting.

RODALE PRESS, INC.
33 E. Minor Street
Emmaus, PA 18098
(800) 527-8200
(610) 967-8962 FAX
Organic Gardening Book Club
(215) 967-5171
Rodale's Home Improvement Book Club
(800) 678-5661

Rodale Press offers a wide line of woodworking and home improvement how-to books, covering both techniques and projects. Most of the books are sold through direct mail, and Rodale usually offers its own credit plan. They've got more than a few good ones on the lists found in the *Organic Gardening Book Club Bulletin* and *Rodale's Home Improvement Bulletin*. Write to the Customer Satisfaction department at the above address, or call for a list of current publications and videos.

SHOPNOTES
Woodsmith Corporation
2200 Grand Avenue
Des Moines, IA 50312
(800) 444-7527

ShopNotes was a new magazine, seeming a bit pricey for length and type, with our first edition. Individual issues are $4.95 at present, a one-year, six-issue subscription is still $19.95. The magazine is in its third year and is pretty sharply defined in aim: You and your woodworking shop, in the form of techniques, tools and projects that assist in the proper use of tools. As the address shows, it's put out by the folks at *Woodsmith*, and it has something of the same classic feel (same editor, Don Peschke, same executive editor, Doug Hicks, and much of the same staff). *ShopNotes* does use some four-color, and more spot color, however. It isn't pricey except on the basis of bulk: You're getting a no-advertising publication here, so all thirty-two pages of it is meat. Currently, one article tells how to build a sliding table for your table

saw, a useful accessory that costs hundreds of dollars, and more, but should assemble at maybe one hundred bucks as shown. The issue includes details on mortising for hinges and a piece on general chisel techniques, which is a handy basics piece that's often ignored. Also featured is a bandsaw circle jig that looks interesting to build and use. The shop tote piece shows a small fastener or other small part carrier built in two levels. Each issue is filled with similar plans and instruction, though Don Peschke says it took six months to simplify the sliding-table design enough to make it sensible. If you've got a use for any of a wide variety of jigs or shop aids, this is the magazine to consider.

SHOW BUSINESS
The Art & Craft Show Guild for the Southeast
P.O. Box 26624
Jacksonville, FL 32226
(904) 757-3913
(904) 751-1437 FAX

Although it's not slick and pretty, it is *the* place to find out about shows and similar goings-on throughout the Southeast—and *Show Business* also skips around a bit. The issue I received from editor and publisher LaVerne Herren covered a lot more than the Southeast: You can find listings from San Francisco; Chicago; St. Paul; West Springfield, Massachusetts; Rosemont, Illinois; Columbus, Ohio; Valley Forge; Dallas; Savannah, Georgia; Greenville, South Carolina; and Jacksonville, Florida. Shows are dated and then rated on the basis of how many attended the preceding year, how many are expected next time, types of crafts and arts, and fees; addresses and phone numbers are provided. A single year is $18 ($19.08 if you live in Florida) for a dozen issues, well worth the expense for anyone involved in craft shows. Listings in *Show Business* are free for shows. The issue I have outlines shows through almost a full year, and I expect any holes will be filled by upcoming issues. There's also a Promoter's Corner for promoters who put on several shows. The classified ads show sources for crafts, including wholesale blanks for various shirts, silk dyes, and a woodworkers craft shop for sale. If you do craft shows in the Southeast or into the Northeast and Midwest and northern California, I don't see how you can do without this collection.

TODAY'S WOODWORKER
P.O. Box 6782
Syracuse, NY 13217-9916

Someday I'll figure out how a magazine produced in

Rogers, Minnesota, is more efficiently mailed from and has its lists handled in Syracuse, New York. Whatever the case, it is a common method today to have the subscription department hundreds or thousands of miles away from the editorial people. At this time, it seems to work, as this sponsored publication (The Woodworker's Store is its parent) booms through its fifth year presenting very clear plans and tips of varying difficulty levels. A single-year subscription price of $21.95 is sometimes discounted for new subscribers (currently $18.95), so check before ordering. The magazine is very nicely done, in full color on slick paper, with at least one (two in the issue I'm looking at) nicely presented and printed, full-sized plan in each issue.

THE TOOL MERCHANT

208 Front Street
P.O. Box 227
Marietta, OH 45750
(614) 373-9973

John Walter owns and runs *The Tool Merchant* and sent me copies of his book and several of his magazines (*Stanley Tool Collector News*). This guy may have forced me into a new hobby—tool collecting. *Stanley Tool Collector News* is a triannual and goes for a single-copy price of $6.95, according to current literature. It costs $20 for a year's subscription. John's book, *Antique & Collectible Stanley Tools*, provides an excellent identification and price guide for Stanley tools that is a read-'em-and-weep sort of history. For example, consider that a set of a dozen 452-socket chisels made in the years 1927 to 1935 is worth as much as $125; the true mental bleeding, however, comes from looking at the selection of tools made over the years and no longer manufactured because of lack of demand. Ouch! Stanley has just begun making the Bailey series of planes again, and in profusion seldom seen on the plane front in recent years: The listings in John Walter's book show items such as the Boston-New Britain models from 1869, as well as many others. If you're at all interested in old tools, the book is $24.95, and there is a recommended book list in brochure form that provides a wide and wild variety of books on old tools. The pocket edition is eleven bucks postpaid, and still covers over one thousand tools, with five hundred illustrations in its one hundred sixty pages. The list is free, and *The Tool Merchant* accepts MasterCard and Visa.

WEEKEND WOODCRAFTS

1320 Galaxy Way
Concord, CA 94520

In this 1992 start-up from EGW Publishing, there are no shop tips or hints, but the forty-eight-page bimonthly (six issues per year, for $14.97 at the moment) offers a string of easily built projects. There are ten in the issue I'm checking, with everything done in color, and full-size "Pull-Out Plans" for some projects. Projects are all simple, or small, enough to be built in a single weekend. It's well worth a check if your interest is in fast projects, particularly those that might prove salable in craft fairs. The crafts projects, let me note, are small, but not necessarily tiny: Seats and toolboxes abound, as do small tables and toys.

WEEKEND WOODWORKING PROJECTS

1716 Locust Street
Des Moines, IA 50336
(800) 678-2666

Subscription price currently is $27.97 for this bimonthly (six issues per year, in January, March, May, July, September and November) from Meredith Corporation. Featuring half-a-dozen easy-to-make, or small, projects every other month, the magazine has presented a collector's cabinet, a bass puzzle, and an Adirondack table and footstool, plus a cutout cottontail box, a lathed letter opener and a stand-up mirror all in a single issue. Using double covers, the staff managed to work in a short tip feature between covers, with other tips (related to included projects) as needed. Nicely done in four colors, with a four-color cover, this is another publication that is well worth a look for those of you interested in small, faster-to-build projects (though I have to admit the collector's cabinet, of cherry and with porcelain knobs, is large enough and complex enough you'd best not be planning on spending major time outside the workshop on the weekend you build it).

WINDMILL PUBLISHING

2147 Windmill View Road
El Cajon, CA 92020
(619) 448-5390

Windmill Publishing doesn't have a big book list, but it does offer two books that may be of interest to many woodworkers, one as a semijoke, and the other for tool collectors. The joke book is Ron Barlow's *The Vanishing American Outhouse*, a look at that once-vaunted form of building, with privy plans enough for any purpose. I love the color shot of the brick seats at the Paxton Brick Factory, built about 1910. Modern sanitary methods are presented with the plans ($15.95 plus $2 postage). Ron also wrote *The Antique Tool Collector's Guide to Value*, a book that presents many old catalog shots and drawings of tools along with current values: Lufkin's tinsmith rule, circa 1890, is worth about $115. Stanley's London 1885 two-foot, fourfold ivory rule brought $275 at auction. A boxwood two-foot, twofold with brass arch joint, circa 1909, is worth $50 ($12.95 plus $2 postage). Other Windmill Publishing books cover running an antique business ($9.95 plus $2 postage), and Victorian housewares, hardware and kitchenware ($19.95 plus $2 postage), plus an illustrated history of the vanishing American barbershop ($16.95 plus $2 postage). Send check or money order; no charge cards are accepted.

WOOD

Wood Customer Service
P.O. Box 55050
Boulder, CO 80322-5050
(800) 374-9663

One of what has become a multitude of very well-done woodworking magazines in recent years, Better Homes & Gardens' *Wood* presents everything from simple projects to complex plans, as well as tips, tool tests, tested jigs, shop hints, on up and down a long list of various useful articles. Some of the project articles are among the most attractive to be found without extra complexity, though the projects are plenty detailed: That is, the plans can be readily followed by most intermediate woodworkers with patience and time to work things out. Some may even be readily accomplished by lower-end intermediate woodworkers, and a few will work for novices. Simpler projects show up in *Wood*'s companion magazine, *Weekend Woodworking Projects*. The magazine completes all project plans in its own shop, described as state-of-the-art. Tool article advice has improved. It started as fact-sheet stuff, but now some use testing and opinion is included. *Wood* is the largest of the woodworking magazines in terms of circulation, having gone past 650,000. Currently running nine issues a year, the magazine's yearly subscription cost is $25. It's best to call to check latest subscription prices.

WOOD STROKES

1320 Galaxy Way
Concord, CA 94520

This bimonthly publication joins *Weekend Woodcrafts* in EGW Publishing's stable of craft magazines (the company also puts out *Veggie Life* and *Tole World*, showing that it's mostly crafts devoted, but not completely . . . at least I don't think vegetable recipes fall under crafts). This one is aimed at those among us who produce woodworking projects that are to be painted. The magazine features designs and patterns for wood painting, with easy instructions

and full-sized patterns. The price for the first six issues is $14.97.

WOODENBOAT MAGAZINE

P.O. Box 492
Mount Morris, IL 61054-9852
(800) 877-5284

The above is the subscription department's address, because this twenty-year-old magazine is edited out of the same complex near Brooklin, Maine, that WoodenBoat Store, WoodenBoat Schools and *Professional Boatbuilder* call home [P.O. Box 78, Brooklin, ME 04616; (207) 359-4651; (207) 359-8920 FAX]. I have been there only once but will go again shortly. I anticipate liking it even more than the first time, when I was very impressed with the abiding interest—bordering strongly on love—in their respective crafts that I perceived in most of the employees. And the place is lovely, with old buildings put to what are now traditional uses. (I'm not a boating nut, though I was born and raised in a waterfront area. If you are interested in woodworking as it bears on making boats, whether it's building a ship's wheel or building a complete boat of wood, you must get this magazine. The issue I am looking at offers a great article on using spruce for spars and a fine review of "Steambending for Woodworkers," a video that could well be of general interest (Northwoods Canoe Co., RFD 3, Box 118, Dover-Foxcroft, ME 04426). There is a final article on building a shellback dinghy, and much else, including a look at San Francisco's wooden tugboats. Tool reviews also run, as do looks at historical wooden boats, balancing boat rigging, planking, wood technology, new designs, and an amazing amount of other material. Subscription price is currently $24.95 for a year that brings six issues.

WOODSHOP NEWS

35 Pratt Street
Essex, CT 06426

An annual subscription price of $12.97, for six issues, brings this working woodshop newspaper, for serious amateurs and professionals alike. The magazine is well worthwhile if your interest in woodworking comes even close to bordering on doing professional work. Check the current subscription price before ordering.

WOODSMITH

Woodsmith Corporation
2200 Grand Avenue
Des Moines, IA 50312
(800) 333-5075

Published bimonthly (six issues per year), *Woodsmith* offers plans, tips and notes for a wide variety of projects. This is another older magazine, with almost fifteen years in business. The back issue I'm staring at right now has a super display-cabinet project and a sewing box. One is large and complex; the other, small and moderate. The magazine tends to offer two, but no more than four, projects per issue, in almost extreme detail. In addition, there will be a number of tip articles, and often a jig or two, all related to the main and subsidiary projects in some way. Tool tips are also offered, though seldom in the form of full-scale tests of tools. Like its companion, *Shop-Notes*, *Woodsmith* offers thirty-two pages of well-done woodworking information, in a lush two-color format (brown is the second color, for a black-and-brown look that, on dark ivory paper, gives the magazine the appearance of a sepia-toned classic). The only advertising is a supplemental catalog in each issue, for supplies for whatever projects are featured in that issue. Usually this involves hardware, but it may include formed plastic parts, tools (especially bits), books, binders, and so on. The catalog portion of the business has grown quite considerably of late, and the catalog supplements also carry material on making shelves, joints, etc., which makes them almost impossible to discard. A single year is $17.95 (call for the latest price information).

WOODWORK

Ross Periodicals, Inc.
33 Redwood Drive
P.O. Box 1529
Ross, CA 94957
(415) 382-0580

Use the post-office-box address above for subscriptions to this bimonthly woodworking magazine of high quality. The magazine offers well-illustrated projects, ranging from small boxes made in various interesting ways to larger projects—a nice looking, easy-to-build daybed is featured in the issue I have. In addition, there are tips, book reviews, and other departments to keep interest high. Instructional articles by Graham Blackburn highlight the issues of *Woodwork*. A subscription costs $17 per year.

WOODWORKER

F&W Publications, Inc.
1507 Dana Avenue
Cincinnati, OH 45207
(800) 925-6241
(513) 531-2690
(513) 531-1843 FAX

Now under the same ownership as *Popular Woodworking*, *Woodworker* is undergoing dramatic improvement. A recent change to full-color throughout and emphasis on clear step-by-step instruction in both words and pictures is sure to be received warmly by beginning to intermediate woodworkers. The projects tend to be the kind easily completed in a weekend or two but are high-quality and will provide a great feeling of accomplishment. New techniques are clearly and thoroughly explained to help woodworkers master the efficient use of time and tools. *Woodworker* also features product and book reviews, idea files, shop notes, an event calendar and resource directory. Subscriptions cost $19.97 for one year (six issues) and $39.94 for two years (twelve issues).

WOODWORKER'S BOOK CLUB

F&W Publications, Inc.
1507 Dana Avenue
Cincinnati, OH 45207
(800) 937-0963
(513) 531-8250
(513) 531-4744 FAX

Each month you'll get a catalog describing up to one hundred books for woodworkers in all areas at all skill levels. Every book is discounted 15 to 20 percent off the retail price, so you can really save some money. Give them a call or drop a line for free information and to find out what the current joining offer is. Currently it's two free books with a third for just $8.95 with no obligation to buy anymore books, which is a great deal for any book club to offer.

WOODWORKER'S JOURNAL

P.O. Box 1790
Peoria, IL 61656

The Woodworker's Journal is one of the oldest of the top woodworking magazines—and it is definitely one of the top group. Currently in its eighteenth year, the magazine presents exceptionally interesting and well-designed projects covering a wide range of interests and skill levels. Drawings are nicely done, and photography is attractive and clear, if not lush (I'd rather have attractive and clear in a magazine presenting do-it-yourself information). The six bimonthly issues cost $19.95. *WWJ* has been recently sold, and is now published by PJS Publications, Inc., at the above address. So far, changes don't seem immense, and the magazine remains one of the clearest and most interesting of an ever-improving group.

WORKBENCH

KC Publishing, Inc.
700 West 47th Street, Suite 310
Kansas City, MO 64112

Workbench is primarily a woodworking magazine, but it often includes other projects for around the house (shingling, drywall and similar projects). Each issue contains several project articles, some easy, some complex: The issue I have in front of me offers four projects, two of which are medium-to-hard and two of which are easy. All appear interesting, with good instructions and clear illustrations. This bi-monthly magazine is nicely done, and has been around for a long time—almost fifty years. There are also tip departments, a problem-solving department and technique articles. *Workbench* also sells an extensive line of books and a large number of its own plans. A one-year subscription costs $12.95.

CATALOGS

ARMOR

P.O. Box 445
East Northport, NY 11731
(800) 292-8296
(516) 462-6228
(516) 462-5793 FAX

John Capotosto writes that, for my readers, he's reducing the standard $1 catalog price to zero. That was the second nice surprise in John's package: The seventy-two-page catalog is not just of plans but also contains many small tools, finishes, furniture trim, hardware and other items, plus four pages of books (in which John has forgone the temptation to include mostly his and brother Rosario's woodworking titles, of which there are many). The book selection, like the plan selection, is very wide for the number of books listed. Clock plans range up to a 77" Washington Hall Clock from a simple outline-cut cowboy boot clock. John also offers a classic rolltop desk plan (with or without his parts kit), cheval mirror, gun cabinets, dry sinks, workbenches, tea carts, cradles, desks, children's outdoor furniture, billiard tables, table soccer plans, lamp plans, rocking horses, toys, vehicles, dollhouses (including kits), and on. Many of the plans are developments for John's articles in top do-it-yourself and craft magazines over the years and are well worth reviewing. The catalog is a must see.

BOB KAUNE

511 West 11th
Port Angeles, WA 98362
(206) 452-2292

Bob presents a selection of scarce, older complete working handtools for collectors and woodworkers. He carries hundreds of ready-to-use pre-1960 tools, including planes, scrapers, spokeshaves, chisels, saws, levels, rules and unusual items. For a current antique and used-tools list, send $3. For a five-list subscription, the cost is $10. Bob Kaune accepts MasterCard and Visa.

BROOKSTONE

5 Vose Farm Road
Peterborough, NH 03458
(800) 846-3000 Customer service
(603) 924-0093 FAX

For a long time, Brookstone has provided odd and interesting items—their catalog is called "Hard To Find Tools," but actually these days it seems to cover more of a hard-to-find anything, or odd items of interest to people who may or may not be so odd. A few things are of direct value to woodworkers, but others require either great imagination or a twisted mind to be classed as woodworking items. I like the catalog and have found the products I ordered to be as represented. An individual catalog costs $3, but if you are included on their mailing list, you will receive them free. Brookstone accepts MasterCard and Visa.

EDMUND SCIENTIFIC

101 East Gloucester
Pike Barrington, NJ 08007
(609) 573-6260

The free catalog from Edmund Scientific offers varied parts that are not woodworking materials or tools but that often are useful in setting up jigs or preparing projects. There is a multitude of small parts, from lenses to latches to almost anything you can imagine that might at some time or another come in handy. It's a gadgeteer's delight.

JAPAN WOODWORKER

1731 Clement Avenue
Alameda, CA 94501
(510) 521-1810
(800) 537-7820

Not only are there extensive lines of Japanese woodworking tools in this catalog (two-year subscription for $1.50), but the book lines for Japanese woodworking concepts are also extensive. The company is the original importer of Japanese woodworking tools and a principal supplier today. There are many top-quality tools of American make in the catalog, too, including Starret measuring tools, Veritas tools, Fein corner

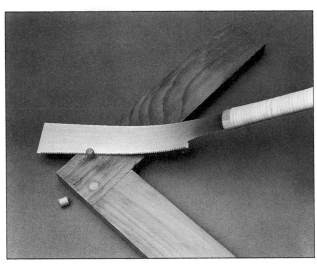

Japanese saws work on the pull stroke, opposite their European-inspired counterparts.

sanders, CMT saw blades, router bits, Radi-Planes and others. You may find yourself selecting from Starrett (truly precise measuring tools, generally meant for machine-shop use but great for woodworking uses as well), Lie-Nielson, Veritas, Akafuji Kanna, Dai, Shizen, Sadakuzura, Hock, Bridge City Tool Works and Razorsaw. I have used enough Japanese tools to be impressed with their superb cutting characteristics, and I've never found anything that begins to come close to Japanese waterstones for sharpening ease and results on almost any edged tool—knives, chisels, plane irons all benefit strongly from a two- or three-step process on the stones. Using the king stone gives a chromelike polish to the tool. The Japan Woodworker takes American Express, MasterCard, Visa and Discover.

KLEIN DESIGN, INC.
17910 Southeast 110th Street
Renton, WA 98059
(206) 226-5937

Klein Design produces two miniature lathes, one of which is a full-pattern lathe with a 12″ bed length. The other is a short bed model. In addition, many jigs and tools are available for the lathes (threading jigs, scroll chuck, custom jaws, indexing system, hole-drilling guides, and so on). This firm also sells videos on lathe use; a series of five covers just about everything you wish to know about miniature turning, down to using unusual materials—horn, bone, cast polyester, mother of pearl, Corian and others—to making turned boxes with threaded lids. Klein Design also offers lathe tools as well as tools for scale modelers. Bonnie lists a number of her tools as perfect for the doll-house builder, but other miniature-makers

also will see some great possibilities in her brochure. Call or drop a note for the latest brochure and price lists. Klein Design takes MasterCard and Visa.

MANNY'S WOODWORKER'S PLACE
602 South Broadway
Lexington, KY 40508
(606) 255-5444

Give Manny a call to check on his list of woodworking books and videos. The list is very extensive, and the catalog costs $2. Manny's takes most credit cards.

NELSON DESIGNS
P.O. Box 422
Dublin, NH 03444
(603) 563-3306

John Nelson recently started offering advanced, full-sized, scroll saw plans, projects and books by mail. His offerings include original 1880 scroll saw patterns from New England: toys, clocks, wall shelves, corner shelves, mirrors and much more. John states that he and his wife, Joyce, have taken most of their patterns from fretwork designs in New England; most of the fretwork dates from the 1880 to 1935 era. I have several of John's books, and if his patterns follow his writing and illustration, they will be excellent and easy to use, though I'll also bet that when he says *advanced*, beginners had best not apply! Pattern prices currently start at $2 for a plant stand and rise to $18 for a merry-go-round with sixteen horses. John also sells a selection of his own books. At the moment, John and Joyce don't take any credit cards, but they hope to reach that stage shortly.

NEMY ELECTRIC TOOL CO.
7635-A Auburn Blvd.
Citrus Heights, CA 95610
(916) 723-1088
(916) 969-1088
(916) 723-1091 FAX

Bill Nemy runs a business that was founded in 1945 and is in its ninth year in its current location. Nemy Electric Tool Company is one of the larger woodworking machinery dealers in northern California. As such, it serves the professional community, the hobbyist, wood-carvers and the cottage-industry woodworker. They also do job-shop work for restoration and antique dealers, and repair tools. Nemy offers classes in woodworking, wood carving, production techniques, stair building and other skills, while also being a local sponsor of *The New Yankee Workshop*, on PBS. Bill has a Woodworks, Volume I, video out, "Arched

Raised Panels," projected as the first of a series of thirteen. The video, which is eighty-three minutes long, details building raised panels with a router and router table. Nemy's catalog is $2.50, and his newsletter, "Woodworker's Bulletin," is free. Nemy Electric Tools accepts Discover, MasterCard and Visa.

RJS CUSTOM WOODWORKING
P.O. Box 12354
Kansas City, KS 66112

My listing for RJS started out noting they had toy carousel plans, but when I received their most recent catalog (printed on recycled paper, with a request that it be recycled after a new catalog arrives), I noted that plans—even excellent full-sized carousel plans and plans for dream-car plaques (if your dream car is a Ferrari or a Rolls)—are only a part of the line. Add books, from Patrick Speilman's varied treatises on scroll saws and routers and their uses to R.J. De Cristoforo's array of power-tool books (Cris's are among the best done to date). Also included are publications on wiring your own home, as well as a great many parts and pieces for projects, plus small tools. There are even stencils of many patterns, words and letters (I believe most of these are Dover patterns).

THE ROCKING HORSE SHOP
9 Spring Street
St. Jacobs, Ontario
Canada N0B 2N0
(519) 664-1661

This is an intriguing catalog—small, but full of information for any rocking-horse enthusiast. The catalog leads with an offer of *The Rocking-Horse Maker*, by Anthony Dew, and you quickly learn that that book is the source for the plans in the catalog. The original company is British, and this Canadian rep sells plans for swinger rocking horses (plain and elaborate), a toddler's rocking horse that can be very simple (cutout head) or more complex (carved head). There are a number of plans for full-carved rocking horses; a video on making rocking horses; accessory kits for all offered plans; and even two dollhouse plans (one Victorian, one Georgian). Other books on rocking horses are offered. John Wombwell claims this St. Jacobs outfit is the most comprehensive supplier of rocking-horse plans, accessories and books, and I see no reason to doubt that statement. All accessories are handmade and include real horsehair manes and tails, cast brass stirrups and other parts, and real leather saddles and reins. In addition, phone help is available to customers. The catalog costs $2.50, and

The Rocking Horse Shop takes American Express, Optima and Visa.

SEYCO
1414 Cranford Drive
Box 472749
Garland, TX 75047-2749
(800) 462-3353
(214) 278-3353

This scroll saw specialist has a $1 catalog that features the Excalibur line of saws, their own line of letter guides, and many books and patterns for scroll saw people. Seyco also offers its own brand of blade clamps, some general accessories such as finishes, glues, blade storage tubes, and turned parts for projects, as well as an extremely extensive line of scroll saw blades. Seyco takes MasterCard and Visa.

SUN DESIGNS
173 East Wisconsin Avenue
Oconomowoc, WI 53066
(414) 567-4255

Sun Designs is a small company producing design books and construction plans for yard and other projects. The Strom Toy is considered a classic of toy design and making and is one of the products from Sun. Janet Strombeck kindly sent along blueprints for the Victoria, a truly lovely sleigh, and a copy of *Timeless Toys in Wood* for me to examine. If I still lived in an area with decent amounts of winter weather—snow, for example—I'd quickly build the Victoria, then go further and produce the Bunker Hill sled. Even without a local winter wonderland, I find a sufficiency of toy plans: The engine and coal car in *Timeless Toys*, for example, are large enough to provide riding models for small children, but they have few enough accessories and other cars that a woodworking parent or grandparent is not too busy to enjoy the child, too. The designs shown in *Gazebos and Other Garden Structures* will keep many a woodworker or carpenter employed for a long period. *Gazebos* is an idea book; plans for the most part are available as extra attractions, at varying prices (birdhouse or feeder plans, for example, are about $5.95 each—buy more, get a discount per plan; gazebo plans are $24.95 each). You'll see drawings in some of the plans, many of which are ornate and correspondingly difficult to build. Others are less ornate and less difficult to erect. The four-color brochure is fifty cents. Sun Designs also mail-orders accessory packages for their toy designs.

TAUNTON PRESS

63 South Main Street Box 355
Newtown, CT 06470
(800) 888-8286 Orders
(203) 426-8171

The Taunton Press offers a line of excellent videos and books, as well as a top woodworking magazine (*Fine Woodworking*). *Fine Woodworking* presents exactly what it says, fine woodworking, in a large-format magazine, often luxuriously photographed (the projects are often luxurious in appearance, too), with sometimes strong emphasis on the artistic edge the craft often enjoys. The tips and hints columns are among the best of all top woodworking magazines, and editing and writing are good. Taunton Press also publishes books that are reprints of articles from *Fine Woodworking* and original books, as well as some of the strongest woodworking videos produced. Free catalogs are available, and Taunton Press takes American Express, MasterCard and Visa.

TREND-LINES

375 Beacham Street
Chelsea, MA 02150
(800) 366-6966 Catalog request number
(800) 767-9999
(800) 877-3338 Automated speed ordering
(617) 889-2072 FAX

Trend-Lines is a discount mail-order house that offers many plans and project books, plus general woodworking books. Their free catalog presents more than 3,000 brand-name products, including power tools and accessories, hand tools, screws, hardware and wood parts in addition to the plans and books. Stan Black always has interesting plans listed, and he often includes some new tools; this catalog packs a lot of interest for woodworkers. Complete satisfaction is guaranteed, and Trend-Lines guarantees also to sell any power tool or accessory for less than any nationally advertised mail-order price. You'll even find contractor's ladder jacks in this catalog! Trend-Lines takes Discover, MasterCard and Visa.

WOODWORKERS' STORE

21801 Industrial Boulevard
Rogers, MN 55374-9514
(800) 279-4441
(612) 428-3200 Orders and customer service
(612) 428-3298 Technical service
(612) 428-8668 FAX

The Woodworkers' Store carries a wide line of plans, books, small power tools, hand tools, woods, fin-ishes, jigs, kits, and a very wide line of hardware, including many porcelain parts, oak and birch carvings, and even briefcase handles in two quality levels (the cheaper is covered in vinyl, the more costly in leather). Plans include dollhouses, whirligigs, desks, rocking toys, entertainment centers, tool centers, cedar chests, and a number of cradles. You'll also find a large line of locks for jewelry boxes, chests, drawers and general cabinets, as well as plenty of knockdown fasteners. Currently unique is their line of workshop knobs in black plastic or aluminum, in five styles, and in many more sizes. The knobs make building your own shop jigs a great deal easier, as do some other new kits in the most recent catalog. The Woodworkers' Store is another company that sends smaller update catalogs with some frequency, so your $3 buys a great deal of information. They accept American Express, Discover, MasterCard and Visa.

WOODHAVEN

5323 West Kimberly Road
Davenport, IA 52806
(800) 344-6657
(319) 391-2386
(319) 391-1275 FAX

Woodhaven is a fairly old (now well past a decade) mail-order house for router bits, tables and general router supplies. The newest catalog is more colorful than the one Brad Witt sent a couple years ago, and it shows a wider line of router tables and tabletops. The claim is now that they offer the widest line of router tables and accessories, and I see no reason to dispute the claim. And Woodhaven now offers a plate inlay template for use with Woodhaven base plates: The plate template is inexpensive and will accept either size of Woodhaven plate, with plate levelers (or you can sand down edges to size another brand of plate). Hinge, lockset and strike plate mortise jigs are also offered, as are fences, angle brackets, and a slew of interesting items for the router-using woodworker. I want to get hold of their video "Frame & Panel Secrets." The catalog is available on video, though it costs $14.99 that way. For circle-cutting jigs, vacuum clamp kits, Keller dovetailing jigs, Beall wood threaders, and an array of other items, this catalog offers much of interest to the woodworker. One such item is the Know-Bit. This is not much more than a pointed metal dowel, with the point set to the top when inserted in a router. It then serves as an exact centering device for router, drill press or lathe. It is machined perfectly straight and round, so it also makes a good run-out check when used with a dial indicator. Chuck it into your drill press or router or lathe, and quickly and simply measure the run-out (wobble). The catalog is free by bulk mail, $3 if you want it sent first class. Woodhaven takes Discover, MasterCard and Visa.

WOODPECKERS, INC.
8318 Manorford Drive
Parma, OH 44129
(800) 752-0725
(216) 888-9463 FAX

Woodpeckers is the sole demonstrator of Incra Jig Products at thirty woodworking shows each year. They are also developers of the heaviest commercially manufactured router table, and they organize Incra classes across the nation. They will send brochures on request, and they take MasterCard, Visa and Discover.

SCHOOLS

THE ARTISANS SCHOOL
P.O. Box 539
Rockport, ME 04856
(207) 236-6071
(207) 236-8367 FAX

The Artisans School specializes in high-quality training for professional artists, builders, and others who wish to become skilled artisans. The two-year associate's degree program uses yacht construction as the focus for an interdisciplinary curriculum the school says integrates manual, small business and academic skills. Emphasis is on woodworking as it relates to boatbuilding and design as it relates to the same goal. There are also year-long, three-year and six-week residencies and internships, in addition to the degree program. The current age range of students is eighteen to forty-six, with students having had to complete high school or its equivalent. The school is college certified by the state of Maine and accepts transfer credits from most schools and colleges. The Artisans School offers a free catalog for a call to the Admissions Office.

BEREA COLLEGE CRAFTS
CPO 2347
Berea, KY 40404

You may write Berea College for more information on their crafts program or send $2 for their color crafts catalog. Berea has long been recognized as one of the top crafts schools, providing a top liberal arts education as well (as my oldest step-daughter can attest,

with her honors degree in Latin). The school offers a special chance for students to experience what it is to work for what one gets: There are no charges for tuition and fees, with expenses, including at least part of room and board, met by student earnings. Every student works at least ten to fifteen hours weekly while carrying a full academic course load. The crafts program began in 1893, with the Fireside Weaving course, and now includes Weaving and Needlecraft, Ceramics, Broomcraft and Wrought Iron. The Woodcraft program is renowned throughout the industry. In all craft courses, students work side-by-side with master craftspersons.

COLLEGE OF THE REDWOODS
440 Alger Street
Fort Bragg, CA 95437
(707) 964-7056

Courses in fine cabinetmaking directed by James Krenov and Michael Burns are featured. Call or write for information.

DAVID ORTH ARCHITECTURAL FURNITURE
1107 Chicago Avenue
Oak Park, IL 60302
(708) 383-4399

Orth offers Chicago-area apprenticeships. This is a furniture studio, and the students are apprenticed for one year, with no tuition and no salary. The concept covers five days a week of woodworking starting in early January and early July, and at the end of a year's apprenticeship, the student will have built at least half-a-dozen furniture projects. To date, all graduates of the program are employed in the woodworking industry. The information packet costs $10.

DOVETAIL JOINT
1332 Harlem Road
Rockford, IL 61103
(815) 965-6677

Write for information on five-day classes in Windsor chair making and Shaker furniture workshops taught by Peter Cullum. Pete didn't provide tuition figures, but he will on your copy of the brochure. Tuition includes five nights' lodging, and meals served at the Cullum home. Pete teaches hand- and foot-operated tool methods, and students get to use his shop full of such tools. Class size is small for maximum one-on-one instruction, so there is no need for students to already be expert woodworkers.

HAYWOOD COMMUNITY COLLEGE
Production Crafts—Wood Dept.
Att.: Wayne Raab, Woodworking Instructor
Freedlander Drive
Clyde, NC 28721
(704) 627-4673

Haywood is a regionally accredited college on an 83-acre campus and even runs its own commercial-sized sawmill and dry kiln; it also has a 320-acre teaching forest. A degree is offered in Production Crafts, which includes woodworking as one of its four curriculum areas: clay, fiber, jewelry, wood. The wood major covers everything from hand tooling and mechanical drawing on to an independent thesis project, after the student has been through framing construction and advanced joinery, chair design and construction, small scale production design, and carcase design and construction. Drop Wayne Raab a note, or give a call and ask for a catalog and other details.

HYMILLER SCHOOL OF FINE FINISHING & HAND JOINERY
Route 2, Box 243A
Sparta, TN 38583
(615) 738-5706

John Hymiller offers an impressive list of references for the school he teaches. From his other advertising, he appears to specialize in restoration of truly messed-up antiques, but he also builds and finishes fine furniture when not teaching. The course offered, fine finishing, repair and hand joinery, is two weeks long, with the first week devoted to everything from marketing through fine finishing in lacquer. The student finishes four miniature tabletops as examples of his or her work. Week two moves from sharpening to cabinet scrapers to hand-cut dovetails, mortises and tenons, and making proper glue joints. Courses are limited to three students for direct, hands-on supervision. Currently, the price is $950 per week, including materials.

JAMES L. COX SCHOOL OF WOODWORKING
RD 2, Beaver Dam Road
Honey Brook, PA 19344
(610) 273-3840

The purpose of the two-day course offered by Jim Cox is to form a basis from which lathe work can be practiced and learned. The class days run from 8:30 A.M. to 5 P.M., and include lathe work; recognition and working characteristics of wood; sharpening techniques for lathe tools; and sanding, finishing and joinery for the project done. The pace is set for the individual student, and there are no more than two students at any one time. The fee is currently $250, with $50 due when the date is requested and the remaining $200 due at time of registration. All needed supplies are included in the fee—unless the student wants an exotic wood—so goggles, wood, lunches, and even coffee breaks are covered. Accommodations are at one of a group of nearby inns and motels. No credit cards are accepted.

JOHN WILSON
500 East Broadway Highway
Charlotte, MI 48813
(517) 543-5325

John is the modern-day torch bearer for Shaker oval boxes, and he offers everything from instruction sheets to the kits to make the boxes, right up to and including the correct kind of toothpicks to use as pegging. A typical Shaker oval-box kit will include materials for the lid, box bands bent to shape, and wood for the bottom, plus an instruction sheet. You need only provide wood glue, a saw that will cut an oval, 120- and 220-grit sandpaper and clear finish. He has his own video, and a line of tools and accessories and patterns that makes the overall job a great deal simpler. John also has a pattern packet that presents more than two dozen oval boxes and carriers, and he offers workshops at specific intervals during the year—and at varied places, so you don't always have to be in Michigan to learn to make oval boxes. Give him a call or drop a note to check prices of current literature and workshops. Check the Woodcraft catalog for some of the kits and products John has specifically designed.

NORTH BENNET STREET SCHOOL
39 North Bennet Street
Boston, MA 02113
(617) 227-0155

North Bennet Street School offers a number of craftsmanship programs, with a stated goal of craftsmanship for all programs. Cabinetmaking and furniture making programs find the student learning of furniture construction with hand and power tools; the course itself is a series of projects. Students start with a set of detail drawings of joints and go on to drawings of full-scale furniture. Bench work and machine operation phases come next, with the student developing fundamental hand skills in use of planes, chisels and lathes. Each student builds a tool chest. The student then goes on to design and build at least one table, a chair, and a piece of case work. Students provide their own hand tools, wood, hardware and finishing materials. All customary power tools and equipment are provided, as are workbenches and wood storage space. There are also carpentry and preservation carpentry courses, as well as violin making and restoration courses. The school has existed since 1885, and it operates out of an early nineteenth-century brick building. Tuition for all courses is broken down into monthly payments, and estimated tool costs are available for each course (currently, the cabinetmaking and furniture making course takes about $1,250 in hand tools and a wood cost of about $1,000, and tuition is $8,800 per year for two years). Violin making and restoration is a three-year course, with some tuition offset by the expected sale of instruments built by the student. Students range in age from seventeen to about seventy, and there are scholarships, Pell Grants, various loan programs, Stafford loans, and other college aid sources available. David Brewster is Director of Admissions, and his office will see that you get a catalog and all relevant material.

NORTHWEST SCHOOL OF WOODEN BOATBUILDING

251 Otto Street
Port Townsend, WA 98368
(206) 385-4948
(206) 385-5089 FAX

The Northwest School of Wooden Boatbuilding offers a variety of one-week seminars and weekend workshops, plus a six-month core program. The six-month program currently lists as $3,950, with a $300 application fee, of which $200 is applied to the tuition and $100 is nonrefundable. Seminars are five to six days long, at $300 each (plus $50 registration and varied text and materials costs). Workshops are listed at $35 each; they cover such subjects as steam bending, oar making, planking, interior joinery, wood turning, spar making, tools and more. (You'll probably never learn more about joinery than when working on a boat, with any boat's odd angles and flowing curves and an ever-present need for extreme conservation of space.) Accreditation is from the Accrediting Commission of Career Schools/Colleges of Technology. If you are going to be or can be in the area for one or more of these workshops or seminars (small-boat construction and wooden boat repair are possibly of most interest to woodworkers), drop a line and ask for their catalog materials. The school takes Discover, Master-Card and Visa.

OREGON SCHOOL OF ARTS & CRAFTS

8245 Southwest Barnes Road
Portland, OR 97225
(503) 297-5544

Woodworking is but a single facet of the Oregon

Both students and instructors work hard on projects at the Oregon School of Arts & Crafts.

School of Arts & Crafts program, but the school offers both an open program and a certificate program in woodworking. Since 1906, the Oregon School has been offering arts and crafts classes and workshops. The Certificate program is one developed by artists, for artists; it takes three years and includes a business practices curriculum along with the arts curriculum. Additional subjects of value to the artist include grant writing and presenting and marketing work. There currently are ten woodworking courses listed, starting with first-year fundamentals and ending with individualized wood study. Write or call for information: Brochures and catalogs are free. Oregon School accepts MasterCard and Visa.

PETERS VALLEY CRAFT CENTER

19 Kuhn Road
Layton, NJ 07851
(201) 948-5200
(201) 948-5202 Craft store and gallery
(201) 948-0011 FAX

Peters Valley offers two- to eight-day woodworking workshops, in June, July and August. The related Peters Valley Craft Fair is now well over two decades old and is open to all original fine contemporary and traditional craft media, plus photography. Workshop room-and-board costs depend on length of stay, starting at $55 for the two-day and going to $410 for the ten-day. Likewise, tuition per course varies, with tuition for John Wilson's Shaker oval boxes course, two days long, being only $135, plus a $35 materials fee and a $15 membership fee (the membership fee exists for all courses). A course on making an acoustic guitar lasts eight days, with a tuition of $305 and a materials fee of $400. The course list seems interesting and well thought out, and if the other craftspersons are of the quality of John Wilson, certainly the expertise for fine teaching is there. Literature is free, and

Peters Valley Craft Center accepts both MasterCard and Visa.

PURDUE UNIVERSITY
Dept. of Forestry and Natural Resources
West Lafayette, IN 47907-1159
(317) 494-3590

Purdue offers a bunch of finishing seminars, lumber grading, workplace efficiency, wood machining, wood manufacturing and other wood and woodworking courses that are sometimes of interest for the hobby woodworker and always of interest to the pro. Give them a call or drop a note to get information on dates and places of various courses. Many of the courses for industrial types might be taken for overall content—it's kind of nice to know what the pros think of water-based polyurethane finishes, and HVLP (high volume, low pressure) spray application systems, particularly now that the price of hobby units has started dropping into a rational range. And there are other subjects that will also match up. If you live within swing distance of Indiana or Michigan (many of the courses are given in cooperation with Michigan State University), you may be interested.

ROCKINGHAM COMMUNITY COLLEGE (RCC)
P.O. Box 38
Wentworth, NC 27375
(910) 342-4261

The RCC fine and creative woodworking program is a two-year, daytime, full-time degree program. Scholarships and other aid are offered. In-state tuition is $15.25 per credit hour at this time, but out-of-state hours go for $109.50 each. Courses are offered in the basics, woods and their properties, right on to shop operation and management, passing through chair construction, furniture construction, fixtures, jigs and forms, and many other options.

SCHOOL OF CLASSICAL WOODCARVING
10 Liberty Ship Way
Sausalito, CA 94965

This school offers one-, two- and twelve-week courses in wood carving and stone carving for furniture and architecture. Write for information on costs and starting dates.

UNIVERSITY OF RIO GRANDE
College of Technology
Rio Grande, OH 45674
(614) 245-5353

The University of Rio Grande was established in 1876 and is an independent four-year university. There is also a community college division, and Ohio residents get a real break because of that during the first two years: Currently, each credit is $45 for residents of a four-county district. Those same credit hours are much more expensive for nonresidents; there's a complex residential setup. The College of Technology is of primary interest to woodworkers, where work through six quarters brings students from the simple introduction to woodworking through the completion of two furniture projects of some complexity. Also studied are production woodworking and small-business management. For anyone interested in woodworking as a career, this seems at least a place to investigate.

Woodenboat School gives in-depth instruction and hands-on experience.

WOODENBOAT SCHOOL
P.O. Box 78
Brooklin, ME 04616
(207) 359-4651
(207) 359-8920 FAX

If your interests cover any part of woodworking that is involved with water, then get the course catalog for this school run from the same complex near Brooklin, Maine, that WoodenBoat Store, *Wooden-Boat* magazine and *Professional Boatbuilder* call home. I have been there once and was impressed with the abiding interest—bordering strongly on love—in their respective crafts that I perceived in most of the employees. And the place is gorgeous, with old buildings put to what are now traditional uses. If you are interested in woodworking as it bears on making boats, you'll find courses ranging from fundamentals of woodworking for women (why not men?) to basic boatbuilding, to lofting, to building various small wooden boats. (The catalog I'm looking at offers courses in a 16' harbor skiff, "The Wee Lassie" [featherweight canoe], "Haven" 12½, DK-14 kayak, "Nutshell Pram" from a kit, Maine guide canoe, dory skiff, Norwegian sailing pram, 12′ fisherman's skiff, and a snipe.) In addition, there are courses in rigging, seamanship, navigation, sail, kayaking, marine mechanics and electronics, astronomy, marine painting and varnishing, basic woodworking for boatbuilding, joinery, and much else. Courses vary a bit in price, but the most costly is $800 for a two-week course (Building the "Haven" 12½), and most others are $450 or $500, plus materials where needed. Some courses have a materials cost, and some offer a raffle for the boat built by students. The maximum number of students in most courses at one time is ten. WoodenBoat also offers off-site courses in San Francisco and in southeast Alaska (Ketchikan). There's much more to tell, but let them do it. Drop a line, or give them a call and ask for the course catalog and brochure. WoodenBoat Schools takes Discover, Master-Card and Visa.

WORCESTER CENTER FOR CRAFTS

25 Sagamore Road
Worcester, MA 01605
(508) 753-8183

Call or write for the Professional Crafts catalog, describing two-year programs in woodworking and other crafts.

YESTERMORROW, INC.

Box 344
Warren, VT 05674
(802) 496-5545

Yestermorrow offers coordinated courses, with students learning design from designers and application from applicators—for example, architects teach building design, and contractors teach construction. Over the years, the original concept has been applied to a growing number of courses, now including a decently wide range of building-related trades and professions, including cabinetmaking, CAD training, shop assembly and other areas. Woodworking curriculum courses are one week long, geared to three levels of ability. Courses such as Cabinetry I, II and III start you at the beginning and may be stacked (II starts the day after I ends, if you want, but may also be taken later, with no delay moving into level III). Tuition and room and board for a week-long course is currently $1,025 (that includes breakfast, brown-bag lunches, and dinners). Faculty lists appear to emphasize design, though there's obviously a great deal of hands-on experience as well (for example, Dick Roberge has a bachelor's in fine arts, but runs his own cabinetmaking and woodworking shop and has studied with Tage Frid. John Connell founded the school in 1980; he holds a master's in architecture, is a licensed architect, and teaches at Yale's architectural school). Sounds very interesting.

Finishing

Finishing

COLOR TOUCH UP

DARWORTH COMPANY
3 Mill Pond Lane
P.O. Box 639
Simsbury, CT 06070
(800) 672-3499
(800) 624-7767
(800) 227-6095 FAX

FI:X Wood Patch and Touch Up Stik are two major products for repair and construction. The color Touch Up Stiks do minor touch-up jobs in a hurry, and the wood patch is made in red oak and white pine, plus ash, maple/alder, white, walnut, natural, pine, oak, dark mahogany/redwood, light mahogany and birch fir. The Wood Patch sands well and accepts stains uniformly. Darworth's new, heavy-duty construction adhesive, PolySeamSeal, works on most woods, drywall, foam boards and paneling. In the past, I've found this type of adhesive excellent for outdoor project reinforcement, which basically means Adirondack chairs and similar projects seem to last a good deal longer when adhesive and nails, or screws, are used, instead of just nails or screws. Call or write for further information.

EQUIPMENT AND TOOLS

ACCUSPRAY
23350 Mercantile Road
Cleveland, OH 44122
(800) 618-6860
(216) 595-6868 FAX

AccuSpray is one of the top makers of high-volume, low-air-pressure (HVLP) finishing equipment and supplies. These are not low-end systems and may be out of reach for most hobby woodworkers, but they might also be considered as rental units for important work. HVLP is becoming more important for small pro shops because of air-standards needs, as well as for eventual economy (much more of the finish ends up on the product, so, in time, the cost of the equipment is amortized there). Some of their guns are designed to be used with standard air compressors, reducing overall cost of stepping up to HVLP if you

AccuSpray's #10 handgun brings high volume, low pressure to shops with only high-pressure air compressors.

already have a compressor. Brochures are available upon request.

OUTDOOR TREATMENT

CUPRINOL PRODUCTS
Customer Service
14 Midland Building
101 Prospect
Cleveland, OH 44115
(800) 424-5837

Cuprinol is a familiar name to many of us who do a lot of outdoor projects. Their finishes are meant for outside, with oil-based siding stain a leader, but also with strong finishes in decks, clearing preservatives, and a new-look wood finish that cleans up with water. Cuprinol's No. 10 Green Preservative is for use on untreated outdoor woods or for treating cut ends of outdoor projects built with pressure-treated woods. For brochures on these and other Cuprinol products, call the 800 number. Cuprinol does not sell direct.

PRESERVATIVES

OSMOSE WOOD PRESERVING, INC.
P.O. Drawer O
Griffin, GA 30224
(404) 228-8431

Osmose is a major manufacturer of wood preservative chemicals, outdoor stains, sealers and cleaners, and it has its own line of deck screws. Osmose produces a wide line of brochures that include many project plans, including a garden bench, mailbox post, planter box, deck (12' × 16' freestanding), sandbox/play pool, gazebo, greenhouse classic picnic table, trash can corral and others. Osmose does not provide these items directly but does send them along to dealers, where you can pick them up.

STAR BRONZE COMPANY
803 South Mahoning
Alliance, OH 44601
(800) 321-9870

Along with Zip-Guard urethane Wood Finish, Star Bronze manufactures sanding eliminators, furniture refinishers, Zip-Strip paint and finish remover for water cleanup, interior and exterior wood stains, and wood preservative. Also available is Dekorator's Enamel in 2-ounce bottles. On request, they'll send a copy of their extensive booklet "Refinishing and Finishing," free of charge. The booklet provides good general information and details the use of many Star Bronze products.

SPRAY SYSTEMS

TIP SANDBLAST EQUIPMENT
7075 Rt. 446
P.O. Box 649
Canfield, OH 44406
(800) 321-9260
(216) 533-3384
(216) 533-2876 FAX

TiP Sandblast Equipment manufactures and sells the widest array of sand and glass blasting gear I've seen in recent years. Obviously, most of their gear is out of a woodworker's need range, but they've got some lighter-duty models that work well for woodworkers who use sandblasting. TiP also produces a turbine painting system that has a low-end model that is right on line with better-quality, low-end models: Another name for turbine spray systems is *high volume, low pressure,* or *HVLP.* HVLP is the coming thing in all types of sprayed finishes: It is actually economical, because there is far less loss of material (about 85 percent actually gets on the target, compared to about ⅓ that with conventional high-pressure spray systems). That makes them safer, too, with less junk in the air your mask must filter. Write for their free, one hundred-page, color catalog of sandblasting and HVLP equipment (there's a lot more, including several brands of air compressors, grinders and MIG welders). TiP takes American Express, Discover, MasterCard and Visa.

Titan Tool manufactures the Pro-Finish 200 high volume, low pressure spray system.

TITAN, INC.
556 Commerce Street
Franklin Lakes, NJ 07417
(800) 526-5362
Titan Tool of Canada, Ltd.
200 Trowers Road, Unit 7B
Woodbridge, Ontario
Canada L4L 5Z8
(800) 565-8665 (Canada only)

For some time now, I've been thoroughly convinced of the superiority of HVLP spray units over standard high-pressure guns: My experience has almost totally been with low-end consumer units, yet the results and ease of use (once you're acclimated) are incredible. Far less finish material is needed. You and your lungs don't end up nearly as badly coated, because something on the order of 80 or 85 percent of the material sticks to the surfaces being sprayed, versus about 10 percent, often less, with high-pressure systems. Titan isn't a system with which I am familiar, but it is a familiar name. Check out the brochure, "Pro-Finish Series HVLP Spraying Systems," which is free for a note or a call.

WAGNER FINECOAT

1770 Fernbrook Lane
Plymouth, MN 55447
(800) 328-8251
(612) 553-7000 (in Minnesota)

For many years, Wagner has been a primary source of airless paint sprayers and power roll-on painters. Now, they produce one of a new array of low-cost HVLP sprayers in addition to their other models. High-volume, low-pressure (HVLP) sprayers work with four pounds per square inch (PSI) of air, instead of up to 2,500 PSI that the conventional systems use. The first real difference you'll note on seeing one is the diameter of the air-supply hose: It is about three times as large as conventional air hoses. HVLP now offers low-cost equipment, low overspray, and general ease of use whether for clear-finish coats or heavier paints. Such sprayers are ideal for the new, water-based poly finishes. Call or write for free information.

STAINS AND FINISHES

AMAZON LUMBER & TRADING CORP., LTD.

P.O. Box 530156
Miami Shores, FL 33153
(800) 832-5645

Amazon makes Amazon's Finishing Oil, a penetrating finish that wipes on easily and is said to provide superb looks and protection. Amazon's is a low-gloss, natural-oil finish that is recommended by the company for even outdoor furniture, cooking utensils and cutting boards, as well as all other woods. It is wiped on, left to penetrate, and after ten minutes the excess is wiped away. It is nontoxic, nonflammable, and does not, according to the company, produce overpowering fumes. Amazon also produces a cedarwood oil enhancer for spraying on old cedar to increase its aromatic output. Free flyers on Amazon's Finishing Oil, Amazon's Cedarwood Oil and a teak cleaner on request. This company accepts MasterCard and Visa.

CLAPHAM'S BEESWAX PRODUCTS, LTD.

324 Le Feuvre Road
Matsqui, BC
Canada V4X 1A2
(800) 667-2939 Orders
(604) 856-2085
(604) 856-5501 FAX

Clapham's business is beeswax, and the list starts with Beeswax Polish, a cream polish for woods, after which you find Clapham's Salad Bowl Finish. The leather dressing is not a polish and is said to be made to conservator standards. Woodworkers have raved about the beeswax polish, and I intend to try some as soon as I have an application. These beekeepers also hand roll candles, and they offer block beeswax, a product I find innumerable shop uses for. Added to the product list is honey soap, hand lotion, body lotion, propolis salve, bio-enzyme barrier cream, and, finally, some specialized woodworking products: pumice rubbing compound, Rottenstone rubbing compound, friction sticks for woodturners. Call for sizes and prices, or drop them a note for their very interesting brochure. Clapham's accepts MasterCard and Visa.

DELTA TECHNICAL COATINGS, INC.

2550 Pellissier Place
Whittier, CA 90601
(800) 423-4135
(800) 553-8940 (in California)
(213) 686-0678

Hallmark Home Decor Antiquing Gel is one of Delta's Home Decor line of water-based stains and finishes. Gel wood stain, liquid wood stain, pickling gel, antiquing gel, neutral gel, transparent pearl glaze gel, gel stain retarder, and an acrylic paint base coat make up most of the line. To make it possible to go from the wood out with the same, compatible, product line, Home Decor products include wood sealer; dimensional stain resist (used to mask areas to be left unstained); water-based interior varnish in matte, satin and gloss; an exterior gloss varnish; and wood filler. Products are generally available in two- and eight-ounce containers. Give them a call and request details.

THE FLECTO COMPANY, INC.

1000 45th Street
Oakland, CA 94608
(800) 635-3286
(510) 655-2470
(510) 652-7135 FAX

Delta Technical Coatings' pickling gel is water based.

Flecto produces Varathane wood stains and finishes, in both oil- and water-based formulations. The newest products are for floors, but there are many of more direct interest to woodworkers. The new Diamond wood stains are water-based, nonyellowing, and have a matching sealer; they finish to prevent problems, from bare wood on out. There is also a line of basic, bright and glossy enamels in water-based styles that dry in a couple of hours, have almost no odor, and work well on toys, among other projects. Call and ask for free brochures on the entire family of products, or on individual products, from stains to floor finishes. The company takes both MasterCard and Visa.

FINE PAINTS OF EUROPE
P.O. Box 419
Woodstock, VT 05091
(800) 332-1556
(802) 457-3984 FAX

Most of the products sold by Fine Paints are from Holland, including Schreuder Brilliant, Schreuder Satin and Schreuder Matte paints, Oborex house paint, and other products. Other products include marine yacht varnish, isotol varnish (interior urethane), marine deck paint, primer, drop cloths, masking tape, and a line of superb paint and varnish brushes. The excel-lent catalog is free, and Fine Paints takes MasterCard and Visa.

FORMBY'S WORKSHOP
Olive Branch, MS 38654

Formby's finishes are designed for safety and ease of use. Formby's offers a full line, from finish removers and accessories (finish remover pads, steel-wool pads, protective plastic covers, refinishing gloves, and so on) to restoring finishes, wood stains, tung oils, and, finally, finish-care products. For further information, see the Thompson & Formby's listing.

GOUGEON BROTHERS
P.O. Box 908
Bay City, MI 48707
(517) 684-7286

The West System 1000 Polyurethane Varnish and epoxy adhesives are available from Gougeon Brothers. West System Epoxy is a two-part adhesive and coating for wood, fiberglass and metal. Strong and waterproof, it doesn't shrink, and it is easily modified with fillers and additives. *EpoxyWorks*, a biannual publication for modern epoxy users, is free, as is the absolutely superb *West System Tech Manual and Product Guide*. There is also a free brochure on epoxy-composite construction and a comprehensive dealer list. If you're unable to find a local dealer, Gougeon Brothers will sell direct; they take MasterCard and Visa.

HYDROCOTE
P.O. Box 160
Tennent, NJ 07763
(800) 229-4937
(908) 257-4344

Hydrocote was one of the earliest companies manufacturing water-based, clear finishes. I've used a number of the new water-based, finishes and I may never go back to those thinned with mineral spirits, but I've yet to try Hydrocote: It does have a very good reputation. Call or write for further information.

MARTIN SENOUR PAINTS
Customer Service
101 Prospect-15 Midland
Cleveland, OH 44115
(800) 542-8468

The Martin Senour catalog reads like a listing of available stains and paints from around the market. It should, for this is one of the larger paint companies around: Of particular interest to woodworkers are the

Tough Coat Enamels, for interior and exterior use. All coatings are lead free, come in semigloss and high-gloss versions, and include a line of high-visibility colors. Super Tough Coat enamels are acrylic water-based enamels, again for exterior and interior uses. There are also exterior stains, wall and trim paints, house paints and latex enamels. The Industrial and Architectural Products Guide also includes surface-prep instructions for most materials. Call for the above products guide and brochures.

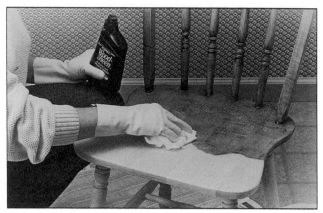

Minwax's Woodsheen rubbing finish is a fast, good-looking, tough, one-step stain and finish.

MINWAX COMPANY, INC.
15 Mercedes Drive
Montvale, NJ 07645

Probably every nonnovice woodworker is familiar with the name Minwax. I surely remember them from some time ago, and I find that their products not only stand up to time but also improve with time. Minwax now offers their version of the new lines of water-based polys, called Polycrylic. Polycrylic offers water cleanup, low odor, fast drying (thirty minutes dry to the touch), nonflammability, and the nonyellowing look that is almost universal among these finishes (so far, I've used four, all excellent and all non-yellowing, leaving wood with a more natural look after finishing). Minwax also offers WoodSheen Frosted Stain & Finish, a one-step, pastel, penetrating oil finish that is really great if you like pastel-look finishes — depending on application, it can be a pickled or a more solid-color look. WoodSheen also comes in a rubbing-oil stain look that just wipes on in seven stains. Of course, Minwax still offers its standard line of stains; polyurethane, tung oil and antique finishes; plus Polyshades, a combined stain and polyurethane finish in one. Minwax's Pastels stains round out the lines, but there is also the Watco line of Danish Oil

finishes. Write and ask for brochures on any of these products.

PARKS CORPORATION
P.O. Box 5
Somerset, MA 02726
(800) 225-8543
(508) 679-5938
(508) 674-8404 FAX

Carver Tripp water-based finishes from Parks cover a wide range of finishing needs. Because they're water-based, solvent vapors aren't a problem, meaning there's less chance of atmospheric poisoning and reduced chance of explosion or fire. Water-based finishes are always the winter-time choice, unless the shop has a great deal of ventilation equipment, and they're often the spring, summer and fall choices as well. Carver Tripp's lines cover polyurethanes, stains, Danish finish (combines pigments and resins for a one-step, wipe-on finish), sanding sealer, and high-gloss polyurethane enamels that go on as easily as anything I've ever tried — and they cover beautifully. Pastel tint bases are also available. Drop them a note or give a call for literature on any of the Carver Tripp products.

PERFORMANCE COATINGS, INC.
P.O. Box 1569
Ukia, CA 95482
(800) 468-8820
(800) 468-8817 (in California)

Call or write for information on penetrating oil finishes, including Penofin.

PERFORMAX PRODUCTS, INC.
112257 Nicollet Avenue S
Burnsville, MN 55337
(800) 334-4910
(616) 895-9922

If you do much wide-board glue-up, the Performax drum sander setup for radial arm saws may be of great interest and help. Because of the one-side-open design, you can sand panels to 44" wide. The Performax is available in models that attach to your radial arm saw and in models that stand on their own. The drum is 5" in diameter by 22" long, of extruded aluminum, machined and balanced. About the only other way to approach the overall width of machine sanding possible is to work with pro machines like ROSS SS-37, and that is not practical for many of us. The line has expanded considerably since the company began in 1986, and it now includes the Pro-Max

III stand alone 1.5 horse model, the Super-Max 37 × 2 closed-end, super-wide sander (the *2* indicates dual drums), the 16-32 stand-alone, the Super-Brush 24, for fine sanding and polishing, and the original Performax. Call or write for brochures and the name of your nearest dealer. Performax has more than one hundred dealers throughout the United States and Canada.

RUST-OLEUM

11 Hawthorn Parkway
Vernon Hills, IL 60061
(800) 323-3584

Rust-Oleum presents Wood Saver as well as a wide line of aerosol paints suitable for use on wood and metal.

STAR BRONZE COMPANY

803 South Mahoning
Alliance, OH 44601
(800) 321-9870

Along with Zip-Guard urethane Wood Finish, Star Bronze manufactures sanding eliminators, furniture refinishers, Zip-Strip paint and finish remover for water cleanup, interior and exterior wood stains, and wood preservative, as well as Dekorator's Enamel in 2-ounce bottles. On request, they'll send a copy of their extensive booklet "Refinishing and Finishing," free of charge. The booklet provides good general information and also details the use of many Star Bronze products.

THOMPSON & FORMBY, INC.

825 Crossover Lane
Memphis, TN 38117
(800) 647-9352

Formby's finishes haven't changed a lot, with staining, refinishing and wood care products being emphasized, but the joining with Thompson's has produced a wider variety of products of interest to woodworkers. Red Devil coatings and enamels are now a part of the mix—and quite a wide one. Red Devil's finishes include gloss polyurethane (oil) enamel; acrylic latex gloss enamel (water); kitchen, bath and trim enamel (water); specialty enamel and lacquer sprays; primers; interior clear polyurethane (oil); exterior clear polys (oil); and clear varnish. Color palettes are reasonably wide in enamels (wider in oils), and there are then wood stains, varnish stains, antiquing kits and removers. New Duratex clear and colors present high-gloss, enamel, hard finishes in clear and colors, exterior grade, with water cleanup. The Formby's line em-

phasizes furniture refinishing, with everything from a plastic paint lifter to gloves including products for removing and cleaning finishes, finish-care products, wood stains, wiping stains, tung-oil finishes, poly finishes and furniture cleaner. Somewhere, in these lines, you will find something to think about. There's also the almost unmentioned Thompson's water protection line for exterior surfaces. Ask for the brochures available, including "Homer Formby's Secrets of Successful Refinishing."

UGL (UNITED GILSONITE LABORATORIES)

P.O. Box 70
Scranton, PA 18501
(800) UGL-LABS

This firm manufactures ZAR wood finishing products, including penetrating wood stains; clear polyurethane varnishes in gloss, satin and flat finishes; and exterior polys in brush-on and spray formulations. They also produce ZAR Aqua, a new line of clear polyurethanes that are water based, hence cutting odors, flammability dangers and solvent-emissions problems. (These nonyellowing finishes also let you clean up with soap and water, and they're formulated for easy brushing: Many of the new water-based polys are formulated primarily for spraying.) ZAR tung oil is a wipe-on (in my experience, an old T-shirt is the best applicator) product that produces a surface resistant to water and most chemicals. Give them a call and they'll ship a free brochure, "The Finishing Touch."

WILLIAM ZINSSER & CO.

39 Belmont Drive, Dept. WSB
Somerset, NJ 08875
(908) 469-4367

Zinsser Bulls Eye Shellac Sealer & Finish comes in a standard three-pound cut, in white and orange (they now call these *clear* and *amber*), in half-pints, pints, quarts, gallons and five-gallon buckets. This past year, Zinsser brought out their Bulls Eye products in 13-ounce spray cans, making them even more near ideal as sealers for knots, spackled areas and similar things. I've also found shellac excellent as sealer for siding nails before painting a house with water-based paints. This is not a mail-order item, so it is found in home centers and hardware stores, but the company will send a free brochure describing the products and their uses: Shellac makes a superb one-coat undercoat for wallpaper, and the wallpaper strips off easily when the time comes for a change. Spackled areas sealed with shellac do not need several coats of paint to kill the flat look. Knots and sap streaks in new wood are nicely sealed with shellac, and woods such as pine take paint more evenly when first given a coat of shellac. Shellac has a lot of good points as a clear finish, too—points we often forget these days. Drop a card to William Zinsser & Company and get an idea of what some of those good points are—or get reminded, if, like me, you used to know. The catalog, product booklets and product information sheets are all free.

STRIPPING

SANSHER CORPORATION
8005 North Clinton Street
Fort Wayne, IN 46825
(219) 484-2000

Sansher Corporation offers Dad's Drip Strip latex paint cleaner that also removes polyurethanes, lacquers, shellacs, varnishes, acrylics, paints and epoxies. The remover is said to cut and dissolve like a liquid while lifting and staying wet like a semigel, so that the stripping job may be stopped at any time, without waste or damage, for later resumption. It comes with its own chemical-resistant sprayer, doesn't need a neutralizer, and is washed off with plain water, leaving no residue. I've not used this particular brand of remover, but if it does most of what is claimed, it will reduce work, odor and mess considerably. Call or write the company for a brochure.

SURFACE PREPARANTS

HYDE TOOLS
54 Eastford Road
Southbridge, MA 01550
(800) USA-HYDE
(508) 764-4344
(508) 765-5250 FAX

For a long, long time, Hyde Tools has produced surface preparation tools—the company was founded in 1875. The tools are found at all fine paint and decorating stores, home centers, hardware stores and similar outlets; they include putty knives, utility knives, wire brushes (including brass for the refinishers out there), and a whole lot more. The company aims at producing the highest possible quality for a reasonable price, and it currently catalogs just over 1,000 products, many of which are of value to woodworkers. If you call, they'll send you free brochures on drywall, masonry, wallcovering, painting, sheet flooring, vinyl tile, wall-to-wall carpet, and ceramic tile. Some of the tools have no application for woodworkers (papering tables, for example), but many do. Check out the brochures and get the name of your local dealer.

STAR BRONZE COMPANY
803 South Mahoning
Alliance, OH 44601
(800) 321-9870

Along with Zip-Guard urethane Wood Finish, Star Bronze manufactures sanding eliminators, furniture refinishers, Zip-Strip paint and finish remover for water cleanup, interior and exterior wood stains, and wood preservative, plus Dekorator's Enamel in 2-ounce bottles. On request, they'll send a copy of their extensive booklet, "Refinishing and Finishing," free of charge. The booklet provides good general information and details the use of many Star Bronze products.

WILLIAM ZINSSER & CO.
39 Belmont Drive, Dept. WSB
Somerset, NJ 08875
(908) 469-4367

Zinsser Bulls Eye Shellac Sealer & Finish comes in a standard three-pound cut, in white and orange (they now call these *clear* and *amber*), in half-pints, pints, quarts, gallons and five-gallon buckets. This past year, Zinsser brought out their Bulls Eye products in 13-ounce spray cans, making them even more near ideal as sealers for knots, spackled areas and similar things. I've also found shellac excellent as sealer for siding nails before painting a house with water-based paints. This is not a mail-order item, so it is found in home centers and hardware stores, but the company will send a free brochure describing the products and their uses: Shellac makes a superb one-coat undercoat for wallpaper, and the wallpaper strips off easily when the time comes for a change. Spackled areas sealed with shellac do not need several coats of paint to kill the flat look. Knots and sap streaks in new wood are nicely sealed with shellac, and woods such as pine take paint more evenly when first given a coat of shellac. Shellac has a lot of good points as a clear finish, too—points we often forget these days. Drop a card to William Zinsser & Company and get an idea of what some of those good points are—or get reminded, if, like me, you used to know. The catalog, product booklets and product information sheets are all free.

WOOD PATCH

DARWORTH COMPANY

3 Mill Pond Lane
P.O. Box 639
Simsbury, CT 06070
(800) 672-3499
(800) 624-7767
(800) 227-6095 FAX

FI:X Wood Patch and Touch Up Stik are two major products for repair and construction. The color Touch Up Stiks do minor touch-up jobs in a hurry, and the wood patch is made in red oak and white pine, plus ash, maple/alder, white, walnut, natural, pine, oak, dark mahogany/redwood, light mahogany and birch fir. The Wood Patch sands well and accepts stains uniformly. Darworth's new heavy-duty Construction Adhesive, PolySeamSeal, works on most woods, drywall, foam boards and paneling. In the past, I've found this type of adhesive excellent for outdoor project reinforcement, which basically means that Adirondack chairs and similar projects seem to last a good deal longer when adhesive and nails, or screws, are used, instead of just nails or screws. Call or write for further information.

WOOD TREATMENTS

VELVIT PRODUCTS COMPANY

P.O. Box 1741
Appleton, WI 54913
(414) 722-8355

Velvit's Chemgard wood treatments include Velvit oil interior finish, Chemgard wood treatments (for wood and logs that won't be sealed for months), and Cabin & Deck Finish for exterior work. Call or write for information.

Hand Tools and Accessories

Hand Tools and Accessories

BRANDING IRONS

BRANDMARK BY F&K CONCEPTS
462 Carthage Drive
Beavercreek, OH 45434-5865
(800) 323-2570
(513) 426-6843

The project branding iron produced by F&K Concepts and called BrandMark is available in several styles. The simplest is the type heated with a torch or hot plate and costs $28. The electric branding iron is more complex and costs $48. Either iron gives you a chance to quickly and permanently mark all your completed projects. The standard first line reads: "Handcrafted By." The second line can have up to twenty spaces, with a ¼" letter height. The first line can be changed, and third and fourth lines and special figures may all be added at extra cost.

NOVA TOOL COMPANY
12500 Finnegan Road
P.O. Box 29341
Lincoln, NE 68529
(800) 826-7606 (except Nebraska)
(402) 464-0511

Many woodworkers like to use a branding iron to let people know just who made a particularly fine piece. The Nova version is solid brass and costs $26 (plus $3 shipping and handling), or you may call or write for the free brochure.

BRUSHES

3M DIY DIVISION
Consumer Relations
515-3N-02
St. Paul, MN 55144-1000

This is the 3M division that handles information on Newstroke snap-off paintbrushes; home-care adhesives; and surface-prep products (hand- and power-sanding materials); paint removers; and personal safety products such as goggles and face masks of both comfort and respirator types. The company makes a wide variety of masks and respirators to reduce the effects of the sandpaper and similar products it also produces. I particularly like their dispos-able general dust and sanding respirator: That's the number 8710, and it comes in contractor packs of twenty, and in packs of two or three. Catalogs are available on request. Specify which product line interests you (listed above).

CALCULATORS

CALCULATED INDUSTRIES
22720 Savi Ranch
Yorba Linda, CA 92687
(800) 854-8075

The Construction Master II (CMII) feet-inch calculator adds, subtracts and divides in feet and inches and with any fraction, from ½ to ¹⁄₆₄, including mixed fractions. The CMII will also convert between feet-inch fractions, decimal feet, inches, yards and metrics, including square and cubic measurements. With all of this, the CMII also works as a standard math calculator, with many functions, including square roots and automatic shutoff. The company distributes and sells direct, and it accepts credit cards.

CHISELS

GARRETT WADE COMPANY
161 Avenue of the Americas
New York, NY 10013-1299
(800) 221-2942
(212) 807-1155

The lush regular catalog is now free and shows about as wide a variety of hand tools and power-tool accessories as it is practical to offer. Certainly there is the widest array of chisels of any company, including their top-of-the-line house brand, often in hard-to-find styles and sizes, including swan neck models, several corner chisels, Sorby's Registered Mortise chisels, dog-leg and other styles. The catalog is replete with color and with tips on tool use: It may have the highest drool factor of any tool catalog because of the excellent photography and layout and the number and variety of tools presented. No place is a one-stop source for all of any woodworker's needs—if it were, there'd be no need for this book—but Garrett Wade fills many needs, from Hydrocote finishes to dozens of books to bow saw kits to Japanese tools. Garrett Wade takes MasterCard and Visa.

SANDVIK CONSUMER TOOLS DIVISION
P.O. Box 2036
Scranton, PA 18501-1220
(800) 632-7297
(800) 877-5687 FAX

Sandvik's small U.S. marketing division is not exactly eager for calls and letters asking for catalogs, so I'd suggest you try your local tool supplier first. They offer a fine line of chisels, coping, fretsaws and handsaws, including hardpoint styles, hammers, and files. Sandvik does not sell direct.

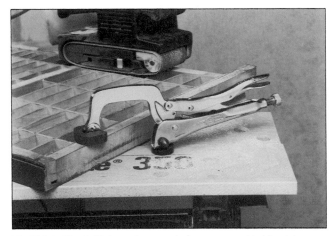

ViseGrip's locking hold down clamp works for many wood holding jobs.

CLAMPS

ADJUSTABLE CLAMP COMPANY
415 North Ashland Avenue
Chicago, IL 60622
(312) 666-0640
(312) 666-2723 FAX

One of the oldest wide-line clamp manufacturers, Adjustable Clamp Company makes Jorgenson and Pony clamps, in styles ranging from light and heavy and medium bar clamps to C-clamps to spring clamps, corner clamps, and E-Z Hold bar clamps, with virtually every other stop in between. Jorgenson clamps are also supplemented by a line of miter boxes, professional woodworkers' vises, and heavy-duty bench vises. (I've tried most of the rest of the Adjustable Clamp lines and love them, but I have yet to try their heavy-duty vises: I expect the quality to be on a par with Jorgenson clamps.) At this time, I believe they're also the only U.S. maker of hand screws. The small "Clamp-It" brochure is free; send $1 for a more extensive brochure.

AMERICAN CLAMPING CORPORATION
P.O. Box 399
Batavia, NY 14021
(800) 828-1004

ACC imports Bessey clamps, which include the K body heavy cabinet clamps—the best I've ever used—and lines of light to heavy bar clamps, specialty clamps and others. They offer free literature.

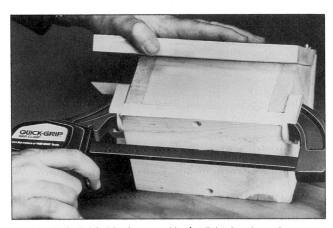

American Tool's Quick-Grip clamp provides fast light clamping action.

AMERICAN TOOL COMPANIES, INC.
301 South 13th Street
Lincoln, NE 68508
(402) 435-3300

Quick-Grip clamps are the tools of woodworker's choice from the makers of Vise Grips, but American Tool also manufactures Pro Snips, Chesco hex tools, Unibits (multisized sheet metal bit) and a variety of other tools. For those who haven't used them, Quick-Grip clamps are real time-savers and well worth investigating if you do any kind of woodworking that calls for bar clamps. They're not production-line tools, but for hobby-shop use, they will last indefinitely. American Tool recently acquired Irwin, so it now has lines of Marathon C4 carbide blades, Forstner bits, Speedbor spade bits, twist bits, and all the other cutting tools, measuring tools, and similar items that Irwin manufactured. Evidently, though, these lines will continue without the Irwin name. Call or write for information on the lines. American Tool does not sell direct.

COLT CLAMP COMPANY, INC.
33 Swan Street
Batavia, NY 14020-3245
(800) 536-8420
(716) 343-8622
(716) 343-8622 FAX

Call, FAX or write for a free catalog of a dozen eccentric clamp styles in aluminum, steel and stainless steel.

DE-STA-CO
P.O. Box 2800
Troy, MI 48007
(800) 245-2759
(313) 589-2008
(313) 644-3929 FAX

A leading maker of toggle clamps, De-Sta-Co offers a free catalog of more than three hundred models. This type of clamp is suitable for most woodworking jigs and fixtures, and allows development of new jigs to aid in your workshop: The catalog is very specific in providing measurements of the clamps and their movements and mounting needs. De-Sta-Co also makes a wide line of pneumatic air clamps designed to work on shop-line pressure: This is not a usual hobby woodworking application, and really, it isn't very often seen in small commercial shops either, but it can be a great boon for certain types of wide-area work, such as laminating large sheets.

LEICHTUNG WORKSHOPS
4944 Commerce Parkway
Cleveland, OH 44128
(800) 321-6840
(216) 464-6764 FAX

Leichtung offers a variety of unusual tools, plus many plans and woodworking supplies in their free catalog. The catalog is digest-sized but sometimes runs more than ninety pages. It presents seasonal plans; some kits (varying with the seasons, but often small boxes and clocks, ships, dollhouses); and parts to help in building some of the plan items. The catalog has many styles of clamps, as well as numerous doweling and jointing jigs, and it is the only tool catalog I've seen where you're as apt to find wildflower seeds by the small sack, rain gauges, barbecue cleaner, rocks, and cowhide gloves as you are Forstner drill bits. I've used a lot of Leichtung's gloves, and I always keep several pair on hand. For the price, they're the best I've seen for light chores, up to and including feeding a planer. The company also has a goodly array of parts bins and jars and hangers for perforated board,

both ¼" and ⅛". They also offer a Woodworker's Guild for a $15 annual membership fee. Leichtung takes American Express, MasterCard, Visa and Discover.

MAPLETEK ENGINEERING, INC.
1016 Morse Avenue #5
Sunnyvale, CA 94089
(800) 425-2677
(408) 377-7992 FAX

MapleTek Engineering produces the Leverclamp and Clamptrax, which they call the most flexible clamping system available. The basic units assemble readily into simple jigs and may be set up in an array to form more complex jigs. Adjustments are instant, as is clamping action. Force of clamping remains the same, regardless of height—force is adjustable. Maple-Tek products are sold through Woodcraft, but they also sell direct. Call for their brochure. The company takes both MasterCard and Visa.

TOOLS ON SALE DIVISION
216 West 7th Street
St. Paul, MN 55102
(800) 328-0457
(612) 224-8263 FAX

Call the toll-free number to see what catalog is available. Tools On Sale presents a huge book, 416 pages long, listing discount prices on tools of virtually all brands. They carry everything from the Bessey clamping system, and many Pony and Jorgenson clamps, to Vise-Grip locking clamps, to Bosch, Black & Decker, DeWalt, Makita, Milwaukee, Hitachi, Campbell Hausfeld, Stanley Bostitch, DeVilbiss, Ryobi, Skil, Porter-Cable, Delta, Freud and Fein, as well as many others, in sanders, circular saws, table saws, radial arm saws, planers, router and shaper bits, Swiss army knives, all sorts of leather belts and pockets and tool holders, Plano toolboxes, Shop-Vac vacuums, and even extension cords. Tools On Sale accepts Discover, MasterCard and Visa.

FILES

SANDVIK CONSUMER TOOLS DIVISION
P.O. Box 2036
Scranton, PA 18501-1220
(800) 632-7297
(800) 877-5687 FAX

This firm offers a fine line of chisels, coping, fretsaws and handsaws (including hardpoint styles), hammers and files. Sandvik's small U.S. marketing division is not exactly eager for calls and letters asking for catalogs, so I'd suggest you try your local tool supplier first. Sandvik does not sell direct.

JAPANESE WOODWORKING TOOLS

HIDA TOOL & HARDWARE, INC.
1333 San Pablo Avenue
Berkeley, CA 94702
(510) 524-3700
(510) 524-3423 FAX

The catalog offered by Hida is rather amateurishly done, but it presents a very nice line of Japanese woodworking hand tools, from marking knives to planes and saws. There is a wide line of waterstones, and hammers and mallets are represented heavily. Here and in other Japanese tool sellers' catalogs, you'll also find the layout tools: The Japanese use a water-based ink to mark snap lines! And the line itself is silk instead of our far more mundane cotton. The short line of Japanese drawer hardware (mostly pulls) looks very interesting. For a free brochure on Japanese saws, drop Hida Tool a line, but for their full catalog, you must send $4. The catalog is expensive but may be worth the investment if you have a solid interest in these hand tools. Hida Tool takes MasterCard and Visa.

Japan Woodworker sells double-sided ryoba saws as well as Razorsaws and other Japanese tools.

JAPAN WOODWORKER
1731 Clement Avenue
Alameda, CA 94501
(800) 537-7820
(510) 521-1810

Not only are there extensive lines of Japanese wood-

working tools in this catalog (two-year subscription for $1.50) but the book lines for Japanese woodworking concepts are extensive. The company is the original importer of Japanese woodworking tools and a principal supplier today. There are many top-quality tools of American make in the catalog, too, including Starret measuring tools, Veritas tools, Fein corner sanders, CMT saw blades, router bits, Radi-Planes and others. You may find yourself selecting from Starrett (truly precise measuring tools, generally meant for machine-shop use but great for woodworking uses as well), Lie-Nielson, Veritas, Akafuji Kanna, Dai, Shizen, Sadakuzura, Hock, Bridge City Tool Works, and Razorsaw. I've used enough Japanese tools to be impressed with their superb cutting characteristics, and I've never found anything that begins to come close to Japanese waterstones for sharpening ease and results on almost any edged tool. Knives, chisels and plane irons all benefit strongly from a two- or three-step process on the stones. Using the king stone gives a chromelike polish to the tool. The Japan Woodworker takes American Express, MasterCard, Visa and Discover.

TASHIRO'S
1024 South Bailey Street
Seattle, WA 98108
(206) 762-8242

Tashiro's has been importing Japanese tools for more than a century, and it offers a solid array of saw blades and handles for almost all wood cutting purposes. The free catalog contains instruction on selecting the right blade for the job and on using the proper handle for the blades needed.

KNIVES

CAPE FORGE
P.O. Box 987
Burlington, VT 05402

This small company success story is unusual in that the Cape Forge is a father and . . . but not father and son. Mike De Punte has as an apprentice his daughter Karyn, who has a B.A. in industrial education and technology. Karyn turns the hardwood handles for the tools and attends to the fit and finish. Mike forges the blades. From the photos Karyn sent, the tools are obviously beautifully made. Most of their tools are for carvers and sculptors, but they do make paring chisels that I can hope to get, in at least one or two sizes, in the future. The catalog costs $1.

CHARLES G.G. SCHMIDT & CO., INC.
301 West Grand Avenue
Montvale, NJ 07645
(201) 391-5300
(201) 391-3565 FAX

Charles G.G. Schmidt manufactures and distributes industrial woodworking knives and cutters for all types of molders, shapers, planers, tenoners and routers. Their products include wing cutters, window-sash cutters, shaper collars, thin knives, cutter heads and custom tooling. Started in 1926, the company produces standard and custom tools of top materials. Their main catalog, "Number 300," is sent at no charge, as is "Knives," their list of standard molding and flooring profiles. Charles G.G. Schmidt & Company accepts Discover, MasterCard and Visa.

NORTH BAY FORGE
Box S
Waldron, WA 98297

As with all hand-forged tools, North Bay's products tend to be pricey as compared to factory-made items. In many senses, that's a matter of choice when selecting tools, though a handmade tool has a greater beauty (and I don't think good machine-made tools are ugly at all, though cheaply made ones sure are) that is often worth the cost. With some makers, the beauty extends into the tool's handling: I can't comment on North Bay's tool handling, but the production is definitely by hand, and in the old manner. North Bay Forge is located on Waldron Island, which has no phones (note the lack of phone number above), and which also lacks electricity! That doesn't mean no machines are used to produce North Bay Forge tools, but it does mean greater attention must be paid to each operation. The catalog, featuring scorps, drawknives and carver's knives, is free.

MEASURING TOOLS

BRIDGE CITY TOOL WORKS
1104 Northeast 28th Street
Suite 200
Portland, OR 97232
(800) 253-3332

Bridge City Tool Works presents some of the most attractive hand measuring tools being made today, with most made of rosewood and brass (where appropriate). The $1 catalog provides much more information and more than a couple of minutes' time looking over true beauty. Bridge City takes American Express, Discover, MasterCard and Visa.

SONIN, INC.
Milltown Office Park
Suite B201, Route 22
Brewster, NY 10509
(800) 223-7511
(914) 725-0202

Sonin produces high-tech linear measuring tools, plumbs and levels and now a new moisture test meter and moisture test tool. These electronic tools give a very rapid indication of moisture present, with the meter measuring levels from 10 percent to 28 percent. Sonin also makes various electronic, and non-electronic, distance-measuring tools, including measuring tapes, and circuit testers that may prove handy around the workshop. Call Sonin's 800 number for a free catalog. Sonin doesn't sell direct.

MOISTURE METERS

DELMHORST INSTRUMENT COMPANY
51 Indian Lane East
Towaco, NJ 07082
(800) 222-0638
(201) 334-2557 (in New Jersey)

Delmhorst moisture meters make up a major line of such meters, and they include a number of models that cover most aspects of testing wood for moisture. I have and use the midrange Delmhorst, and I find it an excellent and accurate measuring tool. For more information, give the company a call or drop them a line.

ELECTROPHYSICS
Box 1143, Station B
London, Ontario
Canada N6A 5K2
(519) 668-2871
(519) 668-2871 FAX

Electrophysics presents several models of wood-moisture meters for home or industrial uses. One of those models, the CT100, is a no-pins version, which means no damaged test samples. A touch-pad probe senses moisture on the interior of the wood, and presents a reading in the range of 0 percent to 30 percent, with a 1 percent accuracy over the range. The unit was designed, and is made, in Canada, and it is small enough to list as pocket-sized, at 2.7" × 4.7" × 1" thick. Lower-cost standard pin models are available, as are more costly, wider-range units. For most small-shop woodworking, a range of 6 percent to 15 percent will suffice, and all the Electrophysics models exceed that, some considerably. For better results, a meter that reads to a top of about 20 percent can be handy, and two Electrophysics models read from 4 percent to 30 percent and 6 percent to 40 percent. The catalog is free, and Electrophysics accepts Visa.

LIGNOMAT USA, LTD.
P.O. Box 30145
Portland, OR 92301
(800) 227-2105
(503) 257-8957
(503) 255-1430 FAX

Lignomat moisture meters are probably the best-known of all such units. A free brochure explains one or more of the many models they produce, with an array starting at the pocket-sized Mini-Lignometer (registering 6 percent to 20 percent, a range adequate for most needs) through the Lignomaster K100 to the G1000. (For the Mini-Lignometer, you'd best have a good-sized free pocket: This is the model I use most often, and I keep it clipped to my belt.) There's a new digital readout Mini-Ligno with a wider range (6 percent to as high as 65 percent). There is an in-kiln model, too, and a newly introduced Thermo-hygrometer for shops and other wood-storage areas. The Thermo-hygrometer may be hand-held, wall mounted, or set on any convenient, flat surface such as a desk. For the person who has everything, including a drying kiln, Lignomat produces a computerized kiln-control system as well. Many of the Lignomat moisture meters are available from various mail-order sources, but the company also sells direct. They take American Express, MasterCard and Visa.

PECO SALES, INC.
P.O. Box 8122
Jackson, MS 39284
(800) 346-6939
(601) 355-5126 FAX

The Protimeter wood-moisture meter from Peco Sales is a wide-ranged unit (6 percent to 60 percent, instead of the more usual 6 percent to 20 or 30 percent). Price is relatively low. The Aquant model has no prongs and uses radio frequency emission technology to determine the moisture content of the wood. Touch the surface being checked and one of sixteen light-emitting diodes comes on. Call for more information on the entire line of moisture meters and the name of a local dealer.

SONIN, INC.
Milltown Office Park
Suite B201, Route 22
Brewster, NY 10509
(800) 223-7511
(914) 725-0202

Sonin produces high-tech linear measuring tools, plumbs and levels and now a new moisture test meter and moisture test tool. These electronic tools give a very rapid indication of moisture present, with the meter measuring levels from 10 percent to 28 percent. Sonin also makes various electronic, and non-electronic, distance-measuring tools, including measuring tapes, and circuit testers that may prove handy around the workshop. Call Sonin's 800 number for a free catalog. Sonin doesn't sell direct.

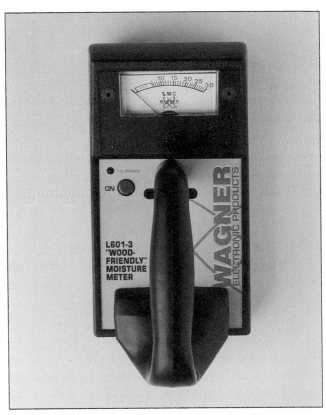

Wagner's L601-3 moisture meter does not have to be driven into wood to measure wood moisture percentage.

WAGNER ELECTRONIC PRODUCTS
326 Pine Grove Road
Rogue River, OR 97537
(800) 944-7078
(503) 582-0541

Wagner makes several wood-moisture meters, the most interesting of which may be the pocket-sized L606. Called the "wood-friendly" model, the L606 uses EMF technology to measure wood moisture content for 6 percent to 30 percent to a wood depth of ¾". No pins are used, so there are no holes left in the wood. The more standard L601-3 moisture meter is larger, and it works over the same range but down to a wood depth of 1", still using EMF instead of pins. This meter comes with a decade-long warranty and features an automatic shutoff to save batteries—it uses four AA cells. Give the company a call for information on either of these moisture meters.

Bill Bartz's MiterRite works well to produce accurate miters.

MITER EQUIPMENT

BILL BARTZ MANUFACTURING COMPANY
854 Arbor Oaks Drive
Vacaville, CA 95687
(707) 451-9104
(707) 451-4666

Bill's MitreRite costs $19.95 plus three bucks shipping, and it works. It's a simple device—series of devices, really—of plastic, including a tool for making four-sided frames, another for making six-sided frames, and a third that works for eight-sided frames, circles and ovals. In essence, it's a flip-over guide that fits in front of the miter gauge on a table saw (it works, with a minor procedure change, with radial arm saws, too). The only requirement for table saws is that the miter gauge slots be parallel to the saw blade, which is a standard setup need, in any case. The MitreRite then produces complementary angles, so you have a good fit. One cut is made, the miter gauge, and the guide is moved to the other gauge slot; then the second cut is made, after flipping the guide over. Any deviation from an accurately angled cut is made up for when the gauge is moved and the guide flipped, so you get gap-free joints. The Mitre-

Rite won the Retailer's Choice Award at the National Hardware Show in August 1992.

GEOFF BROWN
8 Ladbroke Park
Millers Road
Warwick
CV34 5AE United Kingdom
011 44 926 493389
011 44 926 491357 FAX

I'd recommend doing your checking Stateside on the items Geoff Brown exports: He distributes Tormek wet grinder systems (see listing for Tormek U.S.A.), Nobex miter boxes, and Sjobergs joiner's workbenches. The latter two can readily be found in Woodcraft catalogs [(800)535-4482; see listing for Woodcraft]. The Nobex line consists of the Champion Compound Miter Saw, with a 7¼" cutting height, and a few other tools. The Nobex miter square appears of great interest. The Sjobergs joiner's benches are what one might call typical European pattern workbenches, which means that if you've ever become accustomed to them, you hate to use anything else. At the same time, they tend to be exceptionally pricey. Sjobergs benches are also available from Basic Living Products, 1321 67th Street, Emeryville, CA 94608. The phone number there is (800) 829-6300.

JDS COMPANY
800 Dutch Square Boulevard
Suite 200
Columbia, SC 29210
(800) 382-2637
(803) 798-1600

The Accu-Miter free brochure presents a look at an intriguing tool. The Accu-Miter is a replacement miter gauge, with a precision protractor scale, a rigid front fence with telescopic extensions (two sizes, one to 18½" in length and the larger to 24½") and some related accessories, as well as custom parts. It's durable, of die-cast construction, and it offers a stop that may be inserted in either end, for accurate multiple cuts. JDS also makes the Multi-Router machine, which offers quick setup and efficient cutting of many joints, from mortise-and-tenon on through varieties of dovetail, compound-angle tenons, round tenons and more.

POOTATUCK CORP.
P.O. Box 24
Windsor, VT 05089
(802) 674-5984
(802) 674-9330 FAX

Pootatuck is the maker of the Lion miter trimmer, a guillotine-style miter trimmer that is exceptionally accurate and relatively low cost. The tool uses razor-sharp knives to do the trimming, leaving an exceedingly smooth cut. This is the only American-made version of a guillotine miter cutter. Pootatuck sells by mail order, as well as serving as manufacturer and distributor. The company will send a free brochure, on request. Pootatuck takes MasterCard and Visa.

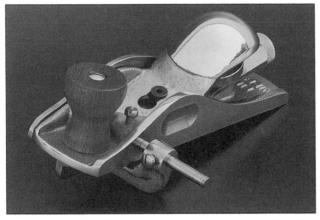

Lie-Nielsen's skew blade block plane is patterned after the Stanley 140 and has a 12 degree blade set for easier crossgrain work.

PLANES

LIE-NIELSEN TOOLWORKS
Route 1
Warren, ME 04684
(800) 327-2520 Orders
(207) 273-2520
(207) 273-2657 FAX

These makers of heirloom-quality hand tools offer a free catalog that is small and short (one tool per page) and a true delight, as are the tools. I've arranged to borrow a Lie-Nielsen plane from another source, and I'm more than a little antsy to give it a try. Lie-Nielsen planes are fairly costly, but considering the materials and care of manufacture, the prices are actually on the low side. As an example, the low-angle jack plane, based on the Stanley 62, is 14″ long with a 2″ iron embedded at 12°. The shoe is movable for mouth adjustment. The plane's body is made from a completely stress-relieved iron casting, and the blade is ³⁄₁₆″ thick and ground to a razor edge. Adjustment is with a knurled stainless captive nut, and the cap iron is bronze. The knob and handle are both cherry in this plane, which was originally designed to plane end grain in such work as flattening butcher blocks. It is costly at $165, but considering the tool,

not outrageously so. Lie-Nielsen has been in business since 1981, and it accepts American Express, Master-Card and Visa.

ROGER K. SMITH
P.O. Box 177
Athol, MA 01331

Roger Smith's book, *Patented Transitional & Metallic Planes in America, Vol. II*, is an 8½″ × 11″ hardcover, with four hundred pages covering planes by L. Bailey, Savage Manufacturing, Worrall, Gladwin, Holly, Phillips, Steers, Taber, Gage, Heald, and a great many others. The 300 line illustrations and 450 photos (44 in color) help the presentation considerably. There is even biographical information on Loughborough, Rodier, Walker, George Evans and other makers, and you'll find more than seventy pages of new data on Stanley planes and their inventors. The book is costly, as most low-circulation, heavily researched books have to be: It is about $80. For plane collectors, there probably isn't much choice. Roger will send information on special offers if you drop him a line. Send a check or money order, and you can't use credit cards.

PLIERS

CHANNELLOCK, INC.
1306 South Main Street
Meadville, PA 16335
(814) 724-8700

Channellock is one company that doesn't require much product description—they designed and produced the original pliers based on resizing the jaw opening with channels on the tool neck. In recent years, the tool has been improved, and the line of pliers has been expanded to include nut drivers, slip joint pliers, end nippers, wire cutters of many types, linemen's and electricians' pliers, long nose pliers, aviation (metal) snips, wiring tools and strippers, adjustable wrenches, and a couple of knives. Write and request their free brochures for further information.

SAWS

HIDA TOOL & HARDWARE, INC.
1333 San Pablo Avenue
Berkeley, CA 94702
(510) 524-3700
(510) 524-3423 FAX

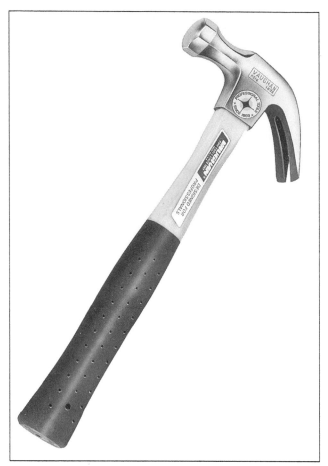

Vaughan & Bushnell's 16-ounce fiberglass handle claw hammer is excellent for general woodworking use.

Hida Tool's catalog is rather amateurishly done, but it presents a very nice line of Japanese woodworking hand tools, from marking knives to planes and saws. There is a wide line of waterstones, and hammers and mallets are represented heavily. Here, and in other Japanese tool sellers' catalogs, you'll also find the layout tools: The Japanese use a water-based ink to mark snap lines! And the line itself is silk, instead of our far more mundane cotton. The short line of Japanese drawer hardware (mostly pulls) looks very interesting. For a free brochure on Japanese saws, drop Hida Tool a line, but for their full catalog, you must send $4. The catalog is expensive, but it may be worth the investment if you have a solid interest in these hand tools. Hida Tool & Hardware takes Master-Card and Visa.

SANDVIK CONSUMER TOOLS DIVISION

P.O. Box 2036
Scranton, PA 18501-1220
(800) 632-7297
(800) 877-5687 FAX

This company offers a fine line of chisels, coping, fret-saws and handsaws (including hardpoint styles), hammers and files. Sandvik does not sell direct. Sandvik's small U.S. marketing division is not exactly eager for calls and letters asking for catalogs, so I'd suggest you try your local tool supplier first.

TASHIRO'S

1024 South Bailey Street
Seattle, WA 98108
(206) 762-8242

Tashiro's has been importing Japanese tools for more than a century, and it offers a solid array of saw blades and handles for almost all wood-cutting purposes. The free catalog contains instruction on selecting the right blade for the job and on using the proper handle for the blades needed.

STRIKING TOOLS

VAUGHAN & BUSHNELL MANUFACTURING COMPANY

11414 Maple Avenue
Hebron, IL 60034
(815) 648-2446
(815) 648-4300 FAX

Vaughan & Bushnell makes a wide line of striking tools, from hickory-handled claw hammers to rawhide and rubber mallets and on to axes and similar items. The line of carpenter's claw hammers is wider than most with head weights as low as 7 ounces and as heavy as 32 ounces and including the standard stops at 13, 16, 20, 24, 28 and 32 ounces (I still know of no other maker of 7- and 32-ounce claw hammers). Handle materials cover the standard hickory, fiberglass, tubular and solid steel. The variety of soft-faced hammers, including rawhide, plastics and rubber, is wide enough to let you drive together any tight joint with no marks on even the softest wood. You might particularly want to try one of their Super-Plastic mallets or one of their rawhide mallets. (Need a hard whack followed by a soft whack? Try Vaughan & Bushnell's copper and rawhide-faced mallet.) Send an SASE for information on striking tools and even some struck tools — they make some chisels and many pry bars, as well as hammers, axes, sledges and hatchets. The company has been around a long time: The catalog I got came with information on their 125th anniversary.

SURFACE PREPARATION

HYDE TOOLS
54 Eastford Road
Southbridge, MA 01550
(800) USA-HYDE
(508) 764-4344
(508) 765-5250 FAX

For a long, long time, Hyde Tools has produced surface preparation tools — the company was founded in 1875. The tools are sold at all fine paint and decorating stores, home centers, hardware stores and similar outlets, and they include putty knives, utility knives, wire brushes (including brass for the refinishers out there), and a whole lot more. The company aims at producing the highest possible quality for a reasonable price, and it currently catalogs just over 1,000 products, many of which are of value to woodworkers. If you call, they'll send you free brochures on: drywall; masonry; wallcovering; painting; sheet flooring, vinyl tile and wall-to-wall carpet; and ceramic tile. Some of the tools have no application for woodworkers (papering tables, for example), but many do. Check out the brochures and get the name of your local dealer.

Materials

Materials

BASKET

ROYALWOOD, LTD.
517 Woodville Road
Mansfield, OH 44907
(419) 526-1630

If you need Shaker tape to complete a project, Royalwood has it. The $1.50 (refundable) catalog from this mail-order house presents extensive arrays of many items of great use in the fields of basket weaving and caning. A Shaper Tape sample card is $2, as is a waxed linen color card; neither is refundable.

FABRICS

DONJER PRODUCTS CORPORATION
Ilene Court
Building 8
Bellemead, NJ 08502
(800) 336-6537

DonJer, a company begun in 1946, presents spray-on suede fibers to be used as linings. Woodworkers find this material most useful for box linings. A new mini-flocker is out, and there are thirty-one colors available. DonJer will mail a brochure for $.50 to cover mailing costs, but that brochure contains a $2-off coupon. DonJer takes MasterCard and Visa.

J.B. DAWN PRODUCTS, INC.
3905 West 64th Place
Chicago, IL 60629
(800) 796-2333
(312) 735-2344

Started in 1950, J.B. Dawn produces self-adhesive felt products using a 70 percent wool, 30 percent rayon felt on a poly film backing with a latex adhesive that is very durable. The company is owned and operated by a woman (something I didn't ask about but that the company obviously cares about, so I mention it). Custom products are available, as are Feltdots, Feltape, Feltabs, Gunpads, and Ricobac, which is available 1/16" and 1/8" thick. Colors are black, brown, white, green and silver gray. J.B. Dawn does not accept credit cards.

GLASS

AMERIGLAS
P.O. Box 27668
Omaha, NE 68127
(800) 927-7877

The AmeriGlas catalog of stained-glass supplies covers tools, materials, books, videos, lamps, bevels, and a great deal more. Cost of the catalog is $1.

EASTERN ART GLASS
P.O. Box 341
Wyckoff, NJ 07481
(800) 872-3458

Eastern Art Glass sells glass and mirror supplies from a new color catalog packed with products that include 250 precut etching stencils, glass etching chemicals, beveled glass and mirror boxes, hanging ornaments, mirror stripping products, gold leaf kits, Diamond Point engraving tools, pattern books, and courses on glass etching. The company has been in business more than fifteen years. If it has to do with glass, this catalog will at least supply you with a lead to it or on it. The catalog is free, and Eastern Art Glass takes American Express, MasterCard, Visa and Discover.

FLORAL GLASS MIRROR, INC.
895 Motor Parkway
Hauppauge, NY 11788
(800) 647-7672
(516) 234-2200

Floral provides beveled mirrors in all shapes and sizes, with ovals and circles in eleven sizes and three colors. Thicknesses up to 1" are available.

WHOLESALE GLASS BROKERS
19785 West Twelve Mile Road, Suite 357
Southfield, MI 48076
(800) 288-6854

For dining- and coffee-table tops, shelves, partitions, cabinet doors, beveled panels, or any rectangles, squares, circles or hole-drilled glass, in clear, bronze or gray, from 1/4" to 1" thick, including tempered glass, call or write to check out the free catalog and price guide. Wholesale Glass Brokers accepts Master-Card and Visa.

INSULATION

LOUISIANA-PACIFIC CORPORATION

111 Southwest Fifth Avenue
Portland, OR 97204
(503) 221-0800

Louisiana-Pacific (L-P) produces all kinds of plywood and other wood products, both as engineered wood products (plywoods, oriented strand boards and waferboards, among others) and as lumber, including redwood and pressure-treated versions. One of their most interesting new products, though peripherally related to woodworking, is a blow-in insulation that works with studs as well as joists — that is, it adheres and stays on vertical surfaces, after which excess is shaved off to give a flat surface. This material, made of 100 percent recycled newspaper, is called Nature Guard. Receive a brochure, free of charge, on request. I am getting ready to build a shop and am now — in the past five minutes — considering trying to locate a source for this insulation when things get to that stage. Louisiana-Pacific also has brochures on their version of Oriented Strand Board, called Waferwood. They also produce a general brochure, more like a catalog, showing the full line of L-P products, including OSB products that cover lap siding, panel siding, flooring and sheathing, interior paneling, Nature Guard insulation, laminated joists, software, windows, patio doors and lumber. The least emphasis seems to be on straight lumber products, with manufactured products getting the most. This firm is responsible for a lot of wood and a lot of literature.

METAL

COUNTRY ACCENTS

P.O. Box 437
Montoursville, PA 17754
(717) 478-4127
(717) 478-2007 FAX

Country Accents offers one of the most expensive catalogs, at $5, but if you build projects that need pierced-metal accents, then you absolutely need to look at this one. Country Accents offers a long list of pierced-tin patterns, both in metal and in patterns of their own. The company designs and manufactures pierced-metal panels in eighteen different metals, for use on cabinets, furniture, appliance fronts and in other areas. Country Accents also flatly states that there are no two of their productions exactly alike, and a good number are attractive in any decor. Various finishes are available, as are various metals, to the point where you might want to order some different-colored finishes to see how what you want is going to look. I truly am enjoying this catalog and will go on doing so. Country Accents takes Master-Card and Visa.

PRAIRIE WOODWORKING

343 Harrison
Oak Park, IL 60304
(708) 386-0603 Phone and FAX

Paul Pezella offers, as a sideline to a business of producing custom radiator covers, metal grill work in several different styles, cut to size, framed or unframed, and in a variety of finishes. Write for literature and more information. Paul does not take credit cards.

Plans and Kits

Plans and Kits

ACCENT SOUTHWEST

P.O. Box 35277
Albuquerque, NM 87176

Santa Fe style furniture plans are offered in the $3 Accents Southwest furniture catalog. The plans are said to be well thought out, with start-to-finish instructions. The catalog shows a good array of useful furniture pieces, including a corner curio cabinet, a choice of dining-table shapes, and a rocking chair. Along the way, there are also sofa and lounge chair plans, plans for a sideboard, and plans for dressers. Prices for plans range from $5 for a wall mirror on up to $20 for the sideboard.

ACCENTS IN PINE

Box 7387
Gonic, NH 03867

In the 1,000 patterns Accents in Pine offers, you will find a package of rack and stand plans, including patterns for a ski rack, coat racks, quilt and blanket stands, and others. Farther along in the catalog, one of the Pro-Paks offers three children's stools. The Pro-Paks are intended as easy-to-make projects for commercial craftspersons, and they feature fewer projects than most packs. Packages run $8 each and usually include at least half a dozen—often more, and sometimes many more—plans (set #16 has eight whirligigs, set #14 has ten bird feeders, and set #19 presents more than thirty Christmas decorations and centerpieces). Patterns, if the sample (moosehead clothes rack) sent to me is true of all, are well done, in blueprint format and easy to read. Each pattern has tips from James C. Olds, Jr., including tips on retailing your results. The catalog is $1.

THE AMERICAN COASTER

7106 Lake Road
Montrose, MI 48457

This firm offers plans for wood coaster wagons, sled wagons and wood wheelbarrows. Plans are $12.95 each, $21.95 for two, or $29.95 for all three, including shipping and handling. A brochure of plans and parts kits is available for $1.

The APA patterns include many things for children, such as this indoor play center.

AMERICAN PLYWOOD ASSOCIATION (APA)

P.O. Box 11700
Tacoma, WA 98411-0700
(206) 565-6600

The APA Handy Plan catalog is $2, and it lists and shows a wide variety of projects built primarily—naturally enough—of plywood in one form or another. The APA also offers many low-cost booklets, brochures and tech sheets that are of great help when larger projects loom and you find a need to buy plywood in large amounts and a variety of types. Ask about a listing of such technical bulletins: They can save money and problems.

AMERICAN WORKSHOP SERIES

4202 Kensington Road, Suite 2
Baltimore, MD 21229
(410) 536-5128
(410) 247-8813 FAX

The American Workshop Series Preindustrial Arts early country furniture plans catalog (no price listed) offers patterns that look more than vaguely familiar to me from the many years I spent in New York's Hudson River Valley. Many of the patterns are similar to pieces I saw at that time, and the plan included with the information package Jack Bucheimer provided closely resembles blanket chests I have seen and used. The plan is a black line (diazo process) drawing of an actual piece, and the detailed construction directions seem excellent. The actual piece is presented as coming from south-central Pennsylvania sometime between 1820 and 1840, while the similar piece I saw was ensconced in a house built around 1839, in Clinton, New York (Duchess County), an area of Dutch settlement. Dovetail patterns in the chest, to retain authenticity, may have to be hand cut, but might also be done on a Leigh or Porter-Cable Omni dovetail jig, allowing for changes in one or the other set (tail angles change as one tail is ½" across the base, with a top width of ⅛", and the other set is ⅜" across the base, with a ⅛" top width. The space between the dovetails is different, too). Most of the plans from the American Workshop Series are not for novices, though with care, I think all but the rawest novice might follow the plan. Plans include the blanket/dower chest, jelly cupboard, paneled-back settle, New England farm table, six-board blanket chest, and others. Plan prices range from six bucks for a five-board foot stool diagram, to $14 for the hooded, paneled-back settle. The American Workshop Series does not accept credit cards.

AMERICANA DESIGNS
3134 Grayland Avenue
Richmond, VA 23221

Americana Designs offers more than one hundred original gingerbread patterns for mantels, shelves, screen doors and gate designs. The catalog is $3.

Anne's Calico Cats include this furry feline, Nutmeg.

ANNE'S CALICO CAT ORIGINALS
Box 1004
Oakdale, CA 95361
(209) 847-9046

For $1, Anne will send a catalog of crafting patterns and cutouts, all of cats, and from the color photos Anne Engert sent, the patterns are attractive and the cuts very nicely done. If we can get them in, the black-and-white shots will give some indication of how the finished cutouts look. There are literally dozens of poses of these unfinished felines, and almost as many varieties of cat. Anne has named them, and she also sells painting packets with coloring instructions. The cats are multipieced and a bit less than life-sized (mostly). The numbers of pieces ranges from as few as three to as many as nine, and unless I misread, the largest size is 13" × 13" (many aren't even close to square, so there are sizes like 19" × 6" for number 13, Blackberry). If you enjoy cats and modest wood-project assembly and finishing, drop Anne a note. She does not take credit cards.

ARMOR
Box 445
East Northport, NY 11731
(800) 292-8296
(516) 462-6228
(516) 462-5793 FAX

John Capotosto writes that, for my readers, he's reducing the standard $1 catalog price to zero. That was the second nice surprise in John's package: The seventy-two-page catalog is not just of plans, but also contains many small tools, finishes, furniture trim, hardware and other items, plus four pages of books (in which John has forgone the temptation to include mostly his and brother Rosario's woodworking titles, of which there are many). The book selection, like the plan selection, is very wide for the number of books listed. Clock plans range up to a 77" Washington Hall Clock from a simple outline-cut cowboy boot clock. John also offers a classic rolltop desk plan (with or without his parts kit), cheval mirror, gun cabinets, dry sinks, workbenches, tea carts, cradles, desks, children's outdoor furniture, billiard tables, table soccer plans, lamp plans, rocking horses, toys, vehicles, dollhouses (including kits), and on. Many of the plans are developments for John's articles in top do-it-yourself and craft magazines over the years and are well worth reviewing. The catalog is a must see.

ASHLAND BARNS
990-WBS Butlercreek
Ashland, OR 97520
(503) 488-1541

The eighty-two barn and minibarn plans offered in Ashland's $5 catalog (refunded with plans order) are supplemented by a second catalog, at $2 (and, again, refunded with order), offering plans for weather vanes and signs, adorned with "critters" as Jay Wallace puts it. The cuts of signs, weather vanes and a barn show interesting design features, so if projects along these lines are in your area of interest, give Jay a call or drop him a note requesting the catalogs.

THE BERRY BASKET
P.O. Box 925
Centralia, WA 98531
(800) 206-9009 Charge orders
(206) 736-7020 Catalog requests
(206) 736-7336 FAX

The Berry Basket is the only company I've seen listing collapsible basket patterns. The company also offers a plans package for a six-building Christmas village, a child-sized bunny-rocker plan, a doll bench, and a series of other plans and patterns. The Berry Basket also carries quartz miniclock inserts, and it offers free patterns with each of those. The digest-sized, full-color catalog is nicely done; it shows doll furniture, shelves, planters, tole-paint projects, and much else already completed. Pattern themes include Southwest, Victorian, Country and several others. All patterns are full-sized, and The Berry Basket offers a thirty-day money-back guarantee. Currently, the catalog is $1 and comes out twice a year. The Berry Basket takes MasterCard and Visa.

BRENDA'S SHOP
P.O. Box 125
Guildford, MO 64457
(816) 652-3731

Brenda Nelson offers intarsia patterns (sort of a bas relief, only done in wood instead of stone or plaster) for the scroll saw people out there. Patterns are full-sized, and a color photograph and detailed instructions come with the patterns. Brenda's patterns are all original, and they include all sorts of animals, such as a lion's head, an owl, a squirrel, a Canadian goose, and a number of others. Her brochure is $2.50, and she doesn't take credit cards.

BOB MEYER
7347 Highway 247 NE
Elgin, MN 55932
(507) 876-2482

Bob sells originally designed wooden-geared clock plans. One of his three uses a 48" main gear and a 36" escarpment gear—of wood! Another plan, for a wooden-geared standing clock, uses wood and bathroom tubing (polished aluminum) for a clock that is 87" tall. The third is a wooden-geared wall clock, 24" long. All gears on the latter are cut from ¾" hardwood-veneer plywood, as are those in the other

clocks, and they may be cut with a jigsaw. Costs of clock plans range from $15 for the wall clock through $25 for the standing clock to $40 for the monster. Bob discounts the plans when you buy more than one, and all three cost $55. He will also send you an information sheet and a photo of each plan for $1 per plan. Bob Meyer doesn't accept credit cards.

This big clock from Bob Meyer uses 40″ and 48″ wooden main gears.

CALIFORNIA REDWOOD ASSOCIATION
405 Enfrente Drive, Suite 200
Novato, CA 94949
(415) 382-0662

For a wide range of literature on types and uses of redwood lumber, the California Redwood Association can't be beat. The emphasis is on outdoor use, as one might expect, though I've found redwood to be an interesting material for large and small indoor projects as well. (I built two redwood bookshelves some time ago: They continue to stand in my dining room, where their appearance often draws comments because redwood is seldom used for such projects. Most indoor redwood projects are architectural, such as wall paneling and molding.) The Association's literature list offers everything from a Design-A-Deck plans kit to nail-use information. Exterior and interior finishes are covered in large brochures, and there are pamphlets on the industry and its harvesting methods, as well as the environmental impact of using redwood. I'd suggest giving the Association a call, or dropping them a note, to request the literature list, at which time you can ask them about shipping costs that are added to literature prices on the list.

CHERRY TREE TOYS, INC.

P.O. Box 369
Belmont, OH 43718
(800) 848-4363
(614) 484-4363
(614) 484-4388 FAX

Cherry Tree Toys may be most notable for the variety and quality of the shaped wood parts it carries, but it also has a good line of accessories, including drill bits, circle cutters, and even Sakura scroll saws, all at competitive prices. Cherry Tree also carries almost four dozen music-box movements, with songs as diverse as "Amazing Grace" and "You Light Up My Life." Also, there are bank-slot melody movements, mobile-holder musical movements, blinking-nose movements, touch movements, and others. The Cherry Tree line of kits includes a Conestoga wagon, a stagecoach, a chuck wagon, and hardware packages for a variety of other plans. There are many door-harp plans, parts and kits, as well as cradle, dollhouse and toy plans. Cherry Tree offers a line of solid brass stencils for letters and patterns that I have seen nowhere else. The sixty-eight-page Cherry Tree Toys catalog, which sells for $1, is a must have for toy builders. Cherry Tree Toys accepts Discover, MasterCard and Visa.

CLARK CRAFT

16 Aqua Lane
Tonawanda, NY 14150
(716) 873-2640
(716) 873-2651 FAX

Clark Craft presents a catalog of boat kits, and plans, for a nonrefundable $5, first-class mail, $2.50 for bulk mail. The catalog order includes a separate boat-building-supply catalog that includes books, more plans, many laminating and finishing tools and supplies, boat nails and screws (silicon bronze is the featured material), fiberglass cloth, mat, woven roving and tape, plus resins, with detailed instructions for the use of epoxy. The boat plan and kit catalog takes you from canoe and a six-foot dinghy on up to a Rob-

erts 64 sailboat. Along the way, there are plans for kayaks, hovercraft, tunnel hull runabouts, racers, houseboats, and even a 70′ steel-hull cruiser. Prices for plans and patterns start as low as $20, and rise to $695 for the 70′ steel-hull cruiser, jumping to $749 for the Roberts 64. Study prints are available at far lower cost ($30 for the Roberts 64, $20 for the steel 70 footer). Boat kits start at $225 for the little dinghy and scamper up to $6,650 for a Crown Cruiser 26′. Larger boats, and many not so large, are available only as plans kits, but some have frame, hull and fastening kits available, too.

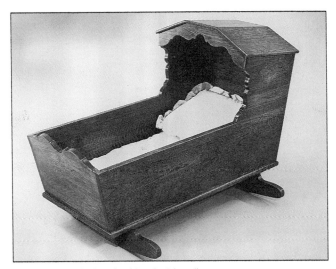

Craft Patterns sells plans for this colonial cradle.

CRAFT PATTERNS

3545 Stern Avenue
St. Charles, IL 60174
(800) 747-1429
(708) 584-3334
(708) 584-3418 FAX

Craft Patterns' 1995 plan catalog offers many items, over five hundred patterns and plans, starting with indoor furnishings in the crate style and going on through most furniture styles, including a rolltop desk, an oak file cabinet, a cheval mirror, a grandmother clock, wall sconces, several dining room table styles, a recycling center, and on to the outdoors and barbecue stands, masonry barbecues, tree seats, swings, gliders, benches, birdhouses, small boats, doghouses, bird feeders, garages, cupolas and rocking horses. There are complex patterns and simple patterns and in-between plans, so that almost all skill levels are served. Craft Patterns also operates a retail store at the above address, has been in business since 1940, and guarantees satisfaction. Hours are eight to five, Monday through Friday, Central Time.

Craft Patterns accepts MasterCard, Visa, Discover and American Express.

CRAFTER'S MART
Box 2342
Greeley, CO 80632

Musical wooden Ferris wheel parts and plans are included in Crafter's Mart's one-dollar catalog. The seventy-two-page catalog is full of projects, parts and supplies. There are more than 350 varieties of varied music box fittings; more than 300 project plans; and bulk pricing on wood turnings such as wheels, spindles, knobs, plugs, pegs, and so on. Many of the plans are said to be proven sales designs at craft fairs. Crafter's Mart takes MasterCard, Visa and Discover.

CUPBOARD DISTRIBUTING
114 South Main Street
P.O. Box 148
Urbana, OH 43078
(800) 338-6388
(513) 652-3338
(513) 652-3898 FAX

Cupboard Distributing presents chunk wood shapes and much else in the way of wood products and supplies. Small carousels and jointed animals are among the offerings, as are small rocking horses (the larger of the two is 6½ × 5"), pull toys, necklace kits, wood bracelets, wheels, buttons, pegs, dowels, smokestacks, axles, gameboards and signs, spindles, finials, table pins, knobs, paints, glues, twine, Christmas ornaments, and resin castings (Santa, grandfather and grandmother, and others). Christmas ornaments include snowmen and angels, and there are miniature desks, blackboards, school bells and books. Cupboard Distributing carries Delta paints, Sakura Pigma pens, 1881 Crackle and much else. The catalog comes out annually and costs $2. Cupboard Distributing accepts Discover, MasterCard and Visa.

DESIGNER FURNITURE PLANS
179 Davidson Avenue, Dept. 4
Somerset, NJ 08873

This plans company was established in 1992 and offers full-sized furniture plans. All plans come with exploded views and parts lists of the piece. The company also includes a separate parts list to make reference to it easier. The catalog is $3, and Designer Furniture Plans does not take credit cards.

EMPEROR CLOCK COMPANY
Emperor Industrial Park
Fairhope, AL 36532
(205) 928-2316

Emperor's clock kits and furniture kits come in solid oak, walnut and cherry; they let you furnish your home at a fraction of the cost of already built furniture before you develop all the skills required for full-scale, and complex, woodworking. All parts are precut, and the frames and doors have already been assembled. Kits are accompanied by a money-back guarantee. The color catalog is free, and Emperor Clock Company takes American Express, MasterCard, Visa and Diners Club.

FAMILY HANDYMAN PLAN SERVICE
P.O. Box 83695
Stillwater, MN 55083
(715) 247-5076

The plans from Family Handyman Plan Service are based on articles in *Family Handyman* magazine, with complete how-to instructions, plenty of step-by-step photos, a shopping list for materials, a cutting list and exploded drawings. Plans include full-sized patterns where curves exist, which helps ease the work of building many projects. The brochure I'm checking out shows a cedar strip canoe, a Colonial pine cradle, a fairly fancy gazebo, a rocking horse, two wood wagons, a playground and a playhouse. Although the plans are not cheap, they aren't exceptionally pricey either; however, there are a couple I'd not pay for plans on no matter how low the price (the cradle and the standard picnic table: Neither adds any complexity to projects that were almost too easy to begin with). Family Handyman Plans Service takes MasterCard and Visa.

FOREST STREET DESIGNS
538 Holiday Drive
Brigham City, UT 84302

Attaché case, coffee table/stereo cabinet, and world-map plans (each continent in a different veneer) are available. Costs are $10.95 for each of the first two, $8.95 for the map, $25.95 for the package, including shipping and a free catalog.

FURNITURE DESIGNS, INC.
1827 Elmdale Avenue
Glenview, IL 60025
(708) 657-7526

Since 1968, interesting furniture plans, including library chair-steps, several blanket chests, a pencil-post bed, a sleigh bed, several corner cabinets, and many cradles have been the forte of Furniture Designs, Inc. Their catalog is $3 and lists more than two hundred full-sized furniture plans over a wide range that even includes rocking horses. Furniture Designs accepts MasterCard and Visa.

GATTO PLAN SUPPLY

Box 1568 R.D. 1
Hamburg, PA 19526

The Gatto plans, from Daniel Gatto, are wheeled models of superb appearance, with great detail. Included are a wood-block backhoe/front-end loader, a farm tractor, a 1930 Ford Model A Roadster (including 16-spoke wheels), an 80-part pickup truck, right down to an opening tailgate, a 50-piece '57 replica car that looks a lot like a '57 Chevy, and a Monster Truck that thoroughly demonstrates the big wheel craze that's been going on for years, including four shock absorbers per wheel and K.C. lights. Many plans include options, and plan prices range from $4.95 to $7.95. Projects are readily built from scrap wood and dowels. The brochure is seventy-five cents.

GILLIOM MANUFACTURING, INC.

P.O. Box 1018
St. Charles, MO 63302
(314) 724-1812

If you have any desire to make your own power tools, kits from Gilliom may be the incentive you need to get started. The list includes a 12″ band saw, an 18″ band saw, a 10″ tilt arbor table saw, a lathe-and-drill-press combination, a 9″ tilt-table table saw, a 6″ belt sander, a spindle shaper, and a circular saw table, at $7.50 each or $25 for the package of eight plans. Gilliom also manufactures kits to help you in building the tools. The descriptive brochure is $2.

HERITAGE BUILDING SPECIALTIES

205 North Cascade
Fergus Falls, MN 56537
(800) 524-4184
(218) 739-9710
(218) 739-5798 FAX

Their plans and materials are currently done in cooperation with major publishers in the woodworking field. In essence, they package the wood precut for projects so that the woodworker can then concentrate on doing the final stages of the work. All wood material is first-grade hardwood to suit the project being built. Heritage takes MasterCard and Visa.

JENNINGS DECOY COMPANY

601 Franklin Ave. NE
St. Cloud, MN 56304
(800) 331-5613
(612) 253-9537
(612) 253-2253 FAX

Jennings Decoy Company presents kits for carving such ducks as the loon, mallard and wood duck, in basswood, tupelo, butternut, and other easily worked woods. Jennings has also a wide line of blanks for songbirds, game birds and Santa figures. Jennings carries Foredom kits, with the foot-controlled Foredom flexible shaft tools. The catalog also covers a great many carving tools, patterns, painting supplies, books and completed carvings and is free for the asking. There are also three sales flyers sent out each year. Jennings Decoy takes MasterCard, Visa and Discover.

JOHN WILSON

500 East Broadway Highway
Charlotte, MI 48813
(517) 543-5325

John is the modern-day torchbearer for Shaker oval boxes, and he offers everything from instruction sheets to the kits to make the boxes, right up to and including the correct kind of toothpicks to use as pegging. A typical Shaker oval box kit will include materials for the lid, box bands bent to shape, and wood for the bottom, plus an instruction sheet. You need only provide wood glue, a saw that will cut an oval, 120- and 220-grit sandpaper and clear finish. He has his own video and a line of tools, accessories and patterns that makes the overall job a great deal simpler. John also has a pattern packet that presents more than two dozen oval boxes and carriers. He offers workshops at specific intervals and at varied places during the year, so you don't always have to be in Michigan to learn to make oval boxes. Give him a call, or drop a note, to check prices of current literature and workshops, or check the Woodcraft catalog for some kits and products John has specifically designed.

KLOCKIT

P.O. Box 636
Lake Geneva, WI 53147
(800) KLOCKIT
(414) 248-9899 FAX

Klockit distributes clock kits, movements, faces and virtually all clock-making accessories. The Klockit emphasis is on quartz battery movements, including some moderately massive chiming-pendulum and dual-pendulum types (not as long or large as truly massive mechanical movements, with a maximum bob diameter of about 3½″ on a 20″-long pendulum). You'll also find mechanicals, with cable-driven movements, bobs over 10″ in diameter, and a wide variety of grandfather and grandmother clock faces, case kits, full kits, cuckoo clocks, fretwork project kits—available ready-to-cut or already laser cut—and on to music box kits with 50-note movements. There is even a two-page spread of wristwatches and a fair assortment of accessories, such as brad-point drill bits, sanding drums, Forstner bits, and wood and brass parts. The catalog is free, and Klockit takes Discover, MasterCard and Visa.

LEICHTUNG WORKSHOPS
4944 Commerce Parkway
Cleveland, OH 44128
(800) 321-6840
(216) 464-6764 FAX

Leichtung offers a variety of unusual tools, plus many plans and woodworking supplies, in their free catalog. The catalog is digest-sized, but sometimes runs over ninety pages. It presents seasonal plans; some kits (varying with the seasons, but often small boxes and clocks, ships, dollhouses); and parts to help in building some of the plan items. The catalog has many styles of clamps, numerous doweling and jointing jigs, and it is the only tool catalog I've seen where you're as apt to find wildflower seeds by the small sack, rain gauges, barbecue cleaner, rocks and cowhide gloves, as you are Forstner drill bits. I've used a lot of Leichtung's gloves and always keep several pair on hand. For the price, they're the best I've seen for light chores, up to and including feeding a planer. The company also has a goodly array of parts bins, as well as jars and hangers for perforated board, both ¼″ and ⅛″. They also offer a Woodworker's Guild for a $15 annual membership fee. Leichtung takes American Express, MasterCard, Visa and Discover.

MASON & SULLIVAN
210 Wood County Industrial Park
P.O. Box 1686
Parkersburg, WV 26102
(800) 225-1153 Order line
(800) 535-4482 Customer service, 8:30 A.M. to 5:00 P.M., Monday-Friday

The Mason & Sullivan line includes antique reproduction clock kits and parts. They also have an extensive line of top-quality chain- and cable-driven clock works for tall clocks and for shorter clocks. The catalog also covers a broad line of clock tools. The catalog is free.

The firm accepts American Express/Optima, Discover, MasterCard and Visa.

MEISEL HARDWARE SPECIALTIES
P.O. Box 70
Mound, MN 55364-0070
(800) 441-9870

Paul Meisel offers a wide variety of plans, with projects shown in an update catalog keyed to Christmas. Once you get on the list, you can expect to look at Christmas projects in the catalog that arrives around the end of July. This allows the woodworker to work up Christmas projects for sale, or for gifts, well in advance of the season. Halloween and Thanksgiving projects are in the same catalog. There is also a 32-page scroll saw catalog included in the subscription cost. Paul's specialties in the plan area are often—far from always, though—cutout patterns for use as lawn ornaments. He also offers simple nativity plans and enough yard-ornament plans to literally cover a huge lawn. Plans are offered as just plans or as combinations of plans and hardware kits. You may also buy the hardware—sleigh bells, wind-streamer material (for Santa's beard), and so on in the Christmas catalog—separately. The 112-page Meisel Hardware Specialties general catalogs offer such items as a slingshot drag racer powered by a rubber band and rocking horse plans that are really fine (the rocking horse can be bought in a number of styles, including with rockers already cut). Meisel Hardware Specialties plans are usually drawn full size, so they can be transferred directly to the wood, simplifying the work. Many of the projects are nearly ideal for beginning and lightly experienced woodworkers. Meisel Hardware takes Discover, MasterCard and Visa.

MINDY'S PUZZLES
Box 176
Elk City, ID 83525
(208) 842-2265

For $5, plus $1.25 postage, Mindy Wiebush will ship you more than twenty puzzle patterns, in sizes ranging from 6″ × 9″ to 10″ × 15″, with the resulting puzzles designed to suit skill levels from two years to more than five years (not for puzzle construction, but for puzzle assembly). A sheet of carbon paper is provided for tracing patterns onto wood, and a six-page tip sheet makes the already simple scroll saw and band saw patterns even simpler and safer to do right. Mindy also sends along a few critter patterns to help reduce scrap wood buildup (kids really do love these simple items), and offers, for an additional $4.50 including shipping, fifty other animal patterns. Ask for the Critter Packet.

MUSICMAKER'S KITS, INC.
P.O. Box 2117
14525 North 61st Street
Stillwater, MN 55082
(800) 432-KITS
(612) 439-9120

Jerry Brown seems to offer about every type of stringed instrument kit that might be of interest. The kit list includes hammered dulcimers, mountain dulcimers, harps, banjos, guitars, mountain mandolins, Renaissance guitar, string bass, panpipes, wooden fife, garden harp, window harp, door harps, a wooden drum, thumb piano, full-sized harps, animal harps (angelfish, anyone?), Celtic harps, and a wild-looking instrument called the hurdy-gurdy. (For those, like me, who haven't got a clue, it sounds like a bagpipe but is played by cranking to vibrate the strings, after which you push keys. Invented in the sixteenth century, it makes a tough project, with lots of small parts.) Also available is a series of special-order kits that includes a Martin classical guitar. In addition, Jerry has bits and pieces for scratch builders, including tuning pins, fret scale graphs, eyelets and much else. To work from plans, get one of his door harp or guitar plans, or any of a couple dozen other plans for everything from a hammer dulcimer to a psaltery (actually, from a banjo to a violin, if we stay alphabetical). He also carries a few items such as flutes, a wooden drum and a Kalimba. Woods, dyes, finishes and clamps are also offered. The catalog sells for $2, and is thirty-six color pages long. Jerry takes most credit cards, including American Express, Optima, Discover, MasterCard and Visa.

NELSON DESIGNS
P.O. Box 422
Dublin, NH 03444
(603) 563-3306

John Nelson recently started offering advanced, full-sized, scroll saw plans and projects and scroll saw books by mail. His offerings include original 1880 scroll saw patterns from New England: toys, clocks, wall shelves, corner shelves, mirrors and much more. John states that he and his wife, Joyce, have taken most of their patterns from fretwork designs in New England; most of the fretwork dates from the 1880 to 1935 era. I have several of John's books, and if his patterns follow his writing and illustration, they will be excellent and easy to use, though I'll also bet that when he says *advanced*, beginners had best not

Shown here is one of the Musicmaker's kits fully assembled.

apply! Pattern prices currently start at $2 for a plant stand, and rise to $18 for a merry-go-round with sixteen horses. John also sells a selection of his own books. At the moment, John and Joyce don't take any credit cards, but they hope to reach that stage shortly.

OSMOSE WOOD PRESERVING, INC.
P.O. Drawer O
Griffin, GA 30224
(404) 228-8431

Osmose is a major manufacturer of wood-preservative chemicals, outdoor stains, sealers and cleaners, and it has its own line of deck screws. Osmose produces a wide line of brochures that include many project plans, including a garden bench, mailbox post, planter box, deck (12' × 16' freestanding), sandbox/play pool, gazebo, greenhouse classic picnic table, trash can corral and others. Osmose does not provide these items directly, but it does send them along to dealers, where you can pick them up.

PINECRAFT PATTERNS
P.O. Box 13186
Green Bay, WI 54307-3186

Lawn ornaments, shelves, birdhouses, porch swings, picnic tables and cabinets make up the 40' plans in Pinecraft's $6.95 package (including shipping and handling).

PLEASURE CRAFTS
Route 2, Box 1485
Mannford, OK 74044

Danny Cheney of Pleasure Crafts produces full-sized, traceable patterns for balancing toys and other wooden mechanical toys, and usable folk-art items. The packages of plans, described in free brochures, present a total of more than 135 patterns. Each book of patterns is $10, or all three are $27, postpaid. Patterns include a mass of toys that are difficult to describe accurately and in terms of apparent actions, but there is a girl on parallel bars, a cowboy with a lariat, a rocking clown, a fisherman catching a fish, a swinging bear, a card-showing magician, a rope-jumping pair, climbing clowns, spice racks, memo holders, coat hangers, and many, many more. Write for the brochures.

QUAKER STATE WOODWORKING SUPPLY
Airport Industries Building #2
RD 9, Box 9386
Reading, PA 19605
(800) 776-5467
(610) 478-9448 (local)
(610) 478-9388 FAX

Quaker State Woodworking Supply offers plans, tools, accessories, and a growing catalog/newsletter, currently at sixteen pages. Drop a card to be added to the list for their quarterly publication. It often comes within a package consisting of the MLCS and Penn State catalogs, and there's a wide variety of offerings from the three outfits. Quaker State itself is a discount tool house, with some emphasis on abrasives, but carrying a goodly line of Porter-Cable tools, some Bosch equipment, Wagner's FineCoat HVLP sprayer, glues, Fas-Tak nail guns, clamps, SECO dust collectors and many other items. They've got a super price on Ryobi's new oscillating spindle sander, too (that, by the way, is a superb tool for home-shop use on curved surfaces: As far as I know, it is the only one on the market with a price under $600, and it's selling for less than a third of that most places). Their showroom is at Reading Airport, and is open Monday through Friday, eight to five, and Saturdays eight to noon. Quaker State will also send you a list of the fifty or more shows they attend annually. Quaker State takes MasterCard and Visa.

RICK EMMANUELLI
4407 Fernhill Road
Wheaton, MD 20906

Rick sells reprints (8½" × 11" size) of old Stanley project design plans. He has three groups for sale: #11, which includes a workbench, tool cabinet, tool chest, saw horse and Adirondack chair; #13, with a circus toy, fireplace bookends, drop-leaf coffee table, end table and wall book shelf; and #16, with a kiddy push car, rocking horse, scooter (that's something for today's kids, who haven't got a clue, even from pictures!), toy wheelbarrow, and toy wagon. Years ago, I built some small projects from old Stanley plans and found them easy to follow and accurate. Rick has a total of nineteen sets of these plans, at $7 per set, and will send you the complete list for an SASE.

RJS CUSTOM WOODWORKING
P.O. Box 12354
Kansas City, KS 66112

RJS piqued my interest when I saw they had toy carousel plans, but when I received their most recent catalog (printed on recycled paper, with a request that it be recycled after a new catalog arrives), I found that plans, including full-sized carousel plans and plans for dream-car plaques (if your dream car is a Ferrari or a Rolls), are only a part of the line. Books range from Patrick Speilman's varied treatises on scroll saws, routers and their uses to his sign-making books to R.J. De Cristoforo's array of power-tool books (Cris's are among the best done to date), on back to wiring your own home. Products also include a great many parts and pieces for projects, as well as small tools. There are even stencils of many patterns, words and letters (I believe most of these are Dover patterns).

THE ROCKING HORSE SHOP
9 Spring Street
St. Jacobs, Ontario
Canada N0B 2N0
(519) 664-1661

This is an intriguing catalog—small, but full of information for any rocking-horse enthusiast. The catalog leads off with an offer of *The Rocking-Horse Maker*, by Anthony Dew, and you quickly learn that book is the source for the plans in the catalog. The original company is British, and this Canadian rep sells plans for swinger rocking horses (plain and elaborate), a toddler's rocking horse that can be very simple (cutout head) or more complex (carved head). There are a number of plans for full-carved rocking horses, a video on making rocking horses, accessory kits for all offered plans, and even two dollhouse plans (one Victorian, one Georgian). Other books on rocking horses are offered. John Wombwell claims that this St. Jacobs outfit is the most comprehensive supplier of rocking-horse plans, accessories and books, and I see no reason to doubt that statement. All accessories are handmade (and include real horsehair manes and tails, cast brass stirrups and other parts, and real leather saddles and reins); also, phone help is available. The catalog costs $2.50, and The Rocking Horse Shop takes American Express, Optima and Visa.

ROYAL SAWDUST COMPANY

2950 Emerson Road
Branchport, NY 14418
(607) 522-4919
(716) 442-6130

The Royal Sawdust Company presents toy plans for larger toys than one usually thinks of when considering wooden toy plans: The $2 catalog starts with a 30"-diameter child's table and chairs, with special detailing on building the curved chair backs. The plans Robert Pearce sent me were of a stove of a size for children to play with without dolls: The plans are well drawn and nicely detailed, and the project is reasonably simple and will take no special tools. There is an entire kitchen full of appliances in plans (stove, refrigerator, sink). Other plans include a vending machine, a block set with its own two-wheeled hand truck, a delivery truck large enough for several children to ride on, a fire truck, a playhouse, a puppet stage, and a multipurpose play table that can serve as a potting bench or an indoor (or outdoor) sandbox. As noted, the catalog is $2, and Royal Sawdust does not accept credit cards.

SCROLLSAW PATTERNS

6060 Spine Road
P.O. Box 55060
Boulder, CO 80323
(800) 678-7300

I'm almost always of two minds about this kind of magazine: It's a foldout, which I don't like to start with; plans are backed up by other plan drawings, so you must copy at least one side of the sheet if you want all the plans; scroll saw plans seem to me to have been severely overdone in recent years. My second wind comes with the fact that I am an occasional scroll saw user who loves fooling with the thing and producing some moderately complex bits (I doubt I've got the patience or skill to do a couple of the items in the Scrollsaw Patterns I have in front of me

as I write this). And I must admit the plans themselves are well done. So, where does that leave us? With the fact that you can always cancel a subscription if you don't like it. Give them a call to check on current subscription prices.

SEYCO

1414 Cranford Drive
Box 472749
Garland, TX 75047-2749
(800) 462-3353
(214) 278-3353

This scroll saw specialist has a $1 catalog that features the Excalibur line of saws, their own line of letter guides, and many books and patterns for scroll saw people. Seyco also offers its own brand of blade clamps, some general accessories such as finishes, glues, blade storage tubes, and turned parts for projects, as well as an extremely extensive line of scroll saw blades. Seyco takes MasterCard and Visa.

SPECIALTY FURNITURE DESIGNS OF MICHIGAN

797 West Remus Road
Mt. Pleasant, MI 48858
(800) 892-4026

Specialty Furniture Designs has six different planter designs, including a planter bench combination, many picnic table plans, chaise lounge and other plans using nominal 2" materials. The plans are full-sized. The color catalog is $2. Specialty Furniture Designs accepts Discover, MasterCard and Visa.

STEWART-MACDONALD

Box 900
Athens, OH 45701
(800) 848-2273
(614) 593-7922 FAX

The 104-page, free catalog from Stewart-MacDonald offers plans for a number of instruments—guitar (solid and acoustic bodies), mandolin and banjo. Stewart-MacDonald also carries many unusual tools and supplies—such products as fret tang nippers, three-corner fret files, bridge pin hole reamers and similar items are, at the least, exotically named. Also offered are video courses in guitar repair, pearl inlay techniques, gluing secrets, guitar finishing, and on. To add to the line of information, Stewart-MacDonald carries many tools other than those already mentioned, and it goes on to carry a lot of familiar supplies (Hydrocote and Behlen finishes, HVLP spray finish outfits, dial calipers, and so on), amongst the bending irons, spool clamps, bridge clamps, bridge saddle routing jigs and much more. They also carry the first actual vacuum tubes for amplifiers that I've seen in longer than I care to think about, as well as a couple of dulcimer kits that look interesting, and not too difficult, to build. If you're interested, there's also a drum maker's catalog, with some interesting products. Full catalog price is $1, and Stewart-MacDonald accepts MasterCard and Visa.

SUN DESIGNS

173 East Wisconsin Avenue
Oconomowoc, WI 53066
(414) 567-4255

Sun Designs is a small company producing design books and construction plans for yard and other projects. The Strom Toys line is considered a classic of toy design and making and is one of the products from Sun. Janet Strombeck kindly sent along blueprints for the Victoria, a truly lovely sleigh, and a copy of *Timeless Toys in Wood* for me to examine. If I still lived in an area with decent amounts of winter weather—snow, for example—I'd quickly build the Victoria, then go further and produce the Bunker Hill sled. Even without a local winter wonderland, I find a sufficiency of toy plans: The engine and coal car in *Timeless Toys*, for example, are large enough to provide riding models for small children, but they have few enough accessories and other cars that a woodworking parent or grandparent is not too busy to enjoy the child, too. The designs shown in *Gazebos and Other Garden Structures* will keep many a woodworker or carpenter employed for a long period. *Gazebos* is an idea book; plans for the most part are available as extra attractions, at varying prices (birdhouse or feeder plans, for example, are about $5.95 each—buy more, get a discount per plan; gazebo plans are $24.95 each). You'll see drawings in some of the plans, many of which are ornate and correspondingly difficult to build. Others are less ornate and less difficult to erect. The four color brochure is fifty cents. Sun Designs also mail-orders accessory packages for their toy designs.

TOMORROW'S HEIRLOOMS

P.O. Box 2D
Hibbing, MN 55746

Peter and Sally Grames began in 1994 offering an extensive selection of toy barn, animal and castle—medieval to modern—plans for children's play time. The plans are full-sized and detailed, including materials lists and instructions, and there are also complete kits for those who wish to do nothing more than finish and assemble. Plans and kits include stencils as well as instructions, and even woods that are shaved to produce a fur look (Sally says bird's-eye maple does well here). Currently, Tomorrow's Heirlooms doesn't accept credit cards, but the $1 for their brochure is refundable with an order for a kit.

TOYS AND JOYS

Box 628
Lynden, WA 98264

The $1 Toys and Joys catalog expands on a list of patterns, wheels, pegs, dowels and kits. The aim is primarily wooden vehicles that are extremely nicely detailed.

TREND-LINES

375 Beacham Street
Chelsea, MA 02150
(800) 366-6966 Catalog request number
(800) 767-9999
(800) 877-3338 Automated speed ordering
(617) 889-2072 FAX

Trend-Lines is a discount mail-order house that offers many plans and project books, plus general woodworking books. In their free catalog, you'll find more than 3,000 brand-name products, including power tools and accessories, hand tools, screws, hardware and wood parts, in addition to the plans and books. Stan Black always has interesting plans listed (often some new tools as well), and he produces a catalog that packs a lot of interest for woodworkers. Complete satisfaction is guaranteed, and Trend-Lines guarantees also to sell any power tool or accessory for less than any nationally advertised mail-order price. You'll even find contractor's ladder jacks in this catalog! Trend-Lines takes Discover, MasterCard and Visa.

TURNCRAFT CLOCKS

P.O. Box 100
Mound, MN 55364-0100
(800) 544-1711

Turncraft Clocks is fairly new, specializing in different and unusual, as well as traditional, clock parts and clock plans. The catalog displays a variety of quartz movements, with and without pendulums and chimes, and an even wider variety of clock faces in sizes from 3¾" up to 12⅜". Drop a line and request the catalog if you're at all interested in making reasonably simple clocks. Turncraft accepts Discover, MasterCard and Visa.

WEEKEND WOODCRAFTS

1320 Galaxy Way
Concord, CA 94520

In this 1992 start-up from EGW Publishing, there are no shop tips or hints, but the forty-eight-page bimonthly (six issues per year, for $14.97 at the moment) offers a string of easily built projects. There are ten in the issue I'm checking, with everything done in color and full-sized Pull-Out Plans for some projects. Projects are all simple or small enough to be built in a single weekend. It's well worth a check if your interest is in fast projects, particularly those that might prove salable in craft fairs. The crafts projects, let me note, are small but not necessarily tiny: Seats and toolboxes abound, as do small tables and toys.

WEEKEND WOODWORKING PROJECTS
1716 Locust Street
Des Moines, IA 50336
(800) 678-2666

Featuring a half dozen easy-to-make or small projects every other month, the magazine has presented a collector's cabinet, a bass puzzle, and an Adirondack table and footstool, plus a cutout cottontail box, a lathed letter opener and a stand-up mirror—all in a single issue. Using double covers, the staff managed to work in a short tip feature between covers, with other tips (related to included projects) as needed. Nicely done in four colors, with a four-color cover, this is another that is well worth a look for those of you interested in small, faster-to-build projects (though I have to admit that the collector's cabinet, of cherry and with porcelain knobs, is large enough and complex enough you'd best not be planning on spending major time outside the workshop on the weekend you build it). Subscription price currently is $27.97 for this bimonthly (six issues per year, in January, March, May, July, September and November) from Meredith Corporation.

WESTERN WOOD PRODUCTS ASSOCIATION
522 Southwest Fifth Avenue
Portland, OR 97204-2122
(503) 224-3930
(503) 224-3934 FAX

Founded more than thirty years ago, in 1964, WWPA presents technical information, grading information, and standards for the species of wood their association emphasizes (Douglas fir, hem-fir, Engelmann spruce, Idaho white pine, lodgepole pine, sugar pine, Ponderosa pine, Western larch, Western cedars and incense cedar), as well as a good series of large and small plans at low cost. I'm looking at a plan for kid-sized storage modules now, their #62: It is easy to build and uses standard lumber sizes. Plan #61 is a mobile workbench that looks no harder to build.

Drop a note (or call, if you wish) asking for the current literature list or a catalog of plans. The list is too long to reproduce here, but it contains a good variety of plans that will almost certainly have one of interest to you. The Association takes MasterCard and Visa.

WINFIELD COLLECTION
112 East Ellen Street
Fenton, MI 48430
(800) 968-3570 Customer service
(800) 927-6447 Orders, catalog requests
(810) 629-7784 FAX

I've got the most recent of the Winfield Collection catalogs in front of me, with a huge assortment of country woodcraft patterns listed and illustrated. The $1 catalog subscription gives you a good chance at finding something you like over time. Projects, from birdhouses to stands and other furniture—and including lawn ornaments and toys—are designed to be quickly and easily made, which adds to fun and makes for a good chance of profit if you're going to do crafts as more than a hobby. Decorative mailboxes are popular now, and there are two color pages of them. Furniture projects, which are designed to use pine or similar low-cost woods (as are all the projects), include a corner country cupboard, a pie safe, a deacon's bench, a child's rocking chair, a hall table, a quilt rack and many others. Patterns are full-sized, set to be traced onto the wood, cut out and assembled. Pattern prices start at $1 and go up to $11.50, with most in the $5 area. And here's a personal tip on traceable patterns: Do not try to do the tracing completely freehand. Use straight edges and french curves as needed to stabilize your tracing so lines will be cleaner and easier to cut accurately. They now carry $5/32$"-thick plywood and have a line of rocking animals as well as many new paints. The Winfield Collection accepts MasterCard, Visa and Discover.

WOOD
Wood Customer Service
P.O. Box 55050
Boulder, CO 80322-5050
(800) 374-9663

One of what has become a multitude of very well-done woodworking magazines in recent years, Better Homes & Gardens's *Wood* presents everything from simple projects on through complex plans, plus tips, tool tests, tested jigs, shop hints, on up and down a long list of useful types of articles. Some of the project articles are among the most attractive to be found without extra complexity, though the projects are plenty detailed: That is, the plans can be readily followed by most intermediate woodworkers with patience and time to work things out. Some may even be readily accomplished by lower-end intermediate woodworkers, and a few will work for novices. Simpler projects show up in *Wood*'s companion magazine, *Weekend Woodworking Projects*. The magazine completes all project plans in its own shop, described as state-of-the-art. Tool-article advice has improved. It started as fact-sheet stuff, but now some use-testing and opinion are included. *Wood* is the largest of the woodworking magazines in terms of circulation, having gone past 650,000. Currently running nine issues per year, the cost is $25. It's best to call to check latest subscription prices.

WOODARTIST

P.O. Box 31564
Charleston, SC 29417

Send an SASE for a list of plans for antique birdhouses.

WOODCRAFTS BY OSCAR HUBBERT

P.O. Box 1415
Fletcher, NC 28732
(704) 687-0350

Oscar Hubbert sells old post-office-box door fronts and banks he makes of those old door fronts. His for-sale collection of door fronts consists of models from twenty-five to more than one hundred years old, and he'll send a price of post-office door supplies available if you'll send him a large (business size or #10) SASE. He operates a store at 16 Jeffrey Lane in Fletcher. He will send a color brochure on completed banks for $1, and he takes MasterCard and Visa.

WOODENBOAT STORE

P.O. Box 78
Brooklin, ME 04616
(800) 273-7447
(207) 359-8920 FAX

The WoodenBoat name tells the story. This store caters to wooden-boat enthusiasts, those who build, buy, sail or row such devices, and the catering is extensive. Books on the subject of wooden boats, both appreciation and construction—and more than a few on use—abound. Plans for model boats, and even kits for model boats, a couple of which are more than three feet long, are offered. There are numerous plans for a wide variety of wooden craft, ranging from a 7'7" pram to a 43' schooner, with the list including daysailers, power launches, rowing shells, kayaks and canoes. There are also boat kits for Nutshell prams in

two sizes (9'6" and 7'7") and the usual batch of logo T-shirts and sweatshirts—the handiest logo item is the WoodenBoat shop apron. Check out the Down East rocker: This rocker is a rowboat shape on massive clear wood rockers. WoodenBoat Store also presents videos and hard-to-find tools. The most fascinating item in the entire catalog, to me, is the Friendship sloop sailing model (Amy R. Payson). This model finishes up at 7'7" along the deck and sails much like a real boat. The original is 29' long. The store is an offshoot of *WoodenBoat* magazine and offers similar quality and interests. If you love boats, this catalog is for you. If you love boats and woodworking, jump on it. WoodenBoat Store takes Discover, MasterCard and Visa.

WOODEN MEMORIES

Route 1, Box 87
Bear Lake, PA 16402
(814) 489-3002

Send $1, and Wooden Memories will send you a color catalog of plans. Plans include full-sized patterns that need only be traced onto the wood, at which time you may cut out the pattern and paste it onto the wood, after painting.

WOOD-MET SERVICES

3314 Shoff Circle
Peoria, IL 61604
(309) 637-9667

Norwood Snowden sent me a pile of material to show how useful the seven hundred or so plans that are included in his $1 (refundable) catalog actually are. No argument there, with over eighty attachments for lathes, drill presses and routers. The preponderance of Wood-Met Services plans tends to lean to the metal working, but there are more than enough woodworking tool and accessory plans to make the catalog worthwhile. Shop equipment, portable power tools, and accessories such as a mobile wood lathe tool holder are very useful. Plans are small scale but clear and nicely dimensioned. Instructions are clear. Snowden spent forty-one years with Caterpillar design, research and development before retiring and starting Wood-Met.

WOOD MOULDING & MILLWORK PRODUCERS ASSOCIATION (WMMPA)

Box 25278
Portland, OR 97225
(503) 292-9288

The WMMPA offers a book with five hundred wood

moulding projects for $5.50. Other consumer literature tells how to work with wood mouldings (the association retains the British spelling), describes the trip from tree to trim, and shows how to remodel homes with wood moulding. Consumer literature prices range from $.50 to above $5.50, and the brochure describing the literature is free.

WOODWORKERS' STORE
21801 Industrial Boulevard
Rogers, MN 55374-9514
(800) 279-4441
(612) 428-3200 Orders and customer service
(612) 428-3298 Technical service
(612) 428-8668 FAX

The Woodworkers' Store carries a wide line of plans, books, small power tools, hand tools, woods, finishes, jigs, kits, and a very wide line of hardware, including many porcelain parts, oak and birch carvings, and even briefcase handles in two quality levels (the cheaper is covered in vinyl, the more costly in leather). Plans include dollhouses, whirligigs, desks, rocking toys, entertainment centers, tool centers, cedar chest, and a number of cradles. You'll also find a large line of jewelry-box, chest, drawer, and general-cabinet locks, as well as plenty of knockdown fasteners. Currently unique is their line of workshop knobs in black plastic or aluminum, in five styles and many more sizes. The knobs make building your own shop

jigs a great deal easier, as do some other new kits in the most recent catalog. The Woodworkers' Store is another company that sends smaller update catalogs with some frequency, so your $3 buys a great deal of information. The Woodworkers' Store accepts American Express, Discover, MasterCard and Visa.

WORKSHOPPE ORIGINALS
P.O. Box 86
Wildomar, CA 92595
(714) 678-9503

Plans consist of full-sized patterns, typically of flat yard designs (Santa's sleigh, Christmas streetlamp, skiing elf, and, to change the season, eighteen vegetable-garden markers. Other plan packages include Christmas ornaments and gifts, more yard patterns for year-round use, and ideas for converting some of the lawn ornament patterns to other uses). Three single-page brochures are done in glossy full color and present fine color suggestions, as well as a good look at the constructed patterns. The catalog, currently of the three brochures, is growing and is $2, refunded on the first order. The one payment enters your name for all succeeding brochures, as well as for the full catalog when it arrives in the near future. Patterns range from $6.50 to $12 per package (the $12 package is the Toyland Express, a 9½' long, four-piece, Christmas train). Patterns come in a 6" × 11" clear plastic package with a full-color cover. The detailed instructions include painting guides.

Power Tools and Accessories

Power Tools and Accessories

AIR COMPRESSORS

CAMPBELL-HAUSFELD
100 Production Drive
Harrison, OH 45030
(800) 634-4793

Campbell-Hausfeld is a leading manufacturer of air compressors, including oilless models. In addition, they have recently come out with a high-volume, low-pressure spray kit that is lower in price than industrial versions and that works very nicely in applying clear and other finishes in a nonproduction setting. Campbell-Hausfeld also makes a line of compressed air nailers and staplers, from heavy framing down to fabric stapling. Their latest is a new, round-head framing nailer, but the preceding one, a lighter-weight stapler, is of more interest to woodworkers. Call and ask for free brochures.

Campbell-Hausfeld's moderate cost high volume, low pressure spray unit brings low pressure, high efficiency spray finishing to almost all shops.

DEVILBISS AIR POWER COMPANY
213 Industrial Drive
Jackson, TN 38301
(901) 423-7000
(901) 423-7900 FAX

The DeVilbiss line of Air America compressors runs the gamut from a small ¾ horse oilless model that

you can almost tuck in your back pocket (it takes a big pocket, but it weighs only 14 pounds without a tank and 25 with) to a monster five-horse, two-stage, industrial model that delivers 175 PSI and weighs 413 pounds. In between, there are Air America models for almost every do-it-yourself or commercial use, with tools to accompany the compressors. The company is the largest volume producer of air compressors, and the products are found in many places, including home centers and other retail outlets. DeVilbiss lists spray guns, air ratchets, dual-action circular sanders, air impact wrenches, air chisels, air staplers, jitterbug air sanders, paint tanks, blow guns, and other tools to go with the Air America line of compressors. Naturally, the compressors will drive finish nailers and similar tools, which DeVilbiss now makes. Write for free brochures.

DRYERS/KILNS

EBAC LUMBER DRYERS
106 John Jefferson Road
Suite 102
Williamsburg, VA 23185
(800) 433-9011
(804) 229-3038
(804) 229-3321 FAX

For the heavy wood user, Ebac presents three lumber-dryer systems that sell for under $3,000, with systems perfected to the point where no experience is needed to get perfectly dried lumber. An example is the TR250, which works on loads from 50 to 250 board feet, drying lumber to 6 percent to 8 percent moisture content (recommended cabinetmaking range). The buyer builds the kiln chamber, which is one reason the price is within reason. Call or write for further information on the kilns and future courses on drying lumber safety. Ebac accepts Master-Card and Visa.

NYLE CORPORATION
P.O. Box 1107
Bangor, ME 04401
(800) 777-NYLE
(207) 989-4335
(207) 989-1101 FAX

Nyle lumber-drying kilns are available in many sizes. The Nyle units are dry-kiln dehumidification systems for kilns with 300 to 300,000 board feet drying capacities. Conventional steam and hot-water kilns are available from 5,000 board feet capacity up. Nyle also makes kiln supplies and moisture meters. Nyle is the only U.S. maker of dehumidification type kilns; it uses a patented system to duplicate conventional kiln-drying times. Call for further information and free brochures. Nyle takes MasterCard and Visa.

WOOD-MIZER PRODUCTS, INC.
8180 West 10th Street
Indianapolis, IN 46214
(800) 553-0182
(317) 271-1542

Wood-Mizer is your company if you're truly sick of paying high prices for good lumber. The company makes portable sawmills of the bandsaw type (generally a bit lower in cost—though far from inexpensive for the good ones, which this is—than circular saw mill setups, as well as being more portable). There are six versions, and the catalog then goes on to describe Solar Dry kilns to finish up the work. Actually, the smallest Solar Dry kiln is not wildly expensive (again, though, it depends on your state of interest, and your wallet: Delivered, it will probably run about $2,250, with a current price of $2,090), and will dry 750 board feet at a time. The third product line is the Dupli-Carver, used to produce three-dimensional wood carving duplicates. The catalog is free, and fascinating.

GENERATORS

GENERAC CORPORATION
P.O. Box 8
Waukesha, WI 53187
(414) 544-4811
(414) 544-4851 FAX

Generac Corporation makes a line of stand-alone generators meant primarily to supplement local power company transmissions during power failures, brownouts and blackouts. The Generac models 3500XL and 2500XL are excellent units; they also provide job-site power where no other power is available (you never really know when such a unit might be handy: The two above are almost light enough [the heavier 3500XL weighs only 110 pounds] to cart around easily). The 3500XL provides more than enough wattage to run a good-sized table saw (25 amperes at 120

volts, with a surge allowance of about 6 more amps). It offers a 30-ampere, 120-volt outlet (surge rated), or a 20-ampere, 240-volt outlet, and its 190cc engine can run for about fifteen hours on its four-gallon fuel load. Most major home-center chains have one or both models, and there is a network of Generac distributors where you can get more information.

GRINDERS

GEOFF BROWN
8 Ladbroke Park
Millers Road
Warwick
CV34 5AE United Kingdom
011 44 926 493389
011 44 926 491357 FAX

I'd recommend doing your checking Stateside on the items Geoff Brown exports: He distributes Tormek wet-grinder systems (see Tormek U.S.A.), Nobex miter boxes, and Sjobergs joiner's workbenches. The latter two can readily be found in *Woodcraft* catalogs [(800) 535-4482; see listing for *Woodcraft*]. The Nobex line consists of the Champion Compound Miter Saw, with a 7¼" cutting height, and a few other tools. The Nobex miter square appears of great interest. The Sjobergs joiners benches are what one might call typical European pattern workbenches, which means that if you've ever become accustomed to them, you hate to use anything else. At the same time, they tend to be exceptionally pricey. Sjobergs benches are also available from Basic Living Products, 1321 67th Street, Emeryville, CA 94608. The phone number there is (800) 829-6300.

TORMEK U.S.A.
14205 West Wisconsin Avenue
Elm Grove, WI 53122
(414) 797-8959 Phone and FAX

Tormek is an interesting-looking wet-grinding system for edged tools. The Tormek 2000 SuperGrind machine is distributed by this company. The tool is a two-wheeled whetstone grinder, using a slow running speed (90 rpm), that uses a series of jigs to sharpen just about everything you can imagine. You can call to request a brochure or to ask for a local or mail-order dealer's name.

HOLE BORING MACHINES

KREG TOOL COMPANY
P.O. Box 367
201 Campus Drive
Huxley, IA 50124
(800) 447-8638
(515) 597-2234
(515) 597-2354 FAX

Kreg Tool Company manufactures a low-cost pocket-hole jig for home workshops and an automated pocket-hole boring machine. Pocket holes, of course, are very useful for making face frames for cabinetry. Kreg Tool also operates as Woodworkers Emporium, selling a line of cabinetmaking supplies. The company takes American Express, Optima, Discover, MasterCard and Visa.

JIGS

KLEIN DESIGN, INC.
17910 Southeast 110th Street
Renton, WA 98059
(206) 226-5937

Klein Design produces two miniature lathes, one of which is a full-pattern lathe with a 12" bed length. The other is a short-bed model. Additionally, many jigs and tools are available for the lathes (threading jigs, scroll chuck, custom jaws, indexing system, hole-drilling guides, and on). Videos on lathe use are also sold, with a series of five covering just about everything you wish to know about miniature turning, down to using unusual materials—horn, bone, cast polyester, mother of pearl, Corian, and others—to making turned boxes with threaded lids. Klein Design also offers lathe tools and videos, as well as tools for scale modelers. Bonnie lists a number of her tools as perfect for the dollhouse builder, but other miniature-makers will see some great possibilities in her brochure as well. Call or drop a note for the latest brochure and price lists. Klein Design takes Master-Card and Visa.

KREG TOOL COMPANY
P.O. Box 367
201 Campus Drive
Huxley, IA 50124
(800) 447-8638
(515) 597-2234
(515) 597-2354 FAX

Kreg Tool Company manufactures a low-cost pocket-

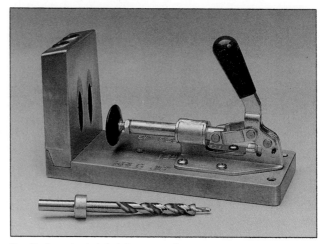

Kreg Tool's pocket hole jig is low cost and easy to use.

hole jig for home workshops and an automated pocket-hole boring machine. Pocket holes, of course, are very useful for making face frames for cabinetry. Kreg Tool also operates as Woodworkers Emporium selling a line of cabinetmaking supplies. The company takes American Express, Optima, Discover, MasterCard and Visa.

LEICHTUNG WORKSHOPS
4944 Commerce Parkway
Cleveland, OH 44128
(800) 321-6840
(216) 464-6764 FAX

Leichtung offers a variety of unusual tools, plus many plans and woodworking supplies in their free catalog. The catalog is digest sized, but it sometimes runs over ninety pages; it presents seasonal plans, some kits (varying with the seasons, but often small boxes and clocks, ships, dollhouses), and parts to help in building some of the plan items. The catalog has many styles of clamps, numerous doweling and jointing jigs, and it's the only tool catalog I've seen where you're as apt to find wildflower seeds by the small sack, rain gauges, barbecue cleaner, rocks and cowhide gloves, as you are Forstner drill bits. I've used a lot of Leichtung's gloves and always keep several pair on hand. For the price, they're the best I've seen for light chores, up to and including feeding a planer. The company also has a goodly array of parts bins and jars and hangers for perforated board, both ¼" and ⅛". They also offer a Woodworker's Guild for a $15 annual membership fee. Leichtung takes American Express, MasterCard, Visa and Discover.

LEIGH INDUSTRIES, LTD.
P.O. Box 357
1585 Broadway Street
Port Coquitlam, BC
Canada V3C 4K6
(800) 663-8932
(604) 464-2700
(604) 464-7404 FAX

Leigh jigs offer an incredible variety of choices in joint making, starting with dovetails: The basic jig gives the ability to cut almost every kind of dovetail, including through, half-blind, sliding, end-on-end, and more, in wood to 1¼" thick. A multiple mortise-and-tenon attachment and a vast array of cutters further assist you in doing what you wish to do. The catalog is free, and beautifully done, and Leigh sells direct, as well as through distributors. Leigh accepts Master-Card and Visa.

TAYLOR DESIGN GROUP
P.O. Box 810262
Dallas, TX 75381
(214) 243-7943
(214) 243-4277 FAX

This outfit is the maker of Incra jigs, which present the best method of producing finger joints I've ever used or heard of, when combined with a good router table. Sooner or later I'll get a chance to check their new professional model, with its larger fence and aluminum (instead of plastic) construction. The line of tools and accessories includes Incra Mike, a master template library, a Miter Slider (runners to allow you to make many table-saw jigs), and wooden hinge plans. This is not the entire line, for there are a variety of accessories for the jigs, and there's a video as well as the template book. A brochure describing the entire line is free for the asking and well worth looking over.

WOODPECKERS, INC.
8318 Manorford Drive
Parma, OH 44129
(800) 752-0725
(216) 888-9463 FAX

Woodpeckers is the sole demonstrator of Incra Jig Products at thirty woodworking shows each year. They are also developers of the heaviest commercially manufactured router table, and they organize Incra classes across the nation. They'll send brochures on request; they take MasterCard, Visa and Discover.

LATHES

CONOVER
Lathe Division
American Woodcraft Tools, Inc.
10420 Kinsman Road
Newbury, OH 44065
(800) 722-5447
(216) 564-9600
(216) 564-9566 FAX

The Conover lathes are justly famous, using as a base a 16" bed design and partial or full kits to produce a lathe with an unlimited length. Leg and other assemblies are of top-grade cast iron, and the bed is shop-produced—your shop—of laminated wood. Call for a free catalog.

DEROSE & COMPANY
Box 150
1125 Hanover Green Drive
Mechanicsville, VA 23111
(804) 746-1705
(804) 746-2556 FAX

This manufacturer of custom lathes offers features that will make a woodturner's mouth water—or hands try to grasp the nearest turning tool. The basic unit has a swing of 25" or 30", with a sliding, rotating head stock (rotation is for outboard turning). The distance between centers can range from 42" (or less) to 102", which is more than sufficient for general use, including bedpost turning—unless you need a bedpost longer than 8½'. A special slow-speed system is optional and can be used to reduce the 550 rpm low speed to 135 rpm (nine speeds from 1,725 rpm down to 135). Information on the DeRose lathe and its options, including lengths greater than 102", can be had for a phone call or a card.

KLEIN DESIGN, INC.
17910 SE 110th Street
Renton, WA 98059
(206) 226-5937

Klein Design produces two miniature lathes, one of which is a full-pattern lathe with a 12" bed length. The other is a short-bed model. Additionally, many jigs and tools are available for the lathes (threading jigs, scroll chuck, custom jaws, indexing system, hole-drilling guides, and on). Videos on lathe use are also sold, with a series of five covering just about everything you wish to know about miniature turning, down to using unusual materials—horn, bone, cast polyester, mother of pearl, Corian, and others—to making turned boxes with threaded lids. Klein Design also offers lathe tools and videos, as well as tools for scale modelers. Bonnie lists a number of her tools as perfect for the dollhouse builder, but other miniature-makers will see some great possibilities in her brochure as well. Call or drop a note for the latest brochure and price lists. Klein Design takes Master-Card and Visa.

RECORD TOOLS, INC.
1915 Clements Road #1
Pickering, Ontario
Canada L1W 3V1
(905) 428-1077

Record is a leading maker of lathes and turning tools, woodturning workbenches, and varied woodturning accessories, but it also turns out a considerable line of top-grade hand tools and accessories. Record planes, chisels and turning gouges, skews chisels, and scrapers are famous worldwide for quality, as is the Marples line of chisels, turning and carving tools made in Sheffield, England, since 1828. The Record line of woodworking vises is justly famed, and other tools produced by Record include hammers (a major source of Warrington—cross peen—hammers), clamps, and some wrenches. Record lathes are quality tools, covering a wide range of sizes, from the single-end bowl lathe, with a 22″ turning capacity, to the Coronet #3, with a 48″ distance between centers and a 12″-diameter swing over the bed (the #3 takes an accessory set that allows a massive, 30″ diameter bowl turning). Call or drop a note for information, or check your local or mail-order woodworking-tool supplier.

WILLIAMS & HUSSEY MACHINE CO., INC.
Riverview Mill
P.O. Box 1149
Wilton, NH 03086
(800) 258-1380
(603) 654-6828
(603) 654-5446 FAX

The W&H molder-planer unit offers quick blade changes and a capacity of almost double blade width because one side is open, allowing double-pass cutting. The unit also takes moulding cutting blades, to double utility. The W&H lathe is relatively low cost and high precision. Write or call for a free information kit.

MULTIPURPOSE TOOLS

DREMEL
4915 21st Street
Racine, WI 53406
(414) 554-1390
(800) 437-3635

Dremel is the manufacturer of the Moto-Tool in all its variations and with all its companion tools. Dremel makes electric power tools, in portable and benchtop versions, with much of its past fame resting on versions of the Moto-Tool. Today, Dremel is quickly gaining more fame for its new scroll saw line (two models) and its band saw, which is said by several people I trust to be the top benchtop band saw now in existence. When our first edition came out, that would have been a very minor distinction, but the entire benchtop tool market has swung to better quality in the past couple of years, and band saws are now following the lead of scroll saws. The ones I've tried, which do not, yet, include the Dremel, are incredibly good for the sizes and prices. Check with Dremel for a copy of their scroll saw blade and speed chart, rotary tool bit guide, and pocket catalog. All are free.

FARRIS MACHINERY COMPANY, INC.
1206 Pavilion Drive
Grain Valley, MO 64029
(800) 872-5489 Phone and FAX
(816) 229-3055

Farris Machinery imports the KITY K5, a multimachine that has a 10″ table saw, a 6″ jointer, a thickness planer, a ¾″ spindle shaper and a mortiser. The K5 is a versatile, multitool workshop that avoids some of the problems of the standard multitool while offering a different selection of tools. The table saw can be bought with an optional attachment for making finger joints, among other features, while the spindle shaper quickly forms inserts for frame and panel construction. The slot mortiser sets up quickly and quickly cuts mortises, and the surface and thickness planer works two ways to edge joint boards and to surface them. The 10-ampere motor has a magnetic starter. Farris also imports the KITY 619 table saw, a 2½″-horse, 220-volt cabinetmaker's saw, with a wide series of options, including a sliding table, rear extension table and side extension table. The base model is priced under some top-line American-made saws, so it might well be worth a look. KITY also makes a jointer/planer; a 12″ band saw, with 1½ horsepower using 110 volts and cutting to an 8″ depth; and a dust collector. The current Farris catalog shows all those, and much more, including Rali bench planes, the

Kreg jig, band saw blades, and a lot of shaper profiles. Farris also imports the Tormek whetstone grinding and honing system, using a low-speed (90 rpm), water-based, grinding system. Low-speed grinding systems cut out problems with ruining blade temper, while also making it harder to make an irretrievable error. Call the company for a catalog. Farris accepts MasterCard and Visa and has its own twelve-month financing plan.

LAGUNA TOOLS
2081 Laguna Canyon Road
Laguna Beach, CA 92651
(800) 234-1976
(714) 494-7006
(714) 497-1346 FAX

Call or write for free details on the Robland X31 one-person shop, an 1,100-pound multitool shop that uses three 3-horse motors to power a 12″ jointer/planer, a 10″ table saw with a 50″ sliding table, and a shaper-mortiser. Cast-iron construction gives accuracy and durability. The table saw has a sliding table with a 50″ capacity, and the jointer and planer share the same three-knife cutterhead, designed for easy knife changes. The Laguna Tools band saw, the LT18, is a 1.8-horsepower, 220-volt single-phase tool that takes a blade to 1″ wide and presents a full 12″ resaw capacity. Laguna tools also has a shaper cutter that accepts different knives, in much the same way molding heads for table saws do. The Laguna Robland tools catalog is on videotape, as is a tape of the Janssen edgebanding machine. These are all top-quality tools, and Laguna Tools takes American Express, Discover, MasterCard and Visa.

SHOPSMITH, INC.
3931 Image Drive
Dayton, OH 45414
(800) 543-7586
(513) 898-6070
(800) 722-3965 FAX

Shopsmith tools take minimal space and quickly convert to different tools: The base unit works as a table saw, lathe, vertical drill press and horizontal borer. This large-tool system takes little space (relatively speaking—actually about 2′ × 6′ for the main unit) when stored, and the basic system has been around since the forties. I've used Shopsmith units and complain only about a few things: the set-up time overall (from tool-to-tool: A minute here and there to change from one use to another isn't much; losing the setup on one tool while you change over to another can be a nuisance) and the difficulty of adjusting the small

additional tables to the main saw table to the same level, making the cutting of larger pieces fairly difficult. There is also a little too much lash in the Mark V lathe I used. For someone wishing to spend modest amounts of money, with little space to spare, the tool is a major answer and has been for over forty years, and add-on tools are available, as are freestanding units, such as a scroll saw, a dust collector and a planer. Shopsmith has consolidated and now offers its own products only, sold through mail and its unique series of shopping-mall demonstrations and classes. Shopsmith accepts MasterCard, Visa, Discover, and its own Shopsmith credit card (you can complete an application toll free over the phone, at the above number).

NAILERS

CAMPBELL-HAUSFELD
100 Production Drive
Harrison, OH 45030
(800) 634-4793

Campbell-Hausfeld is a leading manufacturer of air compressors, including oilless models. In addition, they have recently come out with a high-volume, low-pressure spray kit that is lower in price than industrial versions and that works very nicely in applying clear and other finishes in a nonproduction setting. Campbell-Hausfeld also makes a line of compressed-air nailers and staplers, from heavy framing down to fabric stapling. Their latest is a new round-head framing nailer, but the preceding one, a lighter-weight stapler, is of more interest to woodworkers. Call and ask for free brochures.

DUO-FAST CORPORATION
3702 River Road
Franklin Park, IL 60131
(800) 752-5207

Duo-Fast is an American manufacturer of pneumatic nailers and staplers, with the emphasis on light staplers for furniture, upholstery and case goods. Their DS-Series stapler holds 67 to 134 staples, up to 1½″ long in one version and 2″ in another. Their HFN-880N finish nailer takes 1½″, 1¾″, 2″, 2¼″ and 2½″ finish nails, and they have the widest variety of nailers and staplers I've seen anywhere, including a brad nailer that works with 18-gauge brads from ½″ (or ⅝″ in the other model) to 1¼″. You can find one you can use, if you can use a pneumatic nailer or stapler, in the Duo-Fast line. Duo-Fast also makes glue guns and glue, wood glue (white), adhesives, caulks and seal-

DuoFast presents many stapler models, several of which are useful in small shops.

ants. The catalog is free, and a call will bring you that and the location of your nearest dealer.

STANLEY-BOSTITCH FASTENING SYSTEMS

Route 2, Briggs Drive
East Greenwich, RI 02818
(800) 556-6696
(401) 884-2500
(401) 884-2485 FAX

Stanley-Bostitch air nailers are handy even in the home workshop. Most useful to us as woodworkers are the brad and finishing nailers, though shop construction is a lot easier with framing nailers. Stanley-Bostitch is one of the top-of-the-line brands and, as such, is a bit higher priced than some others, but the tools aren't out of line for the quality. The company also makes its own line of small, high-powered air compressors. Call or write for information.

PRESSES

MERCURY VACUUM PRESSES

P.O. Box 2232
Fort Bragg, CA 95437
(800) 995-4506
(707) 964-7557

Mercury Vacuum presses began manufacturing in 1990, and today makes bag presses in four standard sizes ($4' \times 4'$ to $4' \times 12'$) and custom sizes, self-regulating vacuum pumps and generators, vacuum clamps, and hot and cold membrane presses for production work. Woodworkers and production shops use the presses for laminating veneers to substrates, making bent laminations and similar work. The catalog is free, and Mercury Vacuum Presses also sells direct, accepting MasterCard and Visa.

ROUTERS

BEALL TOOL COMPANY

541 Swans Road NE
Newark, OH 43055
(800) 331-4718
(614) 345-5045
(614) 345-5880 FAX

The Beall wood threader for router use comes in three left-hand and five right-hand sizes. It is one of the tools I've not yet used, and one I'm itching to try. To add to my itch, Judith Beall sent along a copy of their *The Nuts & Bolts of Woodworking*, including twenty projects and a huge amount of information. Write or call for a very informative brochure: Distribution is nearly worldwide, and Beall also sells direct. Beall Tool Company accepts MasterCard and Visa.

CASCADE TOOLS, INC.

P.O. Box 3110
Bellingham, WA 98227
(800) 235-0272
(800) 392-5077 FAX

Cascade Tools imports and distributes the SY line of carbide tools, primarily router bits and shaper cutters. There are many unusual items in both lines, plus some items such as antikickback devices, Magna-Set precision jointer and planer knife setting jigs, rub collars, dust-collection connectors, router bases, roller brackets, and on, including books, videos, Fastak air nailers (brad models), and staplers. The seventy-three-page annual catalog is free and is supplemented by a sixty-four-page spring sale catalog, also free. The 800 number takes orders twenty-four hours a day, and Cascade accepts Visa, MasterCard and Discover.

CMT

5425 Beaumont Center Boulevard, Suite 900
Tampa, FL 33634
(800) 531-5559 (United States)
(813) 886-1819
(813) 888-6614 FAX

Premium router bits are featured in CMT's free catalog. Sets are available—for Incra, JoinTech, Leigh, OmniJig and Keller jigs. Pat Speilman, author of *The Router Handbook*, has done a lot of explanatory text for the catalog, which is a help, especially for beginners and intermediate-level woodworkers, who may be easily confused by the profusion of bit shapes. CMT presents all kinds of top-quality blades, dado sets and other products—their Talon II stack dado set has a good reputation and a low price for a top-of-the-line version. The catalog goes on to present bit sets for specific jigs and jig systems, as above, and now also presents the systems for sale. Other accessories are included, such as acrylic offset router bases, hinge template kits, good-looking Forstner drill bits, and a bunch of other interesting items. The colorful catalog is priced at $2, but you might try just calling and requesting it. It does come with a $10 off offer for your first order.

EAGLE AMERICA CORPORATION

P.O. Box 1099
Chardon, OH 44024
(800) 872-2511 Orders only
(216) 286-7643
(800) 872-9471 FAX

The free Eagle router bit catalog has eighty pages covering large selections of American-made bits, with upwards of eight hundred items. The aim is for American-made products wherever possible, with pro-quality tools. From first-aid kits through JoinTech jigs, Eagle carries a wide array and has even added several pages of books. Unusual router bits include the 14° butterfly spline. Eagle also carries shaper cutters, with a good variety of profiles. Among the tools carried are the Delta and the DeWalt compound miter saws, zero clearance inserts, and multispur bits. Eagle accepts Discover, MasterCard and Visa, and will ship COD (UPS).

EXCALIBUR

210 Eighth Street S
Lewiston, NY 14092
(800) 387-9789
(416) 293-2076 FAX

The Excalibur T-slot saw fence, and its various accessories, is a reasonably easy-to-install replacement and upgrade unit for table saws. I used one for years on my Delta Unisaw and found it met every claim made for it. Accessories include a router table to be built into the saw-fence extension table, router fence brackets, a stock pusher, and guide-rail work stops. Two stock guide-rail lengths are available, allowing rip cuts to the right of the blade of 33" and 62", and two fence lengths, for different-sized saw tables, are available. Excalibur makes its own sliding table for table saws, allowing excellent crosscut accuracy to go with the T-slot fence's great rip cut accuracy. For those who haven't used them, sliding tables on stationary saws add fantastic cutting abilities and accuracy, if well made. The Excalibur comes in two sizes, the EX-SLT30, giving a 28" crosscut depth (to the front of a 10" blade), and the EXSLT60, with a crosscut depth of 37". Excalibur also offers an over-arm blade cover for dust collection. Excalibur also makes some superb scroll saws: Some time ago, up in Hot Air City (DC), I watched Phil Humfrey set a nickel on edge on a running scroll saw and noted that the nickel stayed in place as he cut a small pattern. That is stable! More information is available from Excalibur, and tools are also available from them by mail (UPS), as well as from other retailers. Excalibur takes MasterCard and Visa.

FREUD, INC.

218 Feld Avenue
High Point, NC 27264
(800) 472-7307

Jim Brewer at Freud supplied so much detailed information that, adding it to their three catalogs, I ended up spinning, trying to figure what to include and what to leave out. Their current new router bit catalog offers many pages of top-grade bits—call for a copy of that catalog, or a copy of their saw blade catalog, or a copy of their shaper cutter catalog, or copies of all three. Catalogs are free to readers of this book, so mention it. Some company detail, for those who have never heard of Freud (if any such woodworkers exist), includes the fact the company has been in the U.S. market for upwards of twenty years. They use a special titanium-bonded carbide in their router bits, make their own carbide for best quality control, and provide special computer-controlled grinding to reduce vibration, burn and chatter. I've used Freud bits and blades and a Freud router and found they live up to company claims. Freud blades and bits are a bit pricey but also are durable and well made, which reduces problems with cost. Freud tools remain good value for the money; however, like all costly tools and accessories, they are definitely items to be thought about before purchase. You can find reduced prices if you search through other listings in this book to find a good discount retailer.

MICRO-FENCE

11100 Cumpston Street #35
North Hollywood, CA 91601
(800) 850-4367
(818) 766-4367
(818) 761-3977 FAX

Micro-Fence is a product developed by Richard Wedler, who combines professional woodworking with mechanical engineering. The fence unit for routers uses a center post mechanism to dial in accurate measurements. The laser-cut micrometer dial is graduated in .001" increments and registers fence movement on two stainless-steel shafts. Knurled locking screws lock on guide rods so there's no change of setting during tightening. Precision is what the Micro-Fence is all about, and precision with a time savings is what it is said to deliver. It is made to fit most popular router brands and styles, and it also works on laminate trimmers. There is a thirty-day warranty, with satisfaction guaranteed, so you can return the tool within that time if you don't like the color of the laser-cut dial, or anything else. Micro-Fence also will refund shipping and handling in that period of time. Call or write for their free brochure. Micro-Fence accepts American Express, Carte Blanche, JCB, Diners Club International, MasterCard and Visa, and will ship, cash only, COD through UPS.

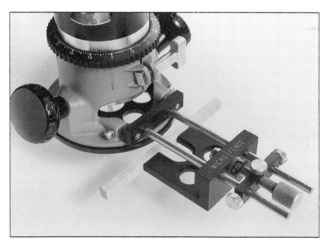

MicroFence is precisely made to provide accuracy during work.

MLCS, LTD.

P.O. Box 4053 C13
Rydal, PA 19046
(800) 533-9298
(215) 938-5067 (local)
(215) 938-5070 FAX

The free MLCS catalog features router bits but also offers other items. The router bits come in a wide variety of profiles, including raised panel, stile and rail, multiform molding makers, French provincial, double ogee, double flute raised panel bits, an ogee raised panel bit with an undercutter, crown molding bits, and a slew of other molding bits, plus standard cove and bead, chamfer, Roman ogee, round over, beading, drawer and finger pull, ogee fillet, and thumbnail bits. There are round nose bits, core box bits, keyhole cutting bits, dish cutters, spiral downcut bits, door lip bits, hinge mortising bits, straight bits, bottom cleaning bits, lock miter bits, finger joint bits, tongue-and-groove bits, flush trimming bits, and others. Other products include Forstner drill bits, from ¼" to 3⅛" in size, shaper cutters, their own router table, an adjustable corner clamp and other items. The forty-page, part-color catalog is definitely worth looking at, inventory is large, and there are experienced woodworkers on staff to help with questions. The MLCS showroom is located at 2381 Philmont Avenue, Huntington Valley, PA, and is open 8:30 A.M. to 5:00 P.M. Monday, Tuesday, Wednesday and Friday; 8:30 A.M. to 7:00 P.M. on Thursday; and 8:00 A.M. to noon on Saturday. MLCS takes Discover, MasterCard and Visa.

MOON'S SAW & TOOL, INC.

2531-39 Ashland Avenue
Chicago, IL 60614
(800) 447-7371
(312) 549-7924
(312) 549-7695 FAX

This Chicago company presents a quarterly sale brochure and a small general-lines catalog, as well as a catalog of Byrom router bits, free and on request. Although the catalog is slender, it presents many edge-forming and other router bits, under Moon's own brand name, plus a full line of saw blades under Moon's name. Moon also carries Wizard Elite and Roadrunner blades, Freud Forstner bits, planer and jointer knives, Freud saw blades, and Morse band saw blades. The spring sale days brochure offers the Freud 3¼" horse router for a very good price and the Fein triangular sander, also for a good price. There are many clamps in the brochure, as well as all sorts of saw blades. The catalog is well worth looking at, as is the sales brochure. Moon's Saw & Tool takes Discover, MasterCard and Visa.

OLDHAM-UNITED STATES SAW
Burt, NY 14028
(716) 778-8588

The Oldham-United States Saw catalog of their saw blades, router bits and abrasive wheels provides some major choices, from ultra-thin kerf carbide blades (Roadrunner series), to carbide tooth nail-cutting blades, on to steel saw blades, then to Wizard and Supreme Wizard premium series (the Wizard series is designed for power mitering and comes in appropriate sizes from 8¼" to 15", while the Supreme Wizard series is for table and radial arm saws: Both series are cutoff styles with sixty or eighty teeth), plus three styles of dado blades, plus masonry and metal cutting abrasive wheels, and then to Viper router bits. A comprehensive array comes from the factory of this company founded in 1857. Literature is free, and Oldham sells only to distributors.

PHANTOM ENGINEERING, INC.
1122 South State Street
Suite 21
Provo, UT 84606
(800) 279-4570
(801) 377-5757
(801) 377-1668

The Woodchuck indexing system works with your router to produce fancy beading, twisted beading, fluting, and all sorts of other shapes, starting with a rough piece of stock, milling on one to thirty-six surfaces. Call or send for free basic information, or send $2 for information and a copy of "The Phantom Woodworker." The full name of the product is the Woodchuck Five Axis Milling System, and some of the projects it can create appear quite startling. "The Phantom Woodworker" has become a monthly newsletter and has dropped its featured project—but the projects will still exist in the Video Project Library. According to Phantom Engineering, the Woodchuck lets you true and size stock and do indexed milling, tapering, circular molding, rope molding, precision joinery, beading and fluting, radial mortising and hollow spirals with your router. Call about details on their new demonstration video. Phantom accepts MasterCard and Visa.

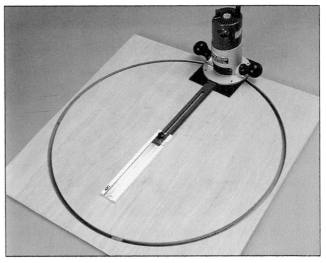
The circle cutting jig is just one of PNI's offerings.

PORTA-NAILS, INC.
P.O. Box 1257
Wilmington, NC 28402
(800) 634-9281
(919) 762-6334

Porta-Nails has a family of woodworking machines that differs in kind from many other tool families. The PNI family revolves around routers but only partially around traditional routers. Their panel template and router arc attachment use standard routers and are described in a free brochure that goes on to describe the Router Mate, which converts a standard router to an overarm precision router; the Ring Master, which cuts rings from wood; and the Dowel Mate, which first clamps the wood, then shoots in two dowel holes. A second product sheet describes the Universal Router Table, which sets up as a router table, joint maker, or pin router, using the same unit and two router motors. Call or write for free brochures and the name of a dealer in your area. PNI sells direct when no dealer is nearby, and takes MasterCard and Visa.

RIDGE CARBIDE TOOL CORPORTION
P.O. Box 497
595 York Avenue
Lyndhurst, NJ 07071
(800) 443-0992
(201) 438-8792 FAX

Ridge Carbide Tool makes custom router bits and shaper cutters from drawings or to fit wood samples. They also make shaper knives, sand-free woodworking saw blades and special dado sets and have a complete sharpening and repair service. RCT emphasizes that they are not just a phone-mail company with stock tools and stock answers. They manufacture tools to custom specifications and to fit special needs. There is a free catalog of standard, stock items, and information is available on custom services and sharpening. RCT accepts MasterCard and Visa.

ROTOZIP TOOL CORPORATION
1861 Ludden Drive
Cross Plains, WI 53528
(800) 521-1817

RotoZip makes the Spira Cut System bits, designed for plunge cutting in drywall materials, cement board, masonry, wood, ceramic tile and other materials. These fit the RotoMite router (and others) and work to force dust out behind the cut, resulting in less cleanup. Originally designed as a drywall tool, the system has become more popular among homeowners and other do-it-yourselfers. The brochure is free and requires only a quick phone call to the company's 800 number above.

WHITESIDE MACHINE COMPANY
4506 Shook Road
Claremont, NC 28610
(800) 225-3982

Whiteside Machine manufactures a professional line of 750 router bits, all carbide or carbide tipped. The company, begun in 1972, moved into bigger quarters in 1985 and makes its own line of bits, plus private-label bits. The catalog, showing or listing all 750 bits, is available for a phone call. The company also makes accessories and will supply you with a dealer's name: Buyers of the Whiteside bits get an 800 number tech support aide, as well as top-quality bits.

WOODHAVEN
5323 West Kimberly Road
Davenport, IA 52806
(800) 344-6657
(319) 391-2386
(319) 391-1275 FAX

Woodhaven is a fairly old (now well past a decade) mail-order house for router bits, tables and general router supplies. The newest catalog is more colorful than the one Brad Witt sent a couple years ago, and it shows a wider line of router tables and tabletops. The claim is now that they offer the widest line of router tables and accessories, and I see no reason to dispute the claim. And Woodhaven now offers a plate-inlay template for use with Woodhaven base plates: The plate template is inexpensive and will accept either size of Woodhaven plate, with plate levelers (or you

can sand down edges to size another brand of plate). Hinge, lockset, and strike plate mortise jigs are also offered, as are fences, angle brackets, and a slew of interesting items for the router-using woodworker. I want to get hold of their Frame & Panel Secrets video. The catalog is available on video, though it costs $14.99 that way. For circle-cutting jigs, vacuum clamp kits, Keller dovetailing jigs, Beall wood threaders, and an array of other items, this catalog offers much of interest to the woodworker. One such item is the Know-Bit. This is not much more than a pointed metal dowel, with the point set to the top when inserted in a router. It then serves as an exact centering device for router, drill press, lathe. It is machined perfectly straight and round, so it also makes a good run-out check when used with a dial indicator. Chuck it into your drill press or router or lathe, and quickly and simply measure the run-out (wobble). The catalog is free by bulk mail, $3 first class. Woodhaven takes Discover, MasterCard and Visa.

WOODPECKERS, INC.
8318 Manorford Drive
Parma, OH 44129
(800) 752-0725
(216) 888-9463 FAX

Woodpeckers is the sole demonstrator of Incra Jig Products at thirty woodworking shows each year. They are also developers of the heaviest commercially manufactured router table, and they organize Incra classes across the nation. They'll send brochures on request. Woodpeckers takes MasterCard, Visa and Discover.

WOODWORKERS' STORE
21801 Industrial Boulevard
Rogers, MN 55374-9514
(612) 428-2199
(612) 428-8668 FAX

Another major mail-order source for many items, Woodworkers' Store carries a wide line of small power tools, hand tools, woods, finishes, plans, jigs, kits, and a very wide line of hardware, including many porcelain parts, oak and birch carvings, and even briefcase handles in two quality levels (the cheaper is covered in vinyl, the more costly in leather). Currently unique is their line of workshop knobs in black plastic or aluminum, in five styles and many more sizes. The knobs make building your own shop jigs a great deal easier, as do some other new kits in the most recent catalog. You'll also find a large line of jewelry-box, chest, drawer, and general cabinet locks, as well as plenty of knockdown fasteners. The Woodworkers' Store is another company that sends smaller update catalogs with some frequency, so your $3 buys a great deal of information. The Woodworkers' Store operates eleven retail outlets in Boston, Chicago, Cleveland, Columbus, Denver, Detroit, Milwaukee, Minneapolis, San Diego, Seattle and Buffalo. The retail stores *do not* accept mail order but may speed access to some items if you happen to be nearby.

SANDERS

CLAYTON ENTERPRISES
2505 West Dewey Road
Owosso, MI 48867

Write for free information on Clayton oscillating spindle sanders: This production oscillating spindle sander is much more expensive than the Ryobi model, but the industrial quality is worth the extra price to many users. Oscillating spindle sanders combine the action of a drum sander, in rotation, with the up-and-down motion of the oscillator. The finish is smooth as a result of the dual action, and buildup of residue on the sleeves is lower.

ECON-ABRASIVES
P.O. Box 865021
Plano, TX 75086
(800) 367-4101
(214) 377-9779

Emphasizing low cost, Econ-Abrasives presents good-to-excellent prices on sanding belts and other tools. They carry a particularly wide line of belts, and offer wet and dry paper to 600-grit, as well as standard grit cabinet and finished papers. Econ-Abrasives also carries discs, router bits, wood glue, wood clamps, flap wheels and other products. The catalog is free for a call or note. Econ-Abrasives accepts MasterCard and Visa.

EXCALIBUR MACHINE CORPORATION
P.O. Box 82
Anderson, MO 64831
(800) 368-ROSS
(417) 223-4031
(417) 223-4034 FAX

Excalibur makes and sells ROSS precision drum sanders and abrasive planers. The ROSS line consists of sanders that go to the SS-37 with a material capacity of 37" wide by 6" tall. ROSS sells through dealers in some areas, and direct in others, throughout the United States, Canada, Mexico, Great Britain, Australia and the far east. All ROSS machines are manufactured in the United States. Literature is free, on request, and Excalibur accepts MasterCard and Visa.

FEIN POWER TOOLS, INC.
3019 West Carson Street
Pittsburgh, PA 15204
(800) 441-9878
(412) 331-2325
(412) 331-3599 FAX

Call for information on Fein's triangular pad sander, for corner work and similar tight spots, and their dust-free sanding systems. The triangular pad sander works nicely in corners, and the tool is nicely balanced and reasonably quiet. Both electric and pneumatic models are available. Fein's dust-free sanding system consists of a vacuum/dust collector unit, and any of several Fein sanders, from half-sheet to random-orbit models. These are not low-cost tools, but the company has a reputation for giving what you pay for, and it has been in business in Germany since 1867. These are production-quality tools, and catalogs on each system (triangular pad and dust-free) are free. Fein accepts American Express, Discover, MasterCard and Visa.

INDUSTRIAL ABRASIVES COMPANY
642 North 8th Street
Reading, PA 19612
(800) 428-2222
(800) 222-2292 (Pennsylvania)

Sanding belts and other abrasive tools are featured in this manufacturer's free catalog. Buy a dozen sanding belts, and get a dozen free.

KLINGSPOR ABRASIVES
P.O. Box 2367
Hickory, NC 28603
(800) 645-5555
(704) 322-3030

Klingspor is an abrasives manufacturer that also sells its products by mail, which makes them ideal for our purposes. Send or call for a free color catalog, which varies in size and content according to sales, possible overstock situations and similar requirements. It is called, sensibly enough, The Sanding Catalogue and is the largest I know of in the abrasives end of the business. Headquartered in Hickory, North Carolina, Klingspor has recently expanded to Ventura, California, to better serve a wider market. Products include belt and disc abrasives with a wide variety of coat styles (open and closed) using a number of different backing materials. Prices are reasonable to low, especially with quantity and special-offering discounts. The catalog offers some tools—random-orbit sanders pop out, as does the Ryobi oscillating spindle sander, Porter-Cable's abrasive plane, and Dremel's belt/disk sander. There is more to abrasives than sanding materials, and Klingspor also carries steel wool, rottenstone, pumice and paraffin oils, along with tack cloths to get the mess off before finishing. Klingspor takes MasterCard, Visa and Discover.

PERFORMAX PRODUCTS, INC.
112257 Nicollet Avenue S
Burnsville, MN 55337
(800) 334-4910
(616) 895-9922

If you do much wide board glue-up, the Performax drum sander setup for radial arm saws may be of great interest and help. Because of the one-side-open design, you can sand panels to 44″ wide. The Performax is available in models that attach to your radial arm saw and in models that stand on their own. The drum is 5″ in diameter by 22″ long, of extruded aluminum, machined and balanced. About the only other way to approach the overall width of machine sanding possible is to work with pro machines like ROSS SS-37, and that is not practical for many of us. The line has expanded considerably since the company began in 1986; it now includes the Pro-Max III stand-alone, 1½ horse model, the Super-Max 37 × 2, closed-end, super-wide sander (the 2 indicates dual drums), the 16-32 stand-alone, the Super-Brush 24, for fine sanding and polishing, and the original Performax. Call or write for brochures and the name of your nearest dealer. Performax has over one hundred dealers throughout the United States and Canada.

QUAKER STATE WOODWORKING SUPPLY
Airport Industries Building #2
RD 9, Box 9386
Reading, PA 19605
(800) 776-5467
(610) 478-9448 (local)
(610) 478-9388 FAX

Quaker State Woodworking Supply offers plans, tools, accessories, and a growing catalog/newsletter, currently in the sixteen-page range. Drop a card to be added to the list for their quarterly publication. It often comes within a package consisting of the MLCS and Penn State catalogs, and there's a wide variety of offerings from the three outfits. Quaker State itself is a discount tool house, with some emphasis on abrasives, but carrying a goodly line of Porter-Cable tools,

some Bosch equipment, Wagner's FineCoat HVLP sprayer, glues, Fas-Tak nail guns, clamps, SECO dust collectors, and many other items. They've got a super price on Ryobi's new oscillating spindle sander, too (that, by the way, is a superb tool for home-shop use on curved surfaces: As far as I know, it is the only one on the market with a price under $600, and it's selling for less than a third of that most places). Their showroom is at Reading Airport, and is open Monday through Friday, eight to five, and Saturdays eight to noon. Quaker State will also send you a list of the fifty or more shows they attend annually. The current list doesn't include any within a sensible distance to my home: I won't drive to Richmond for anything.

SAND-RITE MANUFACTURING COMPANY
321 North Justine Street
Chicago, IL 60607
(800) 521-2318
(312) 997-2200
(312) 997-2407 FAX

Sand-Rite manufactures and sells a line of pneumatic drum sanding machines, abrasive rolls, belts and sleeves in all grits and sizes. Sand-Rite has been around since 1942, and it offers what they call a woodworking-industry sander. It is heavy duty, and the price shows that, but it's not outrageously priced for quality, so it is suitable for even small pro shops as well as the occasional heavily equipped amateur. Sand-Rite also makes their own dust-collection system for use with their sanders. The Sand-Rite combination sander is a larger, more costly version of disc/belt sanders all of us have seen and most of us have used. The 3-horse version weighs 395 pounds and has a 6″ belt and 12″ disc. Sand-Rite takes MasterCard and Visa.

SINGLEY SPECIALTY COMPANY, INC.
P.O. Box 5087
Greensboro, NC 27403
(910) 852-8581
(910) 852-3145 FAX

Singley manufactures its own sleeveless-drum sander that works with paper cut from standard 11″ × 9″ sheets. The Singley drums work on any rotating device, with fittings available for lathes, drill presses, electric drills and small motors. Drums vary in diameter and length from a small ¾″ × 2¼″ model to a 3″ × 6″ version. Discounts are available for volume purchases. The Singley Drum Sanders are made in the United States, and have a lifetime guarantee. Free literature is available for a call or a note, and Singley Specialty takes MasterCard and Visa.

SAWMILLS AND CHAINSAWS

BETTER BUILT CORPORATION
845 Woburn Street, Suite 3
Wilmington, MA 01887
(508) 657-5636

Makers of the RipSaw portable sawmill, Better Built offers a free brochure describing the one-person band saw mill that cuts logs to 20″ diameter, providing boards up to 9″ thick and 14″ wide. The one-person sawmill weighs only 45 pounds and cuts as thin as ⅛″. As far as I can tell, it is the lowest-cost, most easily transported band saw mill in existence: It is almost as low-cost as the Granberg chainsaw mill. Better Built takes Discover, MasterCard and Visa.

ECHO, INC.
400 Oakwood Road
Lake Zurich, IL 60047
(800) 432-ECHO

Give Echo a call if you're mulling over the idea of getting a new chainsaw: The line currently starts with the CS-280E, carrying a 12″ bar, moves on to the new CS-3450 16″, and rises finally to the CS-8000, which comes with a standard 20″ bar but will carry up to a 36″ bar-and-chain combination. Generally, someone cutting their own wood for woodworking isn't going to be satisfied with the lower-end saws and doesn't need the higher-end designs, but Echo has a goodly number in the mid ranges that are of great use. Give them a call for a catalog and the name of your nearest dealer.

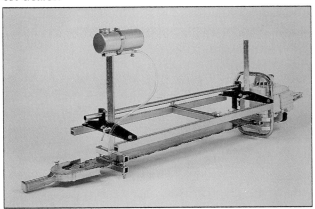

Granberg's two-man chainsaw sawmill works quickly and well, with a heavy duty (5 cubic inch or above) chainsaw.

GRANBERG INTERNATIONAL
P.O. Box 425
Richmond, CA 94807
(800) 233-6499 (outside California)
(510) 237-2099
(510) 237-2099 FAX

Granberg makes a chainsaw lumber mill that appears similar to one I used about twenty years ago: The mill is an attachment for your own chainsaw, and is, thus, about the most economical kind of small sawmill you can find. Elof Granberg is said to have invented the first practical portable chainsaw sharpener before the mill attachment. The company now sells those sharpeners, updated, plus chain-breakers, hedge trimmer attachments for chainsaws, and two models of portable sawmills. The wide-kerf chainsaw cut wastes more wood than do band saw and circular saw mills, and chainsaw mills are more time-consuming to use, but the start-up cost is a tiny fraction of the cost of either of those types. Drop the company a line for their brochure on service tools and accessories for chainsaws.

KASCO
R.R. 3
Box 393
Shelbyville, IN 46176

Write for information on the Kasco Portable Band Saw Mill. Such sawmills tend to be more costly than chainsaw-driven mills, but much cheaper than many circular-saw mills, but also tend to waste far less wood because the band saw blade is so thin the kerf is also thin.

STIHL, INC.
536 Viking Drive
Virginia Beach, VA 23452
(800) 43-STIHL Literature requests
(804) 486-9100

Stihl has long been a name to be counted on for wood-felling gear—chainsaws, since 1926, in fact. For woodworkers who are rolling their own lumber, a good chainsaw is an essential, and Stihl makes a wide line of good chainsaws. They also produce trimmers, brushcutters, vacuums and high-pressure cleaning systems, items probably of less interest to woodworkers. Give Stihl a call and ask for the Chain Saw & Accessories and the Protective Clothing and Forestry Equipment catalogs. They're free, and the latter has some amazing duffel for us amateur woodcutters, including waterproof boots with cut-resistant, nylon-cover steel toes. Stihl will also be delighted to give you the location of the dealer nearest to you.

WOOD-MIZER PRODUCTS, INC.
8180 West 10th Street
Indianapolis, IN 46214
(800) 553-0182
(317) 271-1542

Wood-Mizer is your company if you're truly sick of paying high prices for good lumber. The company makes portable sawmills of the band saw type (generally a bit lower in cost—though far from inexpensive for the good ones, which this is—than circular saw mill setups, as well as being more portable). There are several versions (six), and the catalog then goes on to describe Solar Dry kilns to finish up the work. Actually, the smallest Solar Dry kiln is not wildly expensive (again, though, it depends on your state of interest and wallet: Delivered, it will probably run about $2,250, with a current price of $2,090), and will dry 750 board feet at a time. The third product line is the Dupli-Carver to produce three-dimensional wood carving duplicates. The catalog is free, and it is fascinating.

SLIDING TABLES

MULE CABINETMAKER MACHINE, INC.
334 Chambers Circle
Newmarket, Ontario
Canada L3X 1T2
(905) 898-4110

John Withrow has been in business since 1983, selling his remarkably low-cost and effective sliding table for most of that time, and has now added the Accusquare rip fence to his line. The Accusquare gives you a rip capacity of up to 36″ on either side of the blade. His Mule sliding table is a unit I used for years, and delighted in. It fit with reasonable speed to my Unisaw, and it worked with accuracy with no, or very little, care. The new version is a bit slicker than my early production model and should be better, at about the same price. John also has a router table for a table saw, using a clear, Lexan plate and a two-piece insert. Drop John a note or give him a call (and don't forget that postage to Canada from the United States now costs more). Mule Cabinetmaker Machine takes MasterCard and Visa.

STAPLERS

DUO-FAST CORPORATION
3702 River Road
Franklin Park, IL 60131
(800) 752-5207

Duo-Fast is an American manufacturer of pneumatic nailers and staplers, with the emphasis on light staplers for furniture, upholstery and case goods. Their DS-Series stapler holds 67 to 134 staples, up to 1½″

long in one version and 2″ in another. Their HFN-880N finish nailer takes 1½″, 1¾″, 2″, 2¼″ and 2½″ finish nails, and they have the widest variety of nailers and staplers I've seen anywhere, including a brad nailer that works with 18-gauge brads from ½″ (or ⅝″ in the other model) to 1¼″. You can find one you can use, if you can use a pneumatic nailer or stapler, in the Duo-Fast line. Duo-Fast also makes glue guns and glue, wood glue (white), and adhesives, caulks and sealants. The catalog is free, and a call will bring you that and the location of your nearest dealer.

STATIONARY POWER TOOLS AND ACCESSORIES

A.R.E. MANUFACTURING, INC.
518 South Springbrook Road
Newberg, OR 97132
(800) 541-4962
(503) 538-5148 FAX

The Correct Cut radial arm saw fence replaces your existing fence, provides a precise measuring scale, and has a built-in, hinged stop. It is available in any length. Call or write for further information, in the form of a free brochure. A.R.E. accepts MasterCard and Visa.

AARDVARK TOOL COMPANY
2605 West Alabama Road, #202
Acworth, GA 30101
(404) 427-2414

Aardvark markets SawTrax equipment, including panel saw kits, 30″ crosscut kits, the Cabinet Maker 30″ crosscut kit (voted most revolutionary tool of the year by *Popular Woodworking*), and a few other items made by SawTrax Manufacturing. The rip and crosscut assembly for the panel saw looks like an ideal solution to the $1,000-and-up cost of major panel saws (mostly up), as this one is sturdy looking and can be put together using your saw and lumber that's on hand, probably for under $500, including shipping. Aardvark takes American Express, MasterCard and Visa and will ship COD with a credit-card guarantee of payment. All products are shipped UPS.

ADVANCED MACHINERY IMPORTS
2 McCullough Drive
P.O. Box 312
New Castle, DE 19720
(800) 648-4264
(302) 322-2226

AMI offers Hegner scroll saws, one of the top-of-the-line brands that is excellent, costly, and a lot of fun to use. Information is available on request.

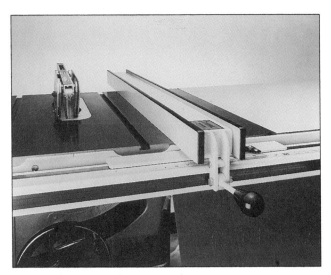

Beisemeyer fences are sturdy, accurate and easy to use.

BIESEMEYER MANUFACTURING
216 South Alma School Road, Suite 3
Mesa, AZ 85210
(800) 782-1831
(602) 835-9300

Biesemeyer manufactures one of the top-of-the-line aftermarket table saw fences and a variety of accessories, in commercial and home-shop versions. I've used the commercial versions enough to regret not having one, but I haven't tried the home-shop versions. The T-Square fence is quick and easy to operate, and not extremely difficult to install, making a fine replacement for most stock rip fences. The system is available in a version that fits to the left of the blade, as well as one to the right: The left-side version lets you miter panels on saws, like the Delta Unisaw, that have blades that tilt to the right. Versions to fit the Biesemeyer sliding tables are also available, as are, naturally, the sliding tables. The standard sliding table gives a cut-off capacity of 25", on a 36"-wide piece. The extended model works on 25" × 68" material. Biesemeyer also offers saw stops, gang stops, radial arm saw precision sets, drill press and blade guards, and a miter saw stop system. Call or write for a brochure and price sheet.

CARTER PRODUCTS COMPANY, INC.
437 Spring Street NE
Grand Rapids, MI 49503
(616) 451-2928
(616) 451-4330 FAX

For those of us who have trouble keeping band saw blades from twisting in their guides, and who have guides that wear out in days instead of years, Carter produces ball-bearing guides that greatly aid precision: These guides are not low-cost, though not outrageous. In my experience, they're worth their price, especially on lower-cost band saws. Carter also produces band saw tires and wheels and a laser guideline light. Free brochures are available on all these products and others that are probably beyond the interest of hobbyist woodworkers—lights for woodworking specialties and a Flip-Pod system to work with CNC production router setups. Carter does not take credit cards, though it does sell direct, either COD or cash with order (in the form of a check or money order, of course). Carter Products items are available through many dealers, too.

D.C. PRECISION TOOLS, INC.
11 Mathews Avenue
Riverdale, NJ 07457
(800) 462-2481

Call for information on the Saw-Mate fence-mounted stock pusher for table saws. The company makes the Hinge Mate as well, and D.C. Precision also sells direct. They accept MasterCard and Visa.

DIANSUPPLY/LABORSABER COMPANY
4505 Green Park Road
St. Louis, MO 63123
(800) 331-6480
(314) 892-8597
(314) 892-6814 FAX

Diansupply/Laborsaber Company will provide a free packet of information on their new, economy-priced, professional-model retractable saw (retractable scroll saw) that works from the bottom up. Diansupply/Laborsaber takes Visa.

DOYEL ENTERPRISES
P.O. Box 315
Yorba Linda, CA 92686-0315
(714) 666-1770

Doyel makes and sells a miter fence system for radial arm saws. The system eliminates the multiple grooves all over the saw table and provides accuracy to within ¼°. Call or write for information.

DREMEL

4915 21st Street
Racine, WI 53406
(800) 437-3635
(414) 554-1390

Dremel is the manufacturer of the Moto-Tool in all its variations, and with all its companion tools. Dremel makes electric power tools, in portable and benchtop versions, with much of its past fame resting on versions of the Moto-Tool. Today, Dremel is quickly gaining more fame for its new scroll saw line (two models) and its band saw, which is said by several people I trust to be the top benchtop band saw now in existence. When our first edition came out, that would have been a very minor distinction, but the entire bench-top tool market has swung to better quality in the past couple of years, and band saws are now following the lead of scroll saws. The ones I've tried, which do not, yet, include the Dremel, are incredibly good for the sizes and prices. Check with Dremel for a copy of their scroll saw blade and speed chart, rotary-tool bit guide, and pocket catalog. All are free.

EDWARD J. BENNETT COMPANY

10378 Fairview #139
Boise, ID 83704
(800) 333-4994 (Twenty-four hours)

The TS-Aligner for table saws is a dial-alignment gauge that rapidly shows whether or not the blade is parallel to the rip fence. Precision is increased, and repeatability is no longer a problem. Test cuts may be reduced or eliminated to prevent wasting wood. Call or write for further information: The free brochure tells the entire story very well. Bennett takes Master-Card and Visa.

EXCALIBUR

210 Eighth Street S
Lewiston, NY 14092
(800) 387-9789
(416) 293-2076 FAX

The Excalibur T-slot saw fence, and its various accessories, is a reasonably easy-to-install replacement and upgrade unit for table saws. I used one for years on my Delta Unisaw and found it met every claim made for it. Accessories include a router table to be built into the saw fence extension table, router fence brackets, a stock pusher, and guide-rail work stops. Two stock guide-rail lengths are available, allowing rip cuts to the right of the blade of 33" and 62", and two fence lengths, for different size saw tables, are available. Excalibur makes its own sliding table for table saws, allowing excellent crosscut accuracy to go with the T-slot fence's great rip cut accuracy. For those who haven't used them, sliding tables on stationary saws add fantastic cutting abilities and accuracy, if well made. The Excalibur comes in two sizes, the EXSLT30, giving a 28" crosscut depth (to the front of a 10" blade), and the EXSLT60, with a crosscut depth of 37". Excalibur also offers an over-arm blade cover for dust collection. The company also makes some superb scroll saws: Some time ago, up in Hot Air City (DC), I watched Phil Humfrey set a nickel on edge on a running scroll saw and noted that the nickel stayed in place as he cut a small pattern. That is stable! More information is available from Excalibur, and tools are also available from them by mail (UPS), as well as from other retailers. Excalibur takes MasterCard and Visa.

EXCALIBUR MACHINE CORPORATION

P.O. Box 82
Anderson, MO 64831
(800) 368-ROSS
(417) 223-4031
(417) 223-4034 FAX

Excalibur makes and sells ROSS precision drum sanders and abrasive planers. The ROSS line consists of sanders that go to the SS-37, with a material capacity of 37" wide by 6" tall. ROSS sells through dealers in some areas, and direct in others, throughout the United States, Canada, Mexico, Great Britain, Australia and the far east. All ROSS machines are manufactured in the United States. Literature is free, on request, and Excalibur accepts MasterCard and Visa.

G&W offers the Wagner Saf-T-Planer for radial arm saws and drill presses. This drill press model is shown surfacing a board.

G & W TOOL COMPANY, INC.

P.O. Box 691464
Tulsa, OK 74169
(918) 486-2761

Free literature describes the Wagner Safe-T-Planer, an accessory that comes in models that fit radial arm saws and drill presses. The planers are made of die-cast aluminum and high-speed steel that is precision ground. Basically, the tools turn a drill press or radial arm saw into a planer, allowing you to cut molding patterns, raised panels, tapered legs, rabbets, tenons and similar patterns. The tool cannot kick back, and is low cost. G&W Tool Company sells directly, and the Wagner Safe-T-Planer is also available from most mail-order houses. Free literature is available for a card or a call, and G&W Tool accepts MasterCard and Visa.

GENERAL MANUFACTURING COMPANY, LTD.
835 Cherrier Street
Drummandville, Quebec
Canada J2B 5A8
(819) 472-1161
(819) 472-3266 FAX

General Manufacturing is maker number three in the top American three of stationary power tools: That means their quality rests right on a par, and some-times, in some tools, above Delta and Powermatic. This Canadian manufacturer is proud of the fact that all tools they manufacture are 100 percent North American. General table saws are the only products I've had hands-on experience with, but they're a worthwhile place to begin: They're great. The basic model in 10″ tilting arbor light production saws is the 350-1, and it comes in about as wide a variety of con-figurations as do the Powermatic models and Delta's Unisaw, in about the same price ranges. General also makes a 14″ table saw, a 14″ radial arm saw, and 14″, 20″ and 24″ stationary planers, as well as jointers, band saws, shapers, sanding stations, lathes, mor-tisers and drill presses, plus accessories. General does not yet produce what might be called hobbyist or lighter-weight trade tools, so all products are light-to-heavy production machines. Give them a call, or drop a note, to request their catalog, and check on lo-cal dealers while you're on the line.

IN-LINE INDUSTRIES
661 South Main Street
Webster, MA 01570
(800) 533-6709
(508) 949-2968

In-Line manufactures and markets the Dubby sliding table cutoff fixture for table saws: The Dubby is the only such fixture that fits right or left of the blade, which makes for many intriguing possibilities — includ-ing working with a pair of the tables. Repetitive accu-racy is said to be within .005″, and adjustments from 2″ to 50″ are quickly made to $\frac{1}{128}$″ accuracy. Models are available for many table saws. In-Line also sells the Paralok rip fence, a table saw tune-up kit and zero clearance inserts. Give them a call or drop a note to get free literature.

MICRO-MARK
340 Snyder Avenue, 1614
Berkeley Heights, NJ 07922
(800) 225-1066
(908) 464-6764

Micro-Mark sells small tools. That said, there's an awful lot missing. There are some reasonably normal tools in the digest-sized, Micro-Mark catalog, includ-ing many by Dremel, but when you start checking out the Microlux tilting arbor table saw, ordinariness goes out the window. This saw uses an eighty-tooth blade to cut balsa to 1″ thick with a 3⅜″ blade diameter. On the facing page are miniature fingers for ships model-ers: These are rigging tools that allow working with fine lines. Palm-grip pliers make work on miniatures easier, as does a specific line of German-made 12-volt/115-volt power tools that are truly tiny: The belt sander fits inside the palm of a hand, and two fingers suffice to run the scroll saw. For the model maker working in wood or other materials, Micro-Mark of-fers easy access to many hard-to-find tools. They also offer some fascinating-appearing ship models and models of aircraft, with books on many kinds of mod-eling also offered (ships, railroads, cars, aircraft, doll-houses, furniture, turned miniatures, cast [metal] min-iatures, dioramas). A four-issue subscription to the eighty-page, full-color catalog costs $1. Micro-Mark takes American Express, Optima, Discover, Master-Card and Visa.

NELSON & JACOBSON, INC.
3546 North Clark Street
Chicago, IL 60657

Nelson & Jacobson makes and sells the Electro band saw brazer, a tool that may seem totally beyond the needs of hobby woodworkers but that is nearly essen-tial to anyone who depends on a band saw for major parts of their woodworking. This inexpensive (still $89.75, FOB factory) brazer allows quick making of new blades from coil band saw stock, and rapid re-pair of broken blades, to ½″ wide and 3/32″ thick. Op-eration is simple, quick, and easy enough to allow use of the band saw for internal sawing, which re-quires breaking and rebrazing the band saw blade. Nelson & Jacobson is a small manufacturer and does not take credit cards, but it will ship on an open account (credit references must accompany order, of course) or postpaid, plus shipping.

RBINDUSTRIES, INC.
1801 Vine Street
P.O. Box 369
Harrisonville, MO 64701
(800) 487-2623
(816) 884-3534
(816) 884-2463 FAX

The RBI Hawk line of scroll saws is a good starting point for the tools made and sold by RBIndustries: These American-made scroll saws are among the best to be found, with throat capacities from 14″ to 26″, with the top three, of four, models produced as free-standing tools. RBI provides a complete line of scroll saw accessories, including a blade rack, diamond blades (for cutting glass and similar hard materials), and a drip tank system for cooling the diamond blade. Further, the price list/catalog has other selections that can add more security. The company does not sell direct but will send a brochure and price list on request.

SAFETY SPEED CUT MANUFACTURING COMPANY
13460 North Highway 65
Anoka, MN 55304
(612) 755-1600

For years in the past, and very likely for years to come, I've wanted a plywood cutting panel saw such as those manufactured by SSC. There are features no hobby woodworker really needs, all of which tend to add to the cost, and these tools are expensive. But the lower-cost models are dropping to within reason as time goes on (or my sense of the dollar's value is getting as warped as a politician's). Most of these are single-purpose machines that do nothing beyond ripping and crosscutting plywood. If you use much plywood, though, the savings in time, materials, energy, and the additions to safety are quickly obvious. The least expensive model will take an 8′-long panel at normal (48″) width and let you rip or crosscut with the panel in a vertical position. That means you're not feeding the heavy, unwieldy plywood panel into a table saw with all that does for inaccurate and unsafe cutting. The only other option is to use a circular saw to cut nearly to size and then to finish cut on the table saw—this is what I mostly do. It wastes material. Most of us use one or both of the above methods, but if you do a great deal of plywood work, give SSC a call or drop them a note and ask for their catalog. They sell directly and through dealers.

SAWTRAX MANUFACTURING COMPANY
2605 West Alabama Road #203
Acworth, GA 30101
(404) 427-2414

SawTrax manufactures a panel saw and router kit that can easily reduce the cost of a full-sized panel saw to under $500, using a saw, or router, and wood you have on hand. The primary unit is a set of paired tubes, designed to crosscut the panels: Two models are made, the SawTrax 68 for panels to 53″ wide (4′ × 8′ sheets) and the SawTrax 80 for panels to 65″ wide (5′ × 10′ sheets). The base unit, for crosscutting only, is currently $299.95 for the smaller kit, and the rip carriage attachment for either panel saw adds $119.95. The company also makes a 30″ crosscut and dado tool for miters and compound cuts, a 10¼″ upgrade for the panel saw and a panel carrier, plus a few other items. The company sells through their merchandising arm, Aardvark Tool Company (see listing). Call or write for brochures.

SEYCO
1414 Cranford Drive
Box 472749
Garland, TX 75047-2749
(800) 462-3353
(214) 278-3353

This scroll saw specialist has a $1 catalog that features the Excalibur line of saws, their own line of letter guides, and many books and patterns for scrollsaw people. Seyco also offers its own brand of blade clamps, some general accessories such as finishes, glues, blade-storage tubes, and turned parts for projects, as well as an extremely extensive line of scrollsaw blades. Seyco takes MasterCard and Visa.

SOLO-SAW
1411 North Fairfield Road
Beavercreek, OH 45432
(800) 861-8484
(513) 848-2800

Solo-Saw manufactures a number of accessory tables for table saws aimed at making it easier for a single person to work with large sheet goods when working alone. These systems fold down on the saw, and present a side feed, and a large run-out table, making it easy, according to Russ Charlton, to slice as little as 1″ off full 4′ × 8′ panel. The 48″ × 44″ × ¾″ tabletop is a low-pressure melamine, and the extendable (up to 45″ from table, side-to-side and 48″ front-to-back) arms are hard maple, and feet are adjustable. This appears to be a good solution to handling problems in

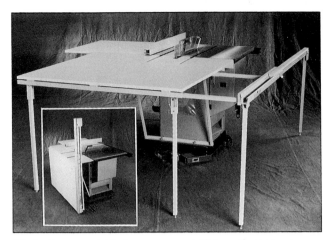

Solo-Saw's accessory tables increase ease and efficiency of one-person operation.

small cabinet and large hobby shops. Solo-Saw takes MasterCard and Visa.

STEUSSY CREATIONS
334 Atherton Avenue
Novato, CA 94945
(415) 897-1457

Steussy has designed the Eze-Angleguide for radial arm saws: That means you don't have to figure angles, or move the radial arm saw's arm to any angle and one for table saws, plus a drill. The Angle-Slide system for table saws lets you dial in a miter on the oversize 18″ dial. The drill-press guide makes repeatability easy, and the radial arm saw unit allows very easy setting and production of angles with no movement of the arm. Brochures on all the items are available at no cost. Steussy doesn't take credit cards but does supply to some mail-order houses that do.

TROJAN MANUFACTURING, INC.
9810 North Vancouver Way
Portland, OR 97217
(800) 745-2120
(503) 285-7731 FAX

Trojan Manufacturing produces a variety of carpentry aides that are also helpful for woodworkers. The Rip Master takes a lightweight table saw, increases ripping capacity to 28″, and makes that saw easily portable: It folds down and forms a cart for transport, but it supports the saw securely when unfolded. Ten inch diameter wheels make all sorts of job-site transport easy. Also of interest to the woodworker is the workcenter miter saw stand: This stand has two sets of legs, accepts a 2 × 6 center bar, and has two roller supports to fit at the ends of the 2 × 6. Miter saws and compound miter saws become more useful when

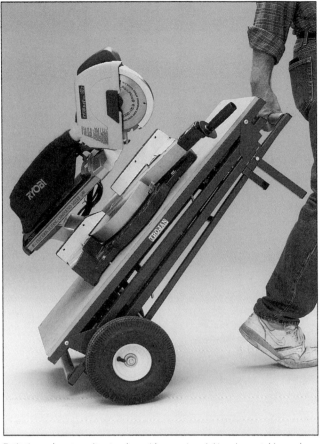

Trojan's workcenter miterstand provides great mobility, plus a stable work platform.

well supported. Trojan also makes a strong series of metal sawhorse legs, in two heights (27″ and 35″) that assemble easily and quickly. Call for free brochures. Trojan sells through three thousand dealers but also sells direct. They accept MasterCard and Visa.

WILKE MACHINERY COMPANY
3230 Susquehanna Trail
York, PA 17402
(717) 764-5000
(717) 764-3778 FAX

Bridgewood woodworking machinery is featured in the Wilke catalog and starts with an emphasis on the big guns, their 24″ × 9″ planer being the lead-off item again. At a net weight of 1,910 pounds, this machine will go through the floor in more than a few shops I know. A few pages on, we run into smaller shop tools with a 20″ economy planer (still 771 pounds), then to the 15″ planer, and on to the 12″ portable model (64 pounds net). Throughout, there is a choice of huge, medium and small shop items (except for those items that aren't at all suitable to small shops, such as 4-side moulders, 3-side planer-moulders, tenoners, and so on). Throughout the catalog, you find Delta, General, Porter-Cable and Bosch tools, DML blades and much else. The catalog is free and well worth checking out. Wilke takes Discover, MasterCard and Visa.

WILLIAMS & HUSSEY MACHINE COMPANY, INC.
Riverview Mill
P.O. Box 1149
Wilton, NH 03086
(800) 258-1380
(603) 654-6828
(603) 654-5446 FAX

The W&H molder-planer unit offers quick blade changes and a capacity of almost double-blade width because one side is open, allowing double-pass cutting. The unit also takes moulding-cutting blades, to double utility. The W&H lathe is relatively low cost

and high precision. Write or call to receive a free information kit.

WOOD CARVERS

KIMBALL SIGN COMPANY
2602 Whitaker Street
Savannah, GA 31401
(912) 232-6561

Ken Kimball's K55 and K66 Woodcarvers are described in a $2 full-color brochure that includes short instruction on how easy the setup is to use, as well as a look at what each model provides. The K55 is the larger unit, and both kits may be had ranging from basic units to fully equipped setups, including routers and dust-collection systems. Ken has been in business since 1952, and he produces machines that use linear ball bushing and carve letters from ½" to 12" high on any length and thickness of wood.

Shop Supplies

Shop Supplies

BAGS

DULUTH TRADING COMPANY
P.O. Box 7007
Duluth, MN 55107
(800) 505-8888
(612) 221-0308
(612) 221-0040 FAX

Duluth Trading Company is an offshoot set up by nondefecting members of Portable Products, Inc., to sell hardgoods made in the Lake Superior region. They feature the Bucket Boss and the rest of the Portable Products line in their catalog, but go on to sell Occidental Leather and other tool belts, Gladstone bags — soft-sided bags with a top that opens to the bag's full width — field bags, a contractor's briefcase (my own personal aim), a medium duffle bag, and a shell bag and purse, all in green or deep olive, with leather trim and solid copper and brass hardware. None of this stuff is cheap, but it does all seem to be fairly priced when compared to similar items sold by other companies (where such similar items exist). The catalog is free for the asking. (You don't even have to pay for the phone call.) Duluth Trading Company accepts Discover, MasterCard and Visa.

Duluth Trading sells the full line of Portable Products, such as this super handy Parachute bag, plus some items of further interest like the contractor's briefcase.

CARTS

RUBBERMAID, INC.
Commercial Products
3124 Valley Avenue
Winchester, VA 22601
(703) 542-8253
(703) 542-8838 FAX

This is the heavy-duty, built-to-be-beaten-on Rubbermaid line. For years, I've used their Brute buckets around the shop and darkroom and their industrial trash cans at one spot or another. Both are incredibly tough and resistant to chemicals. The catalogs that arrived, though, showed me things I had no idea Rubbermaid manufactured, from mops to cafeteria trays to tip-up containers to a wheelbarrow, and some garden carts. For information on heavy-duty cleanup and trash receptacles, check the catalog on Sanitary Maintenance Products. This covers everything from step-on trash cans to mops in more guises and sizes than I believed possible, while also covering utility trucks, hoppers, and a very wide line of push brooms. The Foodservice Products Catalog covers a great many items besides freezer and refrigerator containers, though those are present in profusion. Insulated beverage containers and antifatigue matting may be of interest, as may all-purpose caddies and step stools. The Industrial Products catalog shows hoppers, utility and bushel trucks, a Big Wheel cart, Brute buckets, tubs, parts organizers, and trash cans in sizes from 10 gallons to 55 gallons, round or square. The Agricultural Products catalog shows a tractor cart, wheelbarrow and farm carts. Ask for catalogs or brochures that might have merchandise of interest to you, and ask for the name of your nearest dealer — unlike Rubbermaid's Home Products, these are not found in every store on earth . . . unless you live in a farming community.

SHOPCARTS
A Division of Adapa
P.O. Box 5183
Topeka, KS 66605
(800) 255-2302
(913) 862-4444

The Shopcarts sheet-panel handler would have proved very handy in my latest project, where I had

Shopcart's Panel Skate is an exceptionally handy shop aid for anyone who uses thicker, larger plywood sheets.

to slice four ¾"-thick panels of oak plywood and another of ½" pine, plus a sixth of ¼" lauan. Unfortunately, the shop I'm using is too small for that sort of equipment, as handy as it is. For the home workshop, probably the most useful item made and sold by Shopcarts is the Panel Skate. This is a small unit (it weighs five pounds and is a foot long) with a *V* set between four wheels. This aluminum alloy *V* will let you roll a pretty good sized sheet around the shop with almost no effort. I'll be getting one for my shop very soon. Shopcarts literature is free.

CLEANUP

RUBBERMAID, INC.
Home Products Division
1147 Akron Road
Wooster, OH 44691
(216) 264-6464
(216) 287-2157 FAX

Hard to believe, isn't it? Rubbermaid, though, deserves a listing for woodworkers if for nothing else other than the line of trash cans and brooms they make. Certainly, the Home Products line of clean-up gear isn't as heavy as that listed below for their Commercial Products Division, but there are enough types of trash cans to suit any woodworker. And there are work centers, workbench leg ends, work boxes and toolboxes, as well as all sorts of buckets and spatulas and other tools of interest only when specific jobs come up. Drop a note and ask for literature on Food Storage products (spatulas and food storage products that are great for gluing, and for storage of some finishes and other items); Home Organization (rolling basket carts, lazy susans for finishing without having to lift and turn); Cleaning; Refuse/Recycling (every store you enter has at least one display of these Rub-

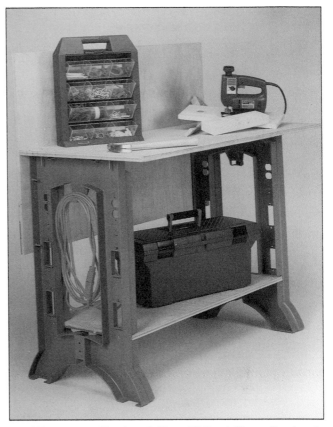

To quickly set up a workbench, try Rubbermaid's Toughsides workbench ends.

bermaid products); Hardware (modular storage cabinets, toolboxes, work boxes, work surfaces [fancy sawhorses], and workbench ends). Probably by the time this book reaches print, there will be other products of interest.

RUBBERMAID, INC.
Commercial Products
3124 Valley Avenue
Winchester, VA 22601
(703) 542-8253
(703) 542-8838 FAX

This is the heavy-duty, built-to-be-beaten-upon Rubbermaid line. For years, I've used their Brute buckets around the shop and darkroom, and their industrial trash cans at one spot or another. Both are incredibly tough and resistant to chemicals. The catalogs that arrived, though, showed me things I had no idea Rubbermaid manufactured, from mops to cafeteria trays to tip-up containers to a wheelbarrow, and some garden carts. For information on heavy-duty cleanup and trash receptacles, check the catalog on Sanitary Maintenance Products. This covers everything from step-on trash cans to mops in more guises and sizes than I believed possible, while also covering utility trucks, hoppers, and a very wide line of push brooms. The Foodservice Products Catalog covers a great many items besides freezer and refrigerator container, though those are present in profusion. Insulated beverage containers and antifatigue matting may be of interest, as may all-purpose caddies and step stools. The Industrial Products catalog shows hoppers, utility and bushel trucks, a Big Wheel cart, Brute buckets, tubs, parts organizers and trash cans in sizes from 10 gallons to 55 gallons, round or square. The Agricultural Products catalog shows a tractor cart, wheelbarrow and farm carts. Ask for catalogs or brochures that might have merchandise of interest to you, and ask for the name of your nearest dealer — unlike Rubbermaid's Home Products, these are not found in every store on earth . . . unless you live in a farming community.

SAVOGRAN

P.O. Box 130
Norwood, MA 02062
(800) 225-9872

Savogran markets a really good and nonpolluting paintbrush cleaner — CleanSafer. Call or write for information.

DOORS

STANLEY DOOR SYSTEMS

1225 East Maple Road
Troy, MI 48084
(313) 528-2500
(313) 528-1424 FAX

Call or write for brochures on Stanley doors, used in garages, residences, shops and everywhere else. Stanley's doors are easy to install, as they are ready to pop into rough openings. Garage doors, of course, make ideal doors for moving in tools and moving out large projects, and Stanley's garage-door openers are great for getting the door open when your back is tired from long, steady work on projects.

GLOVES AND APRONS

GREAT LAKES LEATHER PRODUCTS COMPANY

4022 North 45th Street
Sheboygan, WI 53083
(414) 458-8489

Write or call for free literature on woodworker's leather aprons. Three good-looking designs are cur-

rently offered. One is a classic leather woodworker's apron with waist-height pockets all across the front, and the second is a wood-carver's leather apron, with a different pocket configuration and similar length, while the third is a farrier's (horseshoer's) leather apron, with upper-leg protection. Price for the first two is $49.95, while the farrier's style costs $59.95. The sample of leather Winson Cox sent me is as heavy as in any of my aprons, but they also offer extra-cost options. Aprons are available in short, regular and tall sizes. Great Lakes Leather Products takes MasterCard and Visa.

WELLS LAMONT

6640 West Touhy Avenue
Niles, IL 60714
(708) 647-8200

Starting in 1907, Wells Lamont began manufacturing work gloves and now produces a wide and varied line for all purposes. I've used a number of types of Wells Lamont gloves and remain most attached to the white kidskin model that literally molds itself to your hand. I suggest buying these a size smaller — kidskin stretches very easily — and then washing your hands with mink oil, with the gloves on, until the mink oil disappears. Once that's done, you've got a great pair of gloves for moving almost anything around. There is a canvas-backed, leather-palm pair that is also excellent and works better in real rough stuff like stacking lumber. Call or write for brochures on their work gloves.

LAMPS AND LIGHTING

INTELLECTRON

21021 Corsair Boulevard
Hayward, CA 94545
(510) 732-6790
(510) 732-6910 FAX

Intellectron manufactures motion-detector lighting for consumer-end use: You'll find that their brochure lists everything from Estate Lantern styles to Nautical models with compact fluorescent bulbs. How is any of this of value to woodworkers? Well, basically, I feel motion-detector lights help keep you from stumbling around in front of your shop, looking for the door key and a place to sit down a $20 chunk of wood without creating scratches on the wood. My new shop is under construction at the moment, and I expect to use at least two motion-detector lights on it, and I may use a conversion kit to set up an indoor light for the same action. Intellectron also makes those. Drop a note or give a call for their brochure and a list of dealers. Intellectron does not sell direct.

INTERMATIC
Spring Grove, IL 60081
(815) 675-2321
(815) 675-2112 FAX

This 103-year-old company produces timers, surge protectors, and low-voltage outdoor lighting: Offhand, I cannot think of a major use for timers for woodworkers, but surge protectors and outdoor lighting can both be very handy from time to time. Setting a surge protector in a circuit means that if your radial arm saw or table saw or drill press or other costly tool remains plugged in, as most do, each night, and a surge hits your load center, your chances of total motor loss are reduced by the effectiveness of the surge protector. Naturally, low-voltage lighting makes it easy to set up inexpensive-to-operate outdoor lights. Intermatic products are available from home centers, hardware stores, discount outlets and full-service retailers. You can also call the number above to get the nearest available dealer or to request a Home Protection and Control Products catalog. The catalog is free.

THE LAMP SHOP
P.O. Box 36
Concord, NH 03302
(603) 224-1603

Lamp parts for woodworkers are featured in The Lamp Shop's $2 catalog.

LAMPI
7272 Governors West
P.O. Box 1769
Huntsville, AL 35807
(205) 837-3110
(205) 830-9518 FAX

Lampi makes various lamps useful on projects or around a shop: Most are of the types useful when enclosed in a shelf or cabinet project, or placed nearby. The lamps are available in single quantities at many do-it-yourself centers, but for special orders, you may get in touch with Lampi as above.

ORGANIZATIONAL ITEMS

AKRO-MILS
1293 South Main Street
Akron, OH 44301
(206) 253-5593

Akro-Mils is a forty-five-year-old maker of storage organizers, small-parts cabinets, tool organizers, plastic tool-boxes, and attached-lid general totes. They supply a free annual catalog.

DULUTH TRADING COMPANY
P.O. Box 7007
Duluth, MN 55107
(800) 505-8888
(612) 221-0308
(612) 221-0040 FAX

Duluth Trading Company is an offshoot set up by nondefecting members of Portable Products, Inc., to sell hard goods made in the Lake Superior region. They feature the Bucket Boss and the rest of the Portable Products line in their catalog but go on to sell Occidental Leather and other tool belts, Gladstone bags—soft-sided bags with a top that opens to the bag's full width—field bags, a contractor's briefcase (my own personal aim), a medium duffle bag, and a shell bag and purse, all in green or deep olive, with leather trim and solid copper and brass hardware. None of this stuff is cheap, but it does all seem to be fairly priced when compared to similar items sold by other companies (where such similar items exist). The catalog is free for the asking. (You don't even have to pay for the phone call.) Duluth Trading Company accepts Discover, MasterCard and Visa.

HIRSH COMPANY
8051 Central Park Avenue
Skokie, IL 60076
(800) 872-3279 Customer Service
(708) 673-6610
(708) 673-1412 FAX

Hirsh manufactures a wide line of steel shelving, and stands, sawhorses, workbenches, and similar items of use to woodworkers. Of particular interest to me was their step stool, with tool holder and built in handgrip. They also make organizers designed for use with pegboards, and general tool racks that also mount on pegboards, plus roller-top work supports. It's a varied line. Call or write for Hirsh's free catalog.

PORTABLE PRODUCTS, INC.
58 East Plato Boulevard
St. Paul, MN 55107
(800) 688-2677

This manufacturer of portable products also sells direct, but the lines are carried by many woodworker's catalogs, Sears, K Mart, Target, Hechingers, Ace, Home Depot and other outlets. The company is

Duluth Trading's tool bag is exceptionally handy and durable.

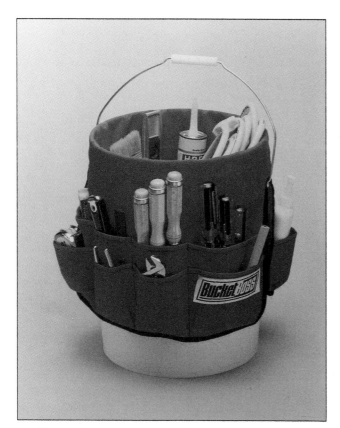

Portable Products may be most noted for their Bucket Boss, a handy carrier that fits over a five-gallon bucket. Portable Products items are designed by tradesmen.

owned and operated by tradesmen. What do they make and sell? The mainstay of the line is the bucket-mounted tool carrier. Having said that, it's necessary to state that there are six of those mainstays, plus a bucket seat (there's also a padded handle for those buckets). The entire line is meant to be mounted on five-gallon plastic buckets and is made in varying patterns with many pockets of heavy material meant to last a long time under extreme conditions (otherwise known as job sites for contractors). The line goes further, into a folding top Parachute Bag to hold small parts (nails, screws and similar items), Chutes a lower-priced version of the full-sized bag, knee pads in three versions, suspenders, and a hobby gardener's line that includes a Garden Boss to fit a bucket, and even a straw hat. There is no pretension whatsoever: Tools are tested by tradesmen, and the catalog is very well done. A related company, Duluth Trading Company, sells retail and carries a wider line of mail-order goods that include canvas briefcases for contractors, and can be reached for catalog requests at (800) 505-8888.

SAFETY, HEALTH AND SECURITY

AIRSTREAM DUST HELMETS
Highway 54 South
P.O. Box 975
Elbow Lake, MN 56531
(800) 328-1792
(218) 685-4457
(218) 685-4458 FAX

Airstream is the distributor for the Racal line of lung and eye protection helmets — respirators — that provide protection from dust, lacquers, glues and strippers. The company also distributes hearing protectors, safety glasses, and a negative (no air pump) respirator for those who don't wish to pay the cost of the positive (pumped air) systems. Mike Nelson tells me their most popular system with woodworkers is the Airmate 3. The Airmate 3 has a hinged visor, optional earmuffs, an eight-hour battery, and an airflow of eight cubic feet per minute. It works especially well on lathes because it has built-in eye protection. This is not a cheap system, but considering what I've done to my hearing over the years and to my lungs, the cost seems reasonable, for this or another quality system. Catalogs are available at no charge, on request. Airstream sells through its own mail-order company and takes MasterCard, Visa and Discover.

DYNAMAT
11440 Lakeland Drive N #101
Minneapolis, MN 55369
(800) 800-2038
(612) 425-4467
(612) 425-4399 FAX

Dynamat makes antifatigue mats that provide industrial quality for the home workshop. The polyvinyl chloride mats are 24″ × 36″ × ⅜″ thick, and they resist water, oil, detergents and sawdust. The mats make concrete floors a great deal easier on one's back and retail for about $19. Since our first edition, I'm informed, Dynamat has come out with a roll product that lets you cut the material to length, up to 60′. Call for information, the name of your nearest dealer and a brochure. Dynamat is sold through home centers and hardware stores nationwide.

ENVIRO-SAFETY PRODUCTS
21344 Avenue 332
Woodlake, CA 93286
(800) 637-6606
(209) 564-8071
(209) 564-8073 FAX

Duane and Peggy Dahlvang have been distributing the Racal Health & Safety product line of dust and chemical helmets/respirators as well as hearing protectors and safety goggles and glasses for nine years. Call or write for free brochures. They ship coast to coast and accept Visa, MasterCard and Discover.

MAG ENGINEERING & MANUFACTURING COMPANY, INC.
15261 Transistor Lane
Huntington Beach, CA 92649
(800) 624-9942
(714) 891-5100

This is another of my oddball companies if we stay tightly in the woodworking context: MAG Engineering sells security products, a couple of which will make your shop—or home—more secure, and help preserve your tools for your use. My main interest in the catalog is the door-reinforcer section. These wraparound plates encase lock, bolt and door. High-security strikes increase the strength of the jamb around the door strike. Combine the two, and any thief has a great deal more work to do to break in. From the list sent to me, I find that combining a reinforcer, for the lockset, and a heavier strike will run less than $30 for suggested list on the fanciest finishes. The MAG price list/catalog has other selections that can add more security. The company does not sell direct but will send a brochure and price list on request.

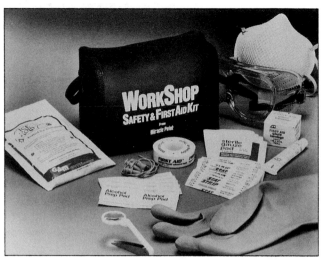

Miracle Point's Safety & First Aid kit holds many worthwhile items.

MIRACLE POINT
P.O. Box 71
Crystal Lake, IL 60014-0071
(815) 477-7713

Miracle Point had a single product a couple years ago, tweezers, at a reasonable cost in a version that specifically suits woodworkers, so no catalog was sent. The Miracle Point Magna-Point is a sharp tweezers combined with a 5× magnifying glass. Cost is $6.95 postpaid if you can't find them locally. They sent a sample, and I used them to remove a splinter. They worked and still do, but Miracle Point has added a very handy workshop first-aid kit to their array, for $25, again postpaid. This first-aid kit includes top brands of dust masks, goggles, ear plugs and gloves, plus the Magna-Point tweezers and a supply of basic first-aid items. It must be emphasized that this is not a truly complete first-aid kit, but it does provide some items of added interest in the woodworking shop and two major safety items in the goggles and dust mask (the mask is a disposable type and will have to be replaced after it clogs).

3M DIY DIVISION
Consumer Relations
515-3N-02
St. Paul, MN 55144-1000

This is the 3M division that handles information on Newstroke snap-off paintbrushes, home-care adhesives, surface-prep products (hand- and power-sanding materials), paint removers, and personal safety products, such as goggles and face masks of both comfort and respirator types to reduce the effects of the sandpaper and similar products 3M produces. I particularly like their disposable general dust and sanding respirator: That's the number 8710, and it

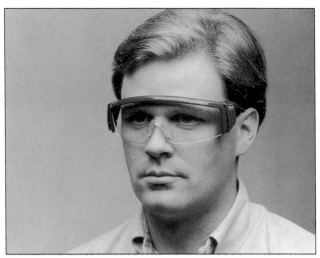

U.S. Safety manufactures Renegade Spectacles.

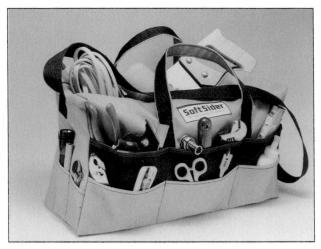

Equally handy is Portable Products' Soft Sider tool bag.

comes in contractor packs of twenty and in packs of two or three. Catalogs are available on request. Specify which product line interests you (listed above).

U.S. SAFETY
8101 Lenexa Drive
P.O. Box 15965
Lenexa, KS 66215
(800) 821-5218
(913) 599-5555
(800) 252-5002 FAX

U.S. Safety designs, develops and manufactures personal protective equipment that includes plain and prescription eyewear, respirators, goggles, faceshields and other protective products. Several types of protective eyewear aid woodworkers' eye safety, including the Renegade Spectagle, which combines the safety and security of a goggle with spectacle styling. The more standard Phoenix and Phoenix II can be had with plain or prescription lenses. The company has been in business almost sixty years. U.S. Safety will send literature on request and accepts Master-Card and Visa.

TOOL CARRIERS

PORTABLE PRODUCTS, INC.
58 East Plato Boulevard
St. Paul, MN 55107
(800) 688-2677

This manufacturer of portable products also sells direct, but the lines are carried by many woodworker's catalogs, Sears, K Mart, Target, Hechingers, Ace, Home Depot and other outlets. The company is owned and operated by tradesmen. What do they make and sell? The mainstay of the line is the bucket-mounted tool carrier. Having said that, it's necessary to state that there are six of those mainstays, plus a bucket seat (there's also a padded handle for those buckets). The entire line is meant to be mounted on five-gallon plastic buckets and is made in varying patterns, with many pockets, of heavy material meant to last a long time under extreme conditions (otherwise known as job sites for contractors). The line goes further, into a folding top Parachute Bag to hold small parts (nails, screws and similar items); Chutes, a lower-priced version of the full-sized bag; knee pads in three versions; suspenders; a hobby gardener's line that includes a Garden Boss to fit a bucket; and even a straw hat. There is no pretension whatsoever: Tools are tested by tradesmen, and the catalog is very well done. A related company, Duluth Trading Company, sells retail and carries a wider line of mail-order goods that includes canvas briefcases for contractors, and Duluth Trading Company can be reached for catalog requests at (800) 505-8888.

UTILITIES

WOODS WIRE PRODUCTS
510 3rd Avenue SW
P.O. Box 2675
Carmel, IN 46032
(800) 428-6168
(317) 844-7261

Woods offers standard extension cords, power block extension cords, surge arrestors and similar items. Does your shop have enough extension cords? Mine doesn't and probably never will. I don't know of a woodworker who does have enough, and if work moves outside, then things get even worse. I particularly like the Woods Yellow Jacket commercial line of extension cords, and their Tool Saver line incorporates circuit breakers. Both are available in 50- and 100-foot lengths with 12-gauge wire, something I consider essential for many of today's high-amperage power tools (don't forget that 13-ampere circular saw or 15 ampere router, is going to overload a 14- or 16-gauge wire in a rush). Call or write for information on add-on surge protectors, as well as extension cords: Surge protectors are often worthwhile additions to shop circuitry, as they stop electrical shocks before the shock can harm a healthy person. Woods also makes work lights in clip-on and drop-light styles. Woods does not sell direct.

VACUUMS

SHOP-VAC CORPORATION
2323 Reach Road
Williamsport, PA 17701
(717) 326-0502
(717) 326-7185 FAX

Drop Shop-Vac a note or give them a call and ask for catalog material on their justly famous line of shop vacuums, to which they've now added the ToolMate shop cleaner. The ToolMate offers two-stage filtering as it picks up directly from your tool's outlet (the ToolMate has a 4" diameter inlet to fit most standard tool dust outlets). The 1.25 horse ToolMate, though, is not nearly as powerful as some Shop-Vacs, which run up to four horsepower in industrial and home models.

SILVER METAL PRODUCTS
2150 Kitty Hawk Road
Livermore, CA 94550
(800) 227-0470

Silver Metal Products fasteners provide many methods for setting up workbenches, shelving and similar projects. The catalog is available for a card or a call and includes many metal products of interest to shop builders and other woodworkers.

WORKBENCHES

ASHMAN TECHNICAL LTD.
351 Nash Road N
Hamilton, Ontario
Canada L8H 7P4
(905) 560-2400
(905) 560-2404 FAX

Ashman Technical is a supplier of shop equipment and tools for government and educational facilities and is able to provide woodworking equipment for different facilities. With woodworking equipment, they're heavy in the General line, and they export the General line to the United States. Ashman also produces a line of workbenches aimed at educational institutions. Ashman Technical accepts MasterCard and Visa.

BASIC LIVING PRODUCTS
1321 67th Street
Emeryville, CA 94608
(800) 829-6300

Among other items carried by Basic Living Products is the Sjobergs line of Swedish workbenches in the European joiners pattern.

GEOFF BROWN
8 Ladbroke Park
Millers Road
Warwick
CV34 5AE United Kingdom
011 44 926 493389
011 44 926 491357 FAX

I'd recommend doing your checking Stateside on the items Geoff Brown exports: He distributes Tormek wet-grinder systems (see Tormek U.S.A.); Nobex miter boxes; and Sjobergs joiner's workbenches. The latter two can readily be found in Woodcraft catalogs [(800)-535-4482, see listing for *Woodcraft*]. The Nobex line consists of the Champion Compound Miter Saw, with a 7¼" cutting height, and a few other tools. The Nobex miter square appears of great interest. The Sjobergs joiners benches are what one might call typical European pattern workbenches, which means that if you've ever become accustomed to them, you hate to use anything else. At the same time, they tend to be exceptionally pricey. Sjobergs benches are also available from Basic Living Products, 1321 67th Street, Emeryville, CA 94608. The phone number there is (800) 829-6300.

Tool Distributors

Tool Distributors

A&I SUPPLY

401 Radio City Drive
North Pekin, IL 61554
(800) 553-5592
(309) 382-2400 (in Illinois)

A&I Supply presents a catalog of woodworking tools
and equipment at discount prices, ranging from a
Delta Unisaw to a Porter-Cable 690 router, with stops
all along the way. The catalog is free, and A&I accepts
MasterCard, Visa and Discover charge cards.

AMERICAN MACHINE & TOOL COMPANY

Fourth Avenue and Spring Street
Royersford, PA 19468-2519
(800) 435-8665 Orders
(800) 435-3279 Customer service, parts, inquiries
(215) 948-0400
(215) 948-5300 FAX

American Machine & Tool Company distributes tools
made for it in Taiwan. The AMT line of low- to
moderate-cost tools and their range of accessories is
shown in a free catalog. Over time, I've used AMT
lathes, jointers and drill presses, plus a number of accessories, and found them excellent representatives
of the moderate part of the price scale for power
tools. I've not had a chance to use their newer lines
of hand tools and accessories, but I expect they'll be
on a par with the other lines. The drill press accepts
an exceptionally wide variety of accessories, all also
sold by AMT. A free catalog is issued seven times a
year. This firm accepts Discover, MasterCard and
Visa.

ATLAS COPCO ELECTRIC TOOLS, INC.

3 Shaw's Cove
New London, CT 06320
(800) 243-0870
(203) 447-4624 FAX

Atlas Copco distributes the AEG line of power tools, a
complete line of power hand tools, from nibblers
through circular saws, and including corded and cordless drills, hammer-drills, slide compound miter saws,
random-orbit sanders (including a unique, at least to
me, cordless model), belt sanders, and on. Their cordless line is more extensive than most, right up to and
including caulking and adhesive guns—AEG chooses

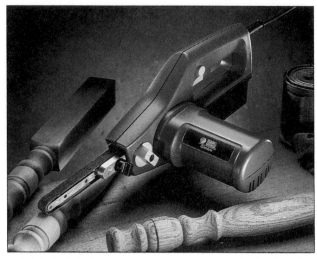

Black & Decker's ½" Quantum belt sander is exceptionally handy in lots of
situations that used to require hand sanding.

to call their battery-powered models "cordfree." A
minicatalog and price list are free for a phone call or
a card.

BLACK & DECKER (U.S.), INC.

Power Tool Division
P.O. Box 798
Hunt Valley, MD 21030

Write for the Black & Decker consumer line catalog
of one of the widest lines of portable power tools
made. The B&D line has been around since 1910,
and it recently was added to with the introduction of
the Quantum series for midrange use. Black &
Decker saw an uncovered opening in the marketplace and went after it with this green-bodied line of
tools that are a step up from consumer models, yet
not as costly as full-stage professional and industrial
tools. I recently got a chance to try many of the tools
and to tour Black & Decker's Easton, Maryland, factory: I enjoyed the way the tools handled and was impressed with the factory, which turns out five million
tools per year, in Black & Decker (both consumer
and full-blown industrial lines carry the Black &
Decker name), Quantum and DeWalt. Black &
Decker can legitimately argue they're in as many
workshops and homes as Sears's Craftsman brand.

BLUE RIDGE MACHINERY & TOOLS, INC.
Box 536-WSB
Hurricane, WV 25526
(304) 562-3538
(304) 562-5311 FAX

The Blue Ridge Machinery catalog of power and hand tools is $1 and covers a wide range, including metal and woodworking machinery, supplies, accessories, books and videos. Blue Ridge carries tools by Jet, Min-Max, Powermatic, and many more, with an array of tools including air compressors, dust collectors, bandsaw blades, drill bits, jointers, lathes, planers, routers, sanders, shapers, and on. Blue Ridge Machinery takes Discover, MasterCard and Visa.

BLUME SUPPLY, INC.
3316 South Boulevard
Charlotte, NC 28209
(800) 288-9200
(704) 523-7811

Blume Supply carries Powermatic and other power tools, and covers sales, repair and rental. In addition, they list everything from angle finders to hand saws to rules to squares to utility knives to wrenches under hand tools. Blume also handles supplies for woodworkers, including wood buttons, plugs and dowels, glues and screws. Call for prices and other details.

COOPER INDUSTRIES
Cooper Hand Tools Division
P.O. Box 30100
Raleigh, NC 27622
(919) 781-7200

Call or drop a note for free brochures on Cooper Tools' varied lines: For those not already familiar with these top lines, that includes Plumb (hammers and similar tools); Nicholson (hand saws, saw blades, files, et al.); Lufkin (measuring tools); Crescent (adjustable wrenches, of course, but also screwdrivers, pliers and other tools); Wiss (scissors, knives, metal snips); Xcelite (small pliers and cutters and electronic assembly and disassembly tools); Weller (soldering tools); H.K. Porter (cable and chain cutters); Turner (propane torches); Campbell (chain, padlocks); and Covert (pulleys, swivels and similar accessories). Cooper recently introduced a new line, tagged as Home Improvement tools after the TV show. The tools seem to be of a midrange quality that should serve well but seem to me to be aimed primarily at getting show watchers to buy tools, and not to be aimed at the serious woodworker, carpenter and general DIYer in the same way Plumb, et al., are. That's fair

Delta's small scroll saw presents a great entry into woodworking.

enough, I guess, for the show is bound to set any real DIYer's teeth on edge. Drop a note for brochures.

DELTA INTERNATIONAL MACHINERY CORPORATION
246 Alpha Drive
Pittsburgh, PA 15238
(800) 438-2486 Consumer hotline

Delta power tools include machines and accessories aimed at home workshops, construction trades, industry and schools. There are now two basic Delta lines, with building trades and home-shop machinery lines paired in a catalog, which you can find at your dealers or get by calling Delta's Consumer Hotline number above. Tools built for contractors and home-shop use differ in some respects (usually being lighter, and less costly, than industrial machines, but not always — no one can class the 12", 33-890 radial arm saw as light or less accurate, except possibly those using the huge industrial machines). Delta also offers an 18", 3-phase, 7½ horse unit that is 745 pounds, which is enough, and then some. The home-shop-machinery catalog is a great deal of fun, and offers just about anything most of us can want, or come close to affording. The industrial-machinery catalog, as noted above, offers truly heavy-duty machinery for the huge jobs where dead-on accuracy is a must on a day-in, day-

Delta's floor model jointers give professional results.

DeWalt's router bits come in many profiles and are carbide tipped or solid carbide.

out basis. For example, the biggest planer in the home-machinery catalog is a 13" (not portable), but Delta's biggest planer is a 24". Delta continually brings out new models including, recently, their Side-kick frame and trim saw (rod-guided compound miter saw, with a cut width of 12" at 90°) and a new dust collector/sweeper. There are several new differentiations in 10" table saws, and a new series of benchtop tools, including a band saw, scroll saw, drill press, table saw, 6" grinder, 6" jointer, and a 12" portable planer. I've used only the jointer but can heartily recommend it for people who are space- and budget-limited in their woodworking shops. One of the top three American (two U.S., one Canadian) stationary tool makers, Delta will send you free a copy of their Building Trades and Home Shop catalog.

DEWALT INDUSTRIAL TOOL COMPANY
626 Hanover Pike
Hampstead, MD 21074
(800) 4-DEWALT

DeWalt is a name that has been around sixty-five-plus years: Today, it denotes Black & Decker's top-grade industrial power tools and accessories, aimed primarily at the construction industry. These tools, including the 12" compound miter saw, the biscuit

joiner, and the big plunge router, are often ideal for serious woodworkers (they're too pricey for the beginner or person who is semi-interested but rationally priced for tools aimed at surviving the day-to-day battering of construction work). DeWalt will be glad to supply a catalog of the entire line (which is expanding with a new line of 14.4-volt cordless drills just hitting the market, alongside a small random-orbit sander). Drop them a note or give the free number a call.

DISSTIM CORPORATION
217 E. Hurffville Road
Deptford, NJ 08096
(609)227-7904
(609) 227-7823 FAX

Disstim produces hand tools, does tool-and-die work and precision grinding, and makes specialty ladders, so they have a very unusual product mix, ranging from Scru-Drill adjustable-screw drill-countersinks to hook-and-hang storage systems, to Driver 21 — a screwdriver with extra tips to handle varied sizes of slot, Phillips and Torx headed screws that is also a multisized nut driver — to a Hol-down drill press clamp to the StepMax folding aluminum and fiberglass ladders that convert immediately from 3' to 6'. Hook 'n Hang storage systems include panels and an assortment of pegboard hooks, of polypropylene, that don't wobble or fall out, according to Disstim's Tim Eichfeld. Literature on these products is available from Disstim, and they accept MasterCard and Visa.

EASTWOOD COMPANY
580 Lancaster Avenue
Malvern, PA 19355
(800) 345-1178
(610) 644-0560 FAX

The Eastwood Specialty Tool catalog contains 180 pages and a slew of tools that are, to say the least, unusual. A partial listing includes rust removers, glass tools, buffing kits, painting supplies, how-to books in many fields, all sorts of hand tools, sandblasting gear and much else. In addition to the sandblasting equipment, Eastwood carries a comprehensive listing of AccuSpray HVLP spraying equipment, which is of great interest to many woodworkers. Most of the rest of the material is for those interested in working on automobiles, but on occasion a tool will cross the line: The in-line air tool oiler is one such item, and there are numerous others. The catalog is free. Eastwood accepts Discover, MasterCard and Visa, and they will accept COD orders from within the continental United States.

GRIZZLY IMPORTS, INC.
West of the Mississippi:
P.O. Box 2069
Bellingham, WA 98227-2069
(800) 647-0801 Customer service
(800) 541-5537 Orders
(800) 225-0021 FAX
East of the Mississippi:
2406 Reach Road
Williamsport, PA 17701
(717) 326-3806 Customer service
(800) 523-4777 Orders
(800) 438-5901 FAX

The Grizzly catalog, a sizable book of 163 color pages, is free from either location, both of which are showroom and warehouse locations (the western address for the showroom is 1821 Valencia Street, Bellingham). Grizzly is a major importer of Taiwanese stationary tools, and has been for more than eleven years. Their catalog shows their line of table saws, planers, dust collectors, sanders, jointers, band saws, and other expected stationary power tools, in which Grizzly specializes. For prospective buyers of these tools, Grizzly will locate Grizzly buyers in that new customer's locale so the new customer can get an opinion on the Grizzly tools from a user. Added to the stationary tools is Grizzly's line of accessories of many kinds, from sanding belts and abrasive discs to mortising attachments and chisels, plus their own line of framing and brad nailers and staplers. In addition, they carry Makita tools and Campbell-Hausfeld

air compressors and accessories, plus a reasonable line of books and videos. There is also European hardware, as well as other supplies and equipment. The catalog is supplemented by a free sixteen-page summer sale brochure each year. Grizzly accepts Visa, MasterCard and Discover.

HARBOR FREIGHT TOOLS
3491 Mission Oaks Boulevard
Camarillo, CA 93011
(800) 423-2567
(805) 445-4900 FAX

Harbor Freight is a mail-order tool company with a colorful catalog—rather, series of catalogs—and a bunch of sale flyers that come out at intervals during the year. I've got their latest sale flyer, which is actually a forty-page color catalog, in front of me, and the variety of tools is wide, and prices are pretty good, even in this day of discount houses. They offer standard brands from Black & Decker, to Bosch to DeWalt to Makita, Milwaukee, Porter-Cable, Ryobi, Skil, Channellock and Stanley, plus many others, over a wide range of products. There are also a slew of less familiar brands, such as Pittsburgh, Central Machinery, and others. Harbor Freight is the only place I've seen honing belts and compound for 1″ × 30″ and 1″ × 42″ belt sanders, and they also offer generators and surge protector strips and models of '92 Dodge Vipers and '57 'Vettes (you figure out what you'd do with them). Call for the catalog. Harbor Freight takes MasterCard, Visa, Discover and American Express.

HARTVILLE TOOL AND SUPPLY
940 West Maple Street
Hartville, IN 44632
(800) 345-2396
(216) 877-4682 FAX

Hartville Tool is a tool and accessories company. Their full-color catalog is seventy to seventy-five pages long and is issued once or twice annually. The company carries most of the Incra line of jigs and accessories; its own router table; Taylor carving tools; Sorby chisels; a line of Japanese chisels; Sorby turning tools; squares; books; abrasives in most styles; glues; adhesives; and finishes, including Watco Oil Finishes, Bartley finishes and Croix HVLP systems. There are dovetail markers; draw knives; bench dogs; dust-collection accessories; clamps; measuring tools; shims; router template bushings; many Porter-Cable tools; some Delta; the Inch Mate calculator; Dozuki saws; spoon bits (for drilling leg holes in Windsor chair bottoms); more clamps; a beading tool; and the DeWalt compound miter saw. This just skims the list, of course, and the catalog does it far more thoroughly. Hartville takes Discover, MasterCard, Visa, American Express and Optima.

HITACHI

3950 Steve Reynolds Boulevard
Norcross, GA 30093
(404) 925-1774
(404) 923-2117 FAX
6219 DeSoto Avenue
Woodland Hills, CA 91365
(714) 891-5330
(714) 898-9096 FAX

Hitachi tools have been in the U.S. market more than a decade now and have earned a reputation for quality. The line consists of more than eighty-five tools, for working wood, concrete, metals and other materials, with the emphasis and interest riding on drills, including the cordless models; circular saws, including miter saws up to 15″ in blade diameter and a well-regarded slide-compound miter saw; routers; planers; jointer-planers; a 12″ table saw; and a 14½″ band saw. The company also produces an exceptionally wide line of pneumatic nailers, including finishing and brad nailers that may be of use to many woodworkers. A new U.S. plant, opened in California in the spring of 1994, aids production and quality control. Hitachi will send a minicatalog on request.

INTERNATIONAL TOOL CORPORATION

1939 Tyler Street
Hollywood, FL 33020
(800) 338-3384
(305) 927-0291 FAX

International Tools is a full-line distributor of quality industrial power tools, featuring Porter-Cable, Bosch, Milwaukee, Hitachi, Skil, Ryobi, Delta, DeWalt, Fein, Panasonic, Freud, Senco, Stanley-Bostitch and many more. After looking through the most recent International Tool catalog, I'd have to say that there are few items they don't offer, and discounts are among the best in the industry. They also manage to cover an awful lot of tools in an eighty-page catalog. This is a must-see catalog if you're in the market for major tool items and know the tools you're looking for. The catalog, done on newsprint, is free, and International Tool takes American Express, Optima, MasterCard, Visa and Discover.

JET EQUIPMENT & TOOLS

P.O. Box 1349
1901 Jefferson Avenue
Tacoma, WA 98401-1477
(206) 351-6000

Jet imports a full line of stationary power tools, many of which are of interest to both the hobby woodworker and the professional. Jet sets up its own specs for the tools and maintains a Taiwanese office to oversee quality. Table saws run up to 16″ in blade diameter, from 10″, and there are lathes, planers, jointers, drill presses, band saws, scroll saws, pneumatic tools—including various nailers and staplers—and air compressors. There are a good number of sanders, shapers and dust collectors. Jet has a large number of dealers and will supply information on different tools if you give them a call. Each year, Jet puts out a full-line catalog, a woodworker's catalog, and various flyers on new products. There is no charge for the literature. As noted, the range is wide: In planers alone, Jet offers a 12″ lightweight; a 15″ heavy-duty; four 20″ (often with larger planers, the major difference is in the power of the motors used, with lighter-duty models using single-phase, 230-volt, and heavy-duty bombers needing three-phase 230- or 460-volt), and a 24″ planer (this uses three-phase, period, with a 10-horse main motor, a 1-horse, feed-roller motor, and a ½-horse power-table motor).

LEICHTUNG WORKSHOPS

4944 Commerce Parkway
Cleveland, OH 44128
(800) 321-6840
(216) 464-6764 FAX

Leichtung offers a variety of unusual tools, plus many plans and woodworking supplies, in their free catalog. The catalog is digest-sized, but sometimes runs more than ninety-pages, and presents seasonal plans, some kits (varying with the seasons, but often small boxes and clocks, ships, dollhouses), and parts to help in building some of the plan items. The catalog has many styles of clamps, numerous doweling and jointing jigs, and is the only tool catalog I've seen where you're as apt to find wildflower seeds by the small sack, rain gauges, barbecue cleaner, rocks and cowhide gloves as you are Forstner drill bits. I've used a lot of Leichtung's gloves and always keep several pair on hand. For the price, they're the best I've seen for light chores, up to and including feeding a planer. The company also has a goodly array of parts bins and jars and hangers for perforated board, both ¼″ and ⅛″. They also offer a Woodworker's Guild for a $15 annual membership fee. Leichtung takes American Express, MasterCard, Visa and Discover.

LIE-NIELSEN TOOLWORKS
Route 1
Warren, ME 04684
(800) 327-2520 Orders
(207) 273-2520
(207) 273-2657 FAX

These makers of heirloom-quality hand tools offer a free catalog that is small and short—one tool per page—and a true delight, as are the tools. I've arranged to borrow a Lie-Nielsen plane from another source, and I'm more than a little antsy to give it a try. Lie-Nielsen planes are fairly costly, but considering the materials and care of manufacture, the prices are actually on the low side. As an example, the low-angle jack plane, based on the Stanley 62, is 14" long with a 2" iron embedded at 12°. The shoe is movable for mouth adjustment. The plane body is made from a completely stress-relieved iron casting, and the blade is ³⁄₁₆" thick and ground to a razor edge. Adjustment is with a knurled stainless captive nut, and the cap iron is bronze. The knob and handle are both cherry in this plane that was originally designed to plane end grain in such work as flattening butcher blocks. It is costly at $165, but considering the tool, not outrageously so. Lie-Nielsen has been in business since 1981 and accepts American Express, MasterCard and Visa.

MAKITA U.S.A., INC.
14930 Northam Street
La Mirada, CA 90638
(714) 522-8088

Makita has recently added 12-volt cordless driver/drills, impact drivers and hammer-drills to their line of cordless tools. This brings the Makita line of cordless power tools in line with other makers who had set 12-volt as the standard for top-of-the-line models. Now, it's a race to see who will have the hottest 14.4-volt tools before 1996 (13.2-volt cordless haven't been totally jumped, but makers found a really solid market in these top-of-the-line cordless tools, so they are going to keep going after it, with more and more models and greater and greater power and utility). Also new from Makita is a cordless stapler that drives as many as 750, ⅞"-long staplers on a single charge. A random-orbit sander helps round out their line of woodworking sanders, so Makita now has a close-to-complete line of power tools, from the cordless to corded drills, circular saws, miter and compound miter saws (I've been using a Makita 10" compound miter saw for some time and find it remarkably good),

generators, portable planers, electric chainsaws, a 14" band saw, a dust collector, a 12" portable planer, a planer-jointer, a couple of table saws, routers and much more: Among the much more is a modest-width line of gas chainsaws. Call or write for dealer's name and a free full-line brochure (really, a catalog).

MCFEELY'S
P.O. Box 3
Lynchburg, VA 24505
(800) 443-7937
(804) 847-7136 FAX

For me, this is about as local as suppliers get, and the catalog is fascinating. If you want instruction in square drive screws, the McFeely catalog is the place to get it. Pages three through five are devoted to telling you everything from reasons for using square drive screws to screw size needs for particular types of work and on to screw head styles and lengths to use. You also learn how a screw is made. A page or two later, the McFeely's catalog presents Warrington hammers, master chuck keys, storage bins, riggers bags, drill bits, gimlets, biscuit joiners, Incra systems, Apollo HVLP spray systems (these are not the relatively low-priced Campbell-Hausfeld and Wagner units but full-scale industrial units, with the cheapest running about 2½ times the price of the Campbell-Hausfeld, which is the least costly of the two lower-priced units currently on the market), Behlen and Watco finishes, toymakers parts, project books, and much else. The catalog spaces information on product quality and use with listings and sales talk about products: Jim Ray tests as many of the products he lists as possible—the first thing you see when you walk in the door is a Unisaw with a Biesemeyer fence mounted. Jim is a woodworker. The catalog is a buck and comes out six times annually. McFeely's accepts Discover, MasterCard and Visa.

MILWAUKEE ELECTRIC TOOL CORPORATION
13135 W. Lisbon Road
Brookfield, WI 53005
(414) 781-3600
(414) 781-3611
Milwaukee Electric Tool (Canada) Ltd.
755 Progress Avenue
Scarborough, ONT
Canada M1H 2W7
(416) 439-4181
(416) 439-6210 FAX

Milwaukee has long been one of the leading wide-line electric tool manufacturers in the hemisphere, to the point where for one of their tools, the name Sawzall

Milwaukee produces top-of-the-line portable electric tools such as this double insulated circular saw.

has almost become a generic term for a reciprocating saw. Ask a plumber or remodeling contractor about a recip saw, and the saw will almost certainly be called the "sawsall." Founded in 1924, the company has been around a long time, and they continue to develop pro-level tools to add to their three hundred-product line. A recent addition to the line is the 10", 15-ampere Magnum miter saw, and the line goes on through a lot of top-quality tools, many of use to woodworkers, including routers, drills, driver-drills, cordless driver-drills, circular saws, grinders, sanders and polishers, random-orbit sanders, heat guns, and a multitude of accessories. The catalog and tool brochures are free.

NEMY ELECTRIC TOOL COMPANY
7635-A Auburn Boulevard
Citrus Heights, CA 95610
(916) 723-1088
(916) 969-1088
(916) 723-1091 FAX

Bill Nemy runs a business that was founded in 1945 and is in its ninth year in its current location. Nemy Electric Tool Company is one of the larger woodworking machinery dealers in north California. As such, it serves the professional community, the hobbyist, wood-carvers, and the cottage-industry woodworker. They also do job-shop work for restoration and antique dealers, and they repair tools. Nemy offers classes in woodworking, woodcarving, production techniques, stair building and other skills, while also being a local sponsor of *The New Yankee Workshop*, on PBS. Bill has a video out, "Woodworks, Volume I: Arched Raised Panels," projected as the first of a series of thirteen. The video is eighty-three minutes

long; it details building raised panels with a router and router table. Nemy's catalog is $2.50, and their newsletter, "Woodworker's Bulletin," is free. Nemy Electric Tools accepts Discover, MasterCard and Visa.

NORTHERN HYDRAULICS
P.O. Box 1219
Burnsville, MN 55378
(800) 533-5545 Orders

Northern Hydraulics's free, 136-page catalog does have a lot of hydraulics equipment and parts, but there's a strong emphasis on hand and power tools, too. Lines carried include Milwaukee, Bosch, Skil, Makita, Channellock, their own NH, Hirsh, Vise-Grip, Homelite, Campbell-Hausfeld, Black & Decker, De-Walt, Ingersoll-Rand, and most others. Also, if you wish to buy 250-pound capacity pneumatic 8" swiveling casters, I know of no other mail-order source. There's a long ton of such stuff, including 1,500-pound industrial-grade casters (I can't even imagine a woodworking need for such things, but probably someone somewhere will). Prices are reasonable, and I've ordered from them often enough to state that their shipping times are also reasonable. Northern takes MasterCard and Visa.

PENN STATE INDUSTRIES
2850 Comly Road
Philadelphia, PA 19154
(800) 377-7997
(215) 676-7609
(215) 938-5067 (showroom only)

Penn State Industries presents a catalog of hobby woodworking machines in the low-to-moderate price range. Three dust-collector sizes are available, including a portable model that has a 760-cubic-feet-per-minute capacity. Other machines include a 12" portable planer, a 6" × 48" belt sander with a 9" disc, a 15" scroll saw, and a pile of other tools and accessories that make the dust to be collected. Penn State has introduced a portable-panel-saw cutting system that looks interesting and affordable, an air-driven carver, and pneumatic-finish nailers. The thirty-two-page, color catalog is free, and interesting. Penn State takes MasterCard and Visa.

PORTER-CABLE
P.O. Box 2468
Jackson, TN 38302
(800) 4-USTOOL
(901) 668-8600
(901) 664-0549 FAX

Porter-Cable's new one-hand random-orbit sanders have a pad control feature for flawless surface preparation.

Porter-Cable manufactures a wide line of router bits, with most having a rust resistant black oxide coating.

Powermatic offers dust collection systems as well as the tools to produce the chips and dust to fill them.

Porter-Cable is one of the smaller of the major U.S. tool manufacturers, but manufactures a wide line of portable power tools with quality second to none. It has been around for eighty-eight years. Circular saws, a laser-guided 10″ miter saw, routers (up to 3¼ horse-power, five-speed monsters, both fixed and plunge, that operate and endure with any routers on the market from anyone), router bits, bayonet saws, the quietest of all biscuit joiners, sanders—belt, orbital, random-orbit, and circular—plus drills in a line that includes several models of the famed Magnaquench cordless, which was one of the first of the 12-volt cordless drills and remains one of the most powerful. Their model 550 pocket cutting kit is probably the best low-cost solution for the small-scale cabinet shop that does a lot of face-frame building. The Porter-Cable tool line goes on through portable band saws, reciprocating saws, the most complete line of laminate trimmers I have seen, shears, grinders, polishers, and on. Their line of router bits is among the widest of all makers' lines, with fifty-one having been added recently. The new black-oxide finish is durable and reduces rust problems. Write for a copy of their free catalog if your interest in hand-held power tools extends to industrial-quality tools over, and beyond, the above range.

POWERMATIC
607 Morrison Street
McMinnville, TN 37110
(615) 473-5551
(800) 248-0144

Powermatic is one of the big three (my classification) in woodworking power tools. It offers top quality for a good price, plus a wide range of tools and power supplies: Table saws, scroll saws, planers, lathes, joiners, shapers, belt and disc sanders, drill presses, band saws, grinders, and others. In recent years, Powermatic has come out with its Artisan series meant for contractors, small shops and hobbyists. These are lower-powered, lower-cost machines that still retain the Powermatic aura. The 6″ Artisan jointer, at 198 pounds, has only its basic existence in common with the 1,350-pound, 17″ jointer and its 108″ long table. Their full-line catalog is definitely worth a look, and it is free for a phone call. Powermatic sells through dealers, not direct.

PRACTICAL PRODUCTS COMPANY

3925 Virginia Avenue
Cincinnati, OH 45227
(513) 561-6560
(513) 561-6778 FAX

Practical Products began business in 1961 and sells primarily to industrial woodworking clients. They present a line of files for plastic and related accessories (aimed at laminate users), edge trimmers (Virutex), and carbide-tipped hinge boring bits, along with plate joiners (Virutex), random orbit sanders (again Virutex), an edge bander, a planer and similar tools. The Virutex machines have the reputation of being second to none, and the brochures show a lot of nice features on the plate joiner and hand edge trimmer, and the planer is a good-looking tool. The company manufactures some of its products, imports others and wholesales most; it has an interesting catalog for woodworkers who also work with laminates on countertops and other areas. Drop a note to get a catalog and brochures on the imported Virutex line. Practical Products does not take credit cards.

QUAKER STATE WOODWORKING SUPPLY

Airport Industries Building #2
RD 9, Box 9386
Reading, PA 19605
(800) 776-5467
(610) 478-9448 (local)
(610) 478-9388 FAX

Quaker State Woodworking Supply offers plans, tools, accessories, and a growing catalog/newsletter, currently in the sixteen-page range. Drop a card to be added to the list for their quarterly publication. It often comes within a package consisting of the MLCS and Penn State catalogs, and there's a wide variety of offerings from the three outfits. Quaker State itself is a discount tool house, with some emphasis on abrasives, but carrying a goodly line of Porter-Cable tools, some Bosch equipment, Wagner's FineCoat HVLP sprayer, glues, Fas-Tak nail guns, clamps, SECO dust collectors, and many other items. They've got a super price on Ryobi's new oscillating spindle sander, too

(that, by the way, is a superb tool for home-shop use on curved surfaces: As far as I know, it is the only one on the market with a price under $600, and it's selling for less than a third of that most places). Their showroom is at Reading Airport, and is open Monday through Friday, eight to five, and Saturdays eight to noon. Quaker State will also send you a list of the fifty or more shows they attend annually. The current list doesn't include any within a sensible distance to my home: I won't drive to Richmond for anything.

RECORD TOOLS, INC.

1915 Clements Road #1
Pickering, Ontario
Canada L1W 3V1
(905) 428-1077

Record is a leading maker of lathes and turning tools, woodturning workbenches, and varied woodturning accessories, but it also turns out a considerable line of top-grade hand tools and accessories. Record planes, chisels and turning gouges, skew chisels and scrapers are famous worldwide for quality, as is the Marples line of chisels, turning and carving tools made in Sheffield, England, since 1828. The Record line of woodworking vises is justly famed, and other tools produced by Record include hammers (a major source of Warrington—cross peen—hammers), clamps and some wrenches. Record lathes are quality tools, covering a wide range of sizes, from the single-end bowl lathe, with a 22″ turning capacity, to the Coronet #3, with a 48″ distance between centers and a 12″ diameter swing over the bed (the #3 takes an accessory set that allows a massive 30″ diameter bowl turning). Call or drop a note for information, or check your local or mail-order woodworking tool supplier.

ROBERT LARSON COMPANY, INC.

33 Dorman Avenue
San Francisco, CA 94124
(800) 356-2195
(415) 821-3786 FAX

Robert Larson Company specializes in woodworking hand tools and sells directly to retail hardware stores, home centers, tool stores, lumberyards, and so on. They distribute Footprint tools, Hirsch carving tools, Stern Forstner bits and many other brands. Their annual catalog is free to resellers and costs $3 for consumers. Because the company does no retail selling, it does not take credit cards.

RYOBI AMERICAN CORPORATION

P.O. Box 1207
Anderson, SC 29625
(800) 525-2579

Ryobi calls their line of power tools the Workaholics:
The company makes a wide variety of products, from
printing equipment through lawn and garden tools to
hardware and sporting goods, but probably the most
relevant other line is an aluminum-die-casting company that has helped them produce lightweight aluminum castings for most of their tools. Ryobi makes
benchtop tools and portable power tools, from a remarkable oscillating spindle sander to a table saw to a
12″ planer and a 9″ saw. From there, you find a scroll
saw, a portable radial arm saw, several miter and compound miter saws, a jointer-planer, cordless tools, a
random-orbit sander, belt and part-sheet sanders,
drills, circular saws, jigsaws, routers and laminate trimmers, power hand planers, a biscuit joiner, and more.
Ryobi also makes a chisel mortiser, one of only three
companies I know of to do so, and a chain mortiser
(I know of no other company to produce a chain mortiser), and many other tools. The Ryobi catalog and
product literature is free, on request, for a free
phone call.

SANDVIK CONSUMER TOOLS DIVISION

P.O. Box 2036
Scranton, PA 18501-1220
(800) 632-7297
(800) 877-5687 FAX

Sandvik's small U.S. marketing division is not exactly
eager for calls and letters asking for catalogs, so I'd
suggest you try your local tool supplier first. They offer a fine line of chisels, coping, fret and handsaws, including hardpoint styles, hammers and files. Sandvik
does not sell direct.

S-B POWER TOOL COMPANY

4300 West Peterson Avenue
Chicago, IL 60646
Attention: Marketing Communications
(312) 286-7330

S-B Power Tool Company combines Skil Corporation
and Bosch Tools to form a true marketing giant, with
a very wide line of tools sold through hardware
stores, home centers, lumberyards and woodworking
outlets. *Skilsaw* almost became a generic term for *circular saw* — which the company fights like the devil.
It's flattering to be so closely tied to a tool your company brought out first, but in later years, it's also limit-
ing. S-B Power Tool Company is now noted for a full

Skil's new random-orbit sander is a two-speed model.

line of corded and cordless portable power tools, and
has recently developed a full line of benchtop stationary tools — a table saw, a drill press, a disc/belt
sander, a scroll saw, a bench grinder. Their Top Gun
12-volt cordless drill is accepted as one of the top
models in that field. Skil joined with Bosch to create
a marketing giant known as S-B Power Tool Company, providing access in two directions to marketing
strategies and tool research. Some interesting
changes have been made in the tool lines of both
companies since the combo started. Ask for brochures.

SEARS ROEBUCK & COMPANY

Check with your local Sears retail store, or call (800)
377-7414 for their free tool catalog. Featuring their
own Craftsman tool line, the catalog also presents
power tools from many other manufacturers, including Ryobi, Makita, Black & Decker and Skil. Craftsman
woodworking tools are the tools everyone loves to
knock, but as the advertising manager of a major industrial and consumer tool company told me some
years ago, "No matter how much you complain about
them, you have to always consider the fact that everyone who uses tools has at least one Craftsman tool!"
The tools are seldom the best but are usually good
enough to do the job at a very low cost, so many mil-
lions of people have bought them over the past century. Craftsman tools are now increasing in quality in
some ranges (and, of course, in price), while the basic Craftsman quality and price also remain as bul-
warks. And Sears now is widening its line of outside
tools even more. This is almost the last of the Sears
Roebuck catalog operations. It is the last that approxi-
mates the company's one-time commitment to true
mail order.

SECO INVESTMENTS COMPANY

315 Cloverleaf Drive #C
Baldwin Park, CA 91706
(818) 333-1799
(818) 333-1899 FAX

Seco manufactures and distributes primarily heavy-duty woodworking machinery, much of which isn't going to interest hobby woodworkers. There are a number of exceptions, including a broad line of dust collectors from a 1-horse, single-phase unit up to a 10-horse, three-phase. Depending on the price, the 20″ band saw might be of interest to some hobbyists, and they also have a good-looking (in the catalog) 10″ table saw—3-horsepower, and single-phase. Most of the rest of the machinery will remain as fantasy materials (many woodworkers would love a wide planer, but imagine the work installing the five-horse, single-phase, 770-pound 20″. All the 24″ models are three-phase, which places them well out of the range of hobby shops. In addition, Seco distributes a good-looking line of stock feeders. Literature is free, and worth asking for if you have any interest in the heavier woodworking machinery.

SEYCO

1414 Cranford Drive
P.O. Box 472749
Garland, TX 75047-2749
(800) 462-3353
(214) 278-3353

This scroll saw specialist has a $1 catalog that features the Excalibur line of saws, their own line of letter guides, and many books and patterns for scroll-saw people. Seyco also offers its own brand of blade clamps, some general accessories such as finishes, glues, blade storage tubes, and turned parts for projects, as well as an extremely extensive line of scroll-saw blades. Seyco takes MasterCard and Visa.

STANLEY TOOLS

600 Myrtle Street
New Britain, CT 06050
(203) 225-5111
(203) 827-5829 FAX

Any woodworker not at least minimally familiar with the Stanley tool line has been on another planet for the past 150 years. Call or write for further information on hammers, screwdrivers, planes, chisels, awls, nail sets, and much, much more. The $4 full-line catalog will stun you with the width and breadth of the Stanley line, but the free Contractor Grade Tool catalog and the new Fine Woodworking

Stanley's woodworking chisels, gouges and rasps are a definite step up to quality.

& Specialty Tool catalog, also free, will be more useful to most of us. The new wood gouges and chisels from Stanley are cases in point: The hardwood handles are hopped at the top to withstand heavy use. Stanley's new top-of-the-line wood chisels are made in Sheffield, England, from special, hardened ball-bearing steel. Bailey planes have returned to Stanley, with fine gray cast-iron bases, and simple adjustments for plane iron alignment, cut depth and mouth size. The venerable Yankee ratcheting screwdriver is also back—something I'm glad to see, as much as I love cordless drills. Stanley tools are available in just about every outlet in the country, but a call or note to Stanley will bring a copy of either of the free catalogs.

STONE MOUNTAIN POWER TOOL CORPORATION

6290 Jimmy Carter Boulevard
Norcross, GA 30071
(404) 446-8390
(404) 416-6243 FAX

The tabloid-sized catalog—my most recent copy runs thirty-two of the large pages—presents an array of small and large power tools from all the major manufacturers (including Delta, Powermatic, Porter-Cable, Makita, Ryobi, Bosch, Panasonic, AccuSpray, Stanley-Bostitch, Hitachi, Williams & Hussey, etc.), plus many accessories, bits and blades. There's a note in the catalog to call if you don't see what you want. Stone Mountain Power Tools also has a retail store (Norcross is just north of Atlanta) and presents a seminar schedule for each of the four seasons, with eight or ten subjects, including projects, processes and tool use (mostly router use in the current catalog).

SUNHILL NIC COMPANY, INC.

500 Andover Park East
Seattle, WA 98188
(800) 929-4321 Orders
(206) 575-4131
(206) 575-3617 FAX

Sunhill imports power feeders, dust collectors, table saws, jointers, planers and band saws under a half dozen brand names, with some machines aimed at the commercial market (unless your shop budget can afford a $3,700, 10" oscillating edge sander, or a 7.5-horse, three phase, 24" × 9" surface planer at $5,650, or, maybe, a four-head 6" × 2¼" molder at $9,985 — in fairness, they also bring in a $359, 6" jointer [on sale], and a 12" portable planer for $299, as well as moderate and low-cost band saws, table saws and other tools). Their 2-horsepower cabinet saw appears interesting, as does the super-heavy-duty, 3-horse, single-phase or five-horse, triple-phase table saw. These are tools that look reasonable for the prices but about which I would want some information from a current user — this is a prudent course with any major mail-order purchase tool. Get the seller to provide a name and address close enough by for you to check the tool out. Write or call for their latest brochure. Sunhill takes Discover, MasterCard and Visa.

TOOL CRIB OF THE NORTH

P.O. Box 1716
Grand Forks, ND 58206
(800) 358-3096
(701) 746-2857 FAX

The colorful Tool Crib catalog shows a wide, wide range of tools, from the AccuMiter to Vega fence systems, with in-between listings for Black & Decker, Freud, Milwaukee, Porter-Cable, Makita, Delta, General, S-K, Vise-Grip, HTC, Porta-Nails (PNI), Ridgid, Jet, Shop-Vac, Elu, DeWalt, Ryobi, and many more, including levels, jigs, HVLP sprayers, glues and more. Tool Crib accepts Discover, MasterCard and Visa.

TOOLS ON SALE DIVISION

216 West 7th Street
St. Paul, MN 55102
(800) 328-0457
(612) 224-8263 FAX

Call the toll-free number to see what catalog is available. Tools On Sale presents a huge book, 416 pages long, listing discount prices on tools of virtually all brands. They carry everything from the Bessey clamping system, and many Pony and Jorgenson clamps to Vise-Grip locking clamps to Bosch, Black & Decker,

DeWalt, Makita, Milwaukee, Hitachi, Campbell-Hausfeld, Stanley, Bostitch, DeVilbiss, Ryobi, Skil, Porter-Cable, Delta, Freud, Fein, and many others in sanders, circular saws, table saws, radial arm saws, planers, router and shaper bits, Swiss army knives, all sorts of leather belts and pockets and tool holders, Plano toolboxes, Shop-Vac vacuums, and even extension cords. Tools On Sale accepts Discover, MasterCard and Visa.

TREND-LINES

375 Beacham Street
Chelsea, MA 02150
(800) 366-6966 Catalog requests
(800) 767-9999 Orders
(617) 884-8951 Tech info
(617) 889-2072 FAX

Trend-Lines is a discount mail-order house and a distributor of the Reliant line of power tools. Their free catalog presents more than 3,000 brand-name products, including power tools and accessories, hand tools, screws, hardware, wood parts, plans, books and more. All popular brand names are carried, from Black & Decker through Porter-Cable, Milwaukee, Delta, Veritas, Stanley-Bostitch, ITW-Paslode, Campbell-Hausfeld, Makita, Skil, Ryobi, DeWalt, Oldham, Freud, Panasonic, and others. In some cases, such as Delta, Trend-Lines comes very close to being a full-line store: Its current two-page display of Delta tools has twenty-four tools listed, plus many, many accessories and variations on the basic tool. For example, they offer four versions of the Delta 3-horsepower Unisaw (different fences) and three mobile base units for those, plus inserts, a special blade, a cutterhead, and several other items. Complete satisfaction is guaranteed, as is lowest price against any nationally advertised price. Trend-Lines takes Discover, MasterCard and Visa.

VERITAS TOOLS

12 East River Street
Ogdensburg, NY 13669
(613) 596-1922
(613) 596-0350 Office
(613) 596-3073 FAX

The variety of interesting and useful tools that comes from Veritas is close to astounding. At the outset, there is a tendency to think of less-expensive, formed plastic tools, such as the center marker, the tool-setting gauge, and the poly gauge. That notion quickly slides away as you note, on moving away from the pair of simple corner rounding tools to the edge trimming block plane, currently at $130, the Veritas shelf drilling jig, at $149.95, or the Tucker vise, at $495. The Tucker vise may need some justification, other than its 13"-wide jaws, 4" throat, 5½"-wide side jaws with 4½" throat, 2¾"-wide carver's chop jaws with 6" throat depth, double ⅞" guide rods, and 12" opening for all jaws, so consider it allows full rotation and tilt, has integral dogs (four 6" round dogs: two in each jaw), pivoting front jaw, automatic opening, quick-release, lined jaws (cork), elevated guide rods, and much more. It is, in fact, the epitome of current woodworkers' vises. Whether or not it's worth five hundred bucks depends on your needs and wants (*Popular Mechanics* presented the Tucker Vise with its Design and Engineering award in January 1992).

WHOLE EARTH ACCESS

822 Anthony Street
Berkeley, CA 94710
(800) 829-6300
(510) 845-8846 FAX

Whole Earth Access offers what they call the best tools on earth, the Elu line (from Black & Decker), which has turned into an elite, hard-to-find (in the U.S.) line of tools. Whole Earth also sells other tools and offers free freight within the continental United States. Give them a call for up-to-date price lists and brochures. Whole Earth accepts Discover, MasterCard and Visa.

WILKE MACHINERY COMPANY

3230 Susquehanna Trail
York, PA 17402
(717) 764-5000
(717) 764-3778 FAX

Bridgewood woodworking machinery is featured in the Wilke catalog and starts with an emphasis on the big guns, their 24" × 9" planer being the lead-off item again. At a net weight of 1910 pounds, this machine will go through the floor in more than a few shops I know. A few pages on, we run into smaller shop tools with a 20" economy planer (still 771 pounds), then to the 15" planer, and on to the 12" portable model (64 pounds net). Throughout, there is a choice of huge, medium and small shop items (except those items that aren't at all suitable to small shops, such as four-side moulders, three-side planer-moulders, tenoners and so on). Throughout the catalog, you find Delta, General, Porter-Cable and Bosch tools, DML blades and much else. The catalog is free and well worth checking out. Wilke Machinery takes Discover, Master-Card and Visa.

WINDSOR FORGE

1403 Harlem Boulevard
Rockford, IL 61103
(815) 964-9590

Located across the street from Pete Cullum's Dovetail Joint school of Windsor chairmaking, the Windsor Forge offers complementary things—the tools with which to make such chairs, and many of the parts already cut. This is a nineteenth-century production blacksmith shop producing tools to make nineteenth century chairs using nineteenth-century techniques, which is what Pete teaches. Paul White is the blacksmith; he makes tools ranging from spoonbit adzes to deep-curve travishers. He also makes slight-curve travishers, which are meant for final finishing of chair seats, while the deep curve tool does the heavy work. Paul also replicates almost any hand tool used in the eighteenth and nineteenth centuries. His brochure is free, and interesting, and prices do not seem out-of-line for quality handmade tools. Paul also is shipping rived wood for Windsor chair seats.

WOODCRAFT

210 Wood County Industrial Park
P.O. Box 1686
Parkersburg, WV 26102-1686
(800) 225-1153 Orders
(800) 535-4482 Customer service
(800) 535-4486 Technical advice

Woodcraft has been around for a long time, starting in 1928. Their catalog is second in lushness to Garrett Wade's only because the photography is a touch less exotic, slanting more to information presentation in top-grade photographs, without exotic lighting. It is just as colorful, just as well photographed, and there are many unusual items, including Brienz carving mallets, lots of brass and other hardware, books, Safety-Mates, Behlen's salad bowl stains, colorwood, ruby slipstones, and other items. Woodcraft emphasizes carving tools more than any other general woodworking catalog with which I am familiar and offers project supplies (hardwood dowels, plugs, wheels, etc.), a wide variety of finishing products, bits and other boring tools, some small power tools (Carba-Tec miniature lathe, Delta 12" portable planer, Delta 2-speed, 16" scroll saw), and a bunch of router and other power-tool accessories, including the Incra Pro jig series. Specific tool brands, such as the Lynx saw from Garlick Saw Company in Sheffield, England, are offered. This handsaw is nearly labor-intensive enough in manufacture to truly deserve the name "handmade" that it is given. Lie-Nielsen reproduction tools are featured in the plane section, though the Clifton

Multiplane takes the honor box: This very, very expensive hand plane with interchangeable blades offers a one-hundred-year-old tradition for handmade tongue-and-groove joints, beading, fillisters, ovolos, rounds, dadoes, rabbets and many others. This is another catalog well worth its cost — in this case, $3. They're now offering second-day delivery at no extra cost (on eligible items; heavy items don't cut it).

WOODWORKERS' STORE

21801 Industrial Boulevard
Rogers, MN 55374-9514
(612) 428-2199
(612) 428-8668 FAX

Another major mail-order source for many items, The Woodworkers' Store carries a wide line of small power tools, hand tools, woods, finishes, plans, jigs, kits, and a very wide line of hardware, including many porcelain parts, oak and birch carvings, and even briefcase handles in two quality levels (the cheaper is covered in vinyl, the more costly in leather). Currently unique is their line of workshop knobs in black plastic, or aluminum, in five styles and many more sizes. The knobs make building your own shop jigs a great deal easier, as do some other new kits in the most recent catalog. You'll also find a large line of jewelry-box, chest, drawer, and general-cabinet locks, as well as plenty of knockdown fasteners. The Woodworkers' Store is another company that sends smaller update catalogs with some frequency, so your $3

buys a great deal of information. The Woodworkers' Store operates eleven retail outlets in Boston, Chicago, Cleveland, Columbus, Denver, Detroit, Milwaukee, Minneapolis, San Diego, Seattle and Buffalo. The retail stores do not accept mail order, but may speed access to some items if you happen to be nearby.

WOODWORKER'S SUPPLY

5604 Alameda Place NE
Albuquerque, NM 87113
(800) 645-9292
(800) 645-9797 Customer service
(505) 821-0578
(505) 821-7331 FAX

Not only does Woodworker's Supply offer a wide variety of tools and project supplies, it offers four different stores, with one in Casper, Wyoming [(307) 577-5272 FAX]; another in Graham, North Carolina [(910) 578-1401 FAX], and another in Seabrook, New Hampshire [(603) 474-3109 FAX]. They offer Woodtek stationary tools in addition to the standard lines from Delta and other makers. The widest catalog line offered is the Woodtek, with machines going right up to professional woodbanding machines, overarm routers, and a moderately priced joint-making machine called Matchmaker. One page of plans contains a number of interesting-looking Southwestern furniture plans, including a Solana bed, Taoseno day bed, bookshelf, nightstand, wardrobe, and table plans. Woodworker's Supply accepts Discover, MasterCard and Visa.

Wood

Wood

ACCENTS

AGRELL & THORPE LTD.
10 Liberty Ship Way #4116
Sausalito, CA 94965
(415) 332-7563
(415) 332-7570

Agrell & Thorpe specializes in hand-carved wood products for architectural uses and for furniture. If you want to build furniture with carved accents but are not a carver, this is one of the places you might check out. All products are carved in pine—and they are hand carved, so there are always slight variations from piece to piece. Categories include garlands, blossoms, brackets, accessories, crowns, and more. They've been in business more than eight years and offer a free brochure of their product line. They also do custom work. Agrell & Thorpe accepts MasterCard and Visa.

CUPBOARD DISTRIBUTING
114 South Main Street
P.O. Box 148
Urbana, OH 43078
(800) 338-6388
(513) 652-3338
(513) 652-3898 FAX

Cupboard Distributing presents chunk wood shapes and much else in the way of wood products and supplies. Small carousels and jointed animals are among the offerings, as are small rocking horses (the larger of the two is 6½″ × 5″), pull toys, necklace kits, wood bracelets, wheels, buttons, pegs, dowels, smokestacks, axles, gameboards and signs, spindles, finials, table pins, knobs, paints, glues, twine, Christmas ornaments, and resin castings (Santa, grandfather and grandmother, and others). Christmas ornaments include snowmen and angels, and there are miniature desks, blackboards, school bells and books. Cupboard Distributing carries Delta paints, Sakura Pigma pens, 1881 Crackle and much else. The catalog comes out annually and costs $2. Cupboard Distributing accepts Discover, MasterCard and Visa.

BOXES, BOWLS AND OTHER OBJECTS

ADVENTURES IN CRAFTS
P.O. Box 6058
Yorkville Station
New York, NY 10128
(212) 410-9793
(212) 348-6124 FAX

Adventures in Crafts primarily offers decoupage prints and supplies, considerations for the box makers among us. Wood accessories include a fairly wide variety of wooden boxes—sanded, unfinished basswood—and some tables, a trunk, a couple of lap desks and a child's chair. The artistically done catalog is also an idea notebook, and there are plenty of ideas to be found in the drawings and photos throughout, with lists of tools, gilding and other decorative substances. Catalog price is listed as $3.50, and Adventures in Crafts takes MasterCard and Visa.

JOHN WILSON
500 East Broadway Highway
Charlotte, MI 48813
(517) 543-5325

John is the modern-day torch bearer for Shaker oval boxes and offers everything from instruction sheets to the kits to make the boxes, right up to and including the correct kind of toothpicks to use as pegging. A typical Shaker oval box kit will include materials for the lid, box bands bent to shape, and wood for the bottom, plus an instruction sheet. You need only provide wood glue, a saw that will cut an oval, 120- and 220-grit sandpaper and clear finish. He has his own video and a line of tools, accessories and patterns that makes the overall job a great deal simpler. John also has a pattern packet that presents more than two dozen oval boxes and carriers, and he offers workshops at specific intervals during the year—and at varied places, so you don't always have to be in Michigan to learn to make oval boxes. Give him a call or drop a note to check prices of current literature and workshops. Or check the Woodcraft catalog for some kits and products John has specifically designed.

TATRO, INC.
7011 Marcelle Street
Paramount, CA
(800) 748-5827
(310) 630-6668 FAX

Tatro's free catalog shows many, many wood turnings and shapes, from the old standards such as Shaker pegs in birch and oak, on to checkers, snowmen, eggs, egg cups, wood scoops, napkin rings, beads — in colors, as well as plain wood — wheels, cargo pieces (barrels, milk cans, milk bottles, drums), stamp boxes, needle boxes, vanity boxes, necklace kits, spindles, finials, fruits and much else. The turnings are American made. Tatro accepts Discover, MasterCard and Visa.

BUILDING SUPPLIES

GEORGIA-PACIFIC (G-P)
Atlanta, GA
(800) BUILD-GP

Georgia-Pacific is probably best described as a full-line building-products company, and a call to their specific and special toll-free number will bring free literature on everything and anything the company manufactures. You can get information on construction lumber, softwood plywood and softwood plywood grading, hardwood plywood and hardwood plywood grading, asphalt base roofing materials, mineral and board insulation, fencing materials, metal roofing and siding, fencing materials — wood and metal, nails, screws — and upward and onward. I'm not presenting you with an address because G-P isn't set up to handle written requests. Just get on the horn and ask for what you need — or ask the person answering the phone what you need. The information will be on the way.

HICKSON CORPORATION
1100 Johnson Ferry Road, NE
Suite 680
Atlanta, GA 30342
(404) 843-2227
(404) 843-3235 FAX

Hickson is one of the largest makers of CCA wood treatment compounds, with their brand names being Wolmanized Pressure Treated Wood, Outdoor Wood, and Dricon Fire Retardant Treated Wood. Various types of treated wood are of interest to woodworkers who build projects that remain outdoors, whether the project is large, as a deck or gazebo, or relatively small, as in table and chairs. Hickson Corporation of-

fers a large number of informative booklets and brochures, plus project ideas, but distributes the material through your local dealer. If you can't locate a dealer, give them a call. If your dealer doesn't have any, or many, of the brochures, ask the dealer to call.

CHAIRS AND ROCKERS

WINDSOR FORGE
1403 Harlem Boulevard
Rockford, IL 61103
(815) 964-9590

Located across the street from Pete Cullum's Dovetail Joint school of Windsor chairmaking, the Windsor Forge offers complementary things — the tools with which to make such chairs and many of the parts already cut. This is a nineteenth-century production blacksmith shop producing tools to make nineteenth-century chairs using nineteenth-century techniques, which is what Pete teaches. Paul White is the blacksmith; he makes tools ranging from spoonbit adzes to deep-curve travishers. He also makes slight-curve travishers which are meant for final finishing of chair seats, while the deep-curve tool does the heavy work. Paul also replicates almost any hand tool used in the eighteenth and nineteenth centuries. His brochure is free, and interesting, and prices do not seem out-of-line for quality handmade tools. Paul also is shipping rived wood for Windsor chair seats.

WOODENBOAT STORE
P.O. Box 78
Brooklin, ME 04616
(800) 273-7447 Shipping
(207) 359-8920 FAX

The WoodenBoat name tells the story. This store caters to wooden boat enthusiasts, those who build, buy, sail or row such devices, and the catering is extensive. Books on the subject of wooden boats, both appreciation and construction — and more than a few on use — abound. Plans for model boats, and even kits for model boats, a couple of which are over three feet long, are offered. There are numerous plans for a wide variety of wooden craft, ranging from a 7'7" pram to a 43' schooner, with the list including daysailers, power launches, rowing shells, kayaks and canoes. There are also boat kits for Nutshell prams in two sizes (9'6" and 7'7"), and the usual batch of logo T-shirts and sweatshirts — the handiest logo item is the WoodenBoat shop apron. Check out the Down East rocker: This rocker is a rowboat shape on massive, clear-wood rockers. WoodenBoat Store also presents videos and hard-to-find tools. The most fascinating item in the entire catalog, to me, is the Friendship sloop sailing model (Amy R. Payson). This model finishes up at 7'7" along the deck and sails much like a real boat. The original is 29' long. The store is an offshoot of *WoodenBoat* magazine, and it offers similar quality and interests. If you love boats, this catalog is for you. If you love boats and woodworking, jump on it. WoodenBoat Store takes Discover, MasterCard and Visa.

CUTOUTS

CUSTOM WOOD CUT-OUTS UNLIMITED
P.O. Box 518
Massillon, OH 44648
(216) 832-2919

The catalog is $2, refundable with your first order. Not only does Custom Wood Cut-Outs make all the scrolled wood cutouts in their catalog, they'll also live up to their name and produce custom cuts from your drawing. Check with them for quantities and prices. Cutouts range from smaller than a tiny pumpkin (1¾" × 1¼") on up to bird houses and feeders, toy wagons, shadow boxes in three sizes and styles, and a sled. Prices range from $.29 for the pumpkin to $30.25 for a 13-piece Nativity set. The catalog shows almost six hundred cutouts, plus Shaker pegs, wheels and paints.

WOODWORKS
4521 Anderson
Ft. Worth, TX 76117
(817) 281-4447

If you need small hardware or wood parts, the one-buck, fifty-six-page catalog contains a sizable listing of each, including eggs, axles, rabbit and other pattern cutouts, candlesticks, spoked wheels, buttons, dowels, spindles and many more. All turnings are American made. Woodworks has been in business over fifteen years and prices items based on volume. All items are bulk packed, and case quantities bring discounted prices. Woodworks accepts Discover, MasterCard and Visa.

DRAWERS AND DOORS

EAGLE WOODWORKING, INC.
1130 East Street
Tewksbury, MA 01876
(800) 628-4849
(508) 640-0077
(508) 640-1501 FAX

Do you need drawers for a project and don't have time or shop tools to build your own? Eagle Woodworking offers dovetailed maple drawers, custom-sized for width and depth, in standard 2", 4", 6", 8" and 10" heights. They use ½"-square edged solid maple, with ¼" maple veneer bottoms, and will build a single drawer or a thousand, as you desire. Special machining on the drawers is available, so you may add hanging files or pencil and pen scoops and other fancy touches. Fully assembled drawers can be shipped sanded or finished. Considering the work in a drawer, Eagle's price list seems reasonable to me, but give them a call to get the current price list and check for yourself. Eagle Woodworking will ship UPS COD, but does not take credit cards, and has been in business more than twenty years.

SCHERR'S CABINETS
5315 Burdick Expressway East
Rt. 5, Box 12
Minot, ND 58701
(701) 839-3384
(701) 852-6090 FAX

Of greatest interest to woodworkers in Scherr's line of cabinetry is the line of custom-made doors and drawer fronts available, all shippable in fifteen days from order date. If your shop isn't equipped to make raised panel doors or drawer fronts, a cabinet shop such as Scherr's can save some major projects. Scherr's offers ten outside-edge profiles and arched top panels (if desired), with a 220-grit finish, on the face, with back, panel profile and edge profiles all finished to 150-grit. The choice of woods is wide, including red oak, birch, maple, cherry, white oak, walnut, ash and white pine, and on to laminates and paints. Scherr's also offers 32mm box components, though to me, 32mm stuff has always seemed like another of those great European discoveries, like our two world wars, that are probably better left undiscovered. Dovetail drawers are also offered, with aromatic cedar added to the list of woods. Drawers are priced per square foot, depending on the wood used. Scherr will send its brochure, and it takes Discover, MasterCard and Visa.

WOODCRAFTS BY OSCAR HUBBERT
P.O. Box 1415
Fletcher, NC 28732
(704) 687-0350

Oscar Hubbert sells old post-office-box door fronts and banks he makes of those old door fronts. His for-sale collection of door fronts consists of models from twenty-five to more than one hundred years old, and he'll send a price list of post-office-door supplies available if you'll send him a large (business size or #10) SASE. He will send a color brochure on completed banks for $1, and he takes MasterCard and Visa. He operates as a store at 16 Jeffrey Lane in Fletcher.

FLOORING

BRUCE HARDWOOD FLOORS
16803 Dall Parkway
Dallas, TX 75248
(800) 722-4647 Dealer referral hotline
(214) 931-3100

Bruce is the largest manufacturer of hardwood flooring in the United States, with six manufacturing facilities producing maple, oak and hickory flooring in plank, strip and parquet styles. Bruce has unfinished flooring as well as factory-finished material. It may seem odd to add a flooring manufacturer to a woodworker's sourcebook, but give it some thought, and you'll realize there are areas where flooring might make an ideal material to finish a project. Bruce's Design Idea Catalog is a buck, and about the only thing it doesn't tell you is how to install the various types. Bruce's Product Information Brochure is free.

CATSKILL MOUNTAIN LUMBER COMPANY
P.O. Box 450
Swan Lake, NY 12783
(800) 828-9663

The free catalog from Catskill Mountain Lumber presents paneling, flooring, white pine and hardwoods direct from the sawmill. Measurement is done after drying, with hardwoods offered in "Select & Better," which combines the top three grades of the National Hardwood Lumber Association. Number 1 Common presents shorter, narrower lengths, with less clear lumber. All lumber is dried to a moisture content of 6 percent to 8 percent, furniture industry standard. CTL offers ash, basswood, beech, hard maple, cherry, birch, red maple, red oak, yellow poplar, white oak, and Eastern white pine. Prices appear well within the normal range for this date and time, possibly a few cents to the lower side. In addition to lumber, CTL presents an array of router bits and some other tools, plus an interesting looking group of educational videos on the lumber industry, machinery, and other aspects of manufacturing wood. Catskill Mountain accepts MasterCard and Visa.

INSTAFLOOR
LignoTrade
4430 NE 148th Avenue
Portland, OR 97230
(800) 227-2105
(503) 257-3708
(503) 255-1430 FAX

This is another example of finished flooring that may be useful for projects: InstaFloor features laminated flooring planks, and goes on especially easily over all types of subfloor. This goes down as a floating floor and is not nailed to the subfloor, making it exceptionally easy to install. It is available in various hardwoods, with some emphasis on oak. InstaFloor comes in eight-bundle packs, and each plank is 8' long × 7½" wide × ⅝" thick. Give them a call for more details.

LEGS

ADAMS WOOD PRODUCTS L.P.
974 Forest Drive
Morristown, TN 37814
(615) 587-2942
(615) 586-2188 FAX

The Adams catalog shows legs for projects from complex Queen Anne to tapered simplicity in enough detail to make me wish one of my current or immediately upcoming projects needed such legs. Stock items include Queen Anne legs, table bases and table-and-chair kits, in walnut, cherry, oak, mahogany and maple. Tilt-top table kits look great. Carved knees may be added to many Queen Anne legs, as may claw and ball feet. Bun and tapered feet are also available, as are pencil, rice and turned bedposts, and cannonball posts, all in stock. Prices vary widely, depending on your needs. Obviously, more costly woods mean more costly parts, as do longer and larger parts. Leg length varies from 8" to 29½", with a box of forty-eight for the smaller legs and a box of a dozen for the longer. Part box prices are the highest, so if you foresee using a dozen long legs over the years, buy the box and save a bit over 10 percent. Turned table legs are less costly, until you get into fluted types, of which Adams Wood Products carries a wide variety. The idea of not having to band saw Queen Anne style legs makes the prices very reasonable: Overall, the products open out the project possibilities for those of us without band saws and lathes. Oak table columns and feet are available. Their catalog is free, and they accept Discover, MasterCard and Visa.

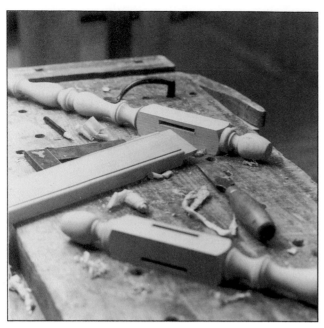

Matthew Burak's table legs are ready to be installed on your project, and they are available in various woods and styles.

The grace and elegance of Matthew Burak's Queen Anne leg design (shown here) is evidence of excellent craftsmanship which also shines through in Burak's other designs.

MATTHEW BURAK, FURNITURE
P.O. Box 279
Danville, VT 05828
(802) 684-2156
(802) 684-9626 FAX

For the past eleven years, Matthew Burak has produced and sold classic legs for tables. The legs are fully grain matched and mortised and are available in cherry, walnut, tiger maple, oak and mahogany. The styles include Queen Anne cabriole leg styles and a turned Queen Anne style; Hepplewhite tapered legs are available, and come in two sizes; Country Sheraton turned legs convey elegant simplicity; Tuscan legs move the visual point of balance downward, with clean lines that blend well in several styles; William and Mary styles are turned more ornately, and are offered in coffee and dining heights, designed and mortised to take a stretcher base. Maple and cherry legs are stocked, and are usually shipped with in twenty-four hours. Call or write or FAX for a free brochure that is updated annually. Matthew Burak Furniture takes MasterCard and Visa.

MILLWORK/MOULDING

ORNAMENTAL MOULDINGS
3804 Comanche Road
Archdale, NC 27263
(800) 779-1135
(910) 431-9120

Ornamental Mouldings isn't hiding a thing with its name. That's exactly what they produce, in large variety and great profusion, distributing the results throughout the United States, Canada and on to other areas. The company makes solid hardwood architectural mouldings (they prefer the British spelling, so why not, at least here) and specialize a bit in dentil and embossed mouldings. They also make accessories such as corner blocks, plinth blocks, baseboard connectors, door pediments, carved corbels and more. The line covers decorative wood trim and ornaments for shelf and full surround mantels and door and window casings, as well as Esitrim miterless system materials. All mouldings come in white hardwood, and most also in red oak, with corner blocks in pine, oak, poplar and banak. Other decorative wood trim comes in basswood, ornaments in tupelo, and corbels and pilasters in beech. Ornamental Mouldings will send you a free copy of Sweet's Catalog insert, which is an eight-page color brochure of some gorgeous work savers for woodworkers who are producing ornate furniture pieces, paneling rooms, or any of dozens of other things. The company does not sell retail but supplies local retailers.

SILVERTON VICTORIAN MILLWORKS
P.O. Box 2987
Durango, CO 81302
(303) 259-5915
(303) 259-5919 FAX

Silverton Victorian Millworks does just what its name states, supplies Victoriana in the form of millwork. All Victorian millwork is available in pine and oak, with four types of crown molding offered, and various case and baseboard molding styles, plus chair rails, corner blocks, corner beads, door and window caps, Victorian gingerbread (in poplar), and carvings in poplar and oak. Their Country Millwork brochure shows similar patterns, in simpler designs (but, as in the case of some of the country corner blocks and case moldings, carved with moderate ornateness). Country gingerbread is also offered, as are carvings. A third line of arch moldings is offered in a separate catalog. If you've got a project that might be enhanced by molding and you are unable or don't wish to produce your own, check out Silverton's free brochures. Silverton takes Discover, MasterCard and Visa.

MINIATURES

BEAR WOODS SUPPLY COMPANY
Box 40, Dept. U
Bear River, Nova Scotia
Canada B0S 1B0
(800) 565-5066
(902) 467-3703
(902) 467-3637 FAX

The unfinished wood items in Bear Woods' free catalog include the only milk bottle and holder array I've seen, in addition to oodles of the usual, and hordes of the not-so-usual, wood parts. Other miniatures include books and hurricane lamps and bean pots and butter churns, bowling pins and bats, yo-yos, bells, needle boxes and thimbles, large bean pots and apple boxes, spindles of many kinds, towel bars, and ball knobs, plus mushroom knobs and sidegrain knobs, cribbage pegs, checkers, dowel caps, spools, blocks, eggs and finials, plus all the usual, and some unusual, wheels. The catalog is a buck's worth of fun, and prices are reasonable: Prospective U.S. customers had better check on conversions and shipping. For Canadians, shipping is free. Bear Woods takes MasterCard and Visa.

MICRO-MARK
340 Snyder Avenue, 1614
Berkeley Heights, NJ 07922
(800) 225-1066
(908) 464-6764

Micro-Mark sells small tools. That said, there's an awful lot missing. There are some reasonably normal tools in the digest-sized Micro-Mark catalog, including many by Dremel, but when you start checking out the Microlux tilting arbor table saw, ordinariness goes out the window. This saw uses an eighty-tooth blade to cut balsa to 1″ thick with a 3⅜″ blade diameter. On the facing page are miniature fingers for ships modelers: These are rigging tools that allow working with fine lines. Palm-grip pliers make work on miniatures easier, as does a specific line of German-made 12-volt/115-volt power tools that are truly tiny: The belt sander fits inside the palm of a hand, and two fingers suffice to run the scroll saw. For the model maker working in wood, or other materials, Micro-Mark offers easy access to many hard-to-find tools. They also offer some fascinating ship models, and models of aircraft, with books on many kinds of modeling also offered (ships, railroads, cars, aircraft, dollhouses, furniture, turned miniatures, cast [metal] miniatures, and dioramas). A four-issue subscription to the eighty-page, full-color catalog costs $1. Micro-Mark takes American Express, Optima, Discover, MasterCard and Visa.

WOOD-N-CRAFTS, INC.
P.O. Box 140
Lakeview, MI 48850
(800) 444-8075
(517) 352-8075
(517) 352-6792 FAX

Wood-N-Crafts catalog presents an array of wooden miniatures, including washboards, Coke bottles, mice, rolling pins, barrels and much else, animal cutouts, jointed animals, pegs, buttons, boxes, candlesticks, toy parts, axle pegs, spindles, thimbles, buckets (from ¾″ tall to 2″ tall), cubes, knobs, dowels, and much of the line of Brainerd hardware. The catalog comes out annually and is free for the asking. Wood-N-Crafts takes MasterCard, Visa and Discover, and they will also ship COD.

SHINGLES

SHAKERTOWN 1992, INC.
P.O. Box 400
Winlock, WA 98596
(206) 785-3501
(206) 785-3076 FAX

Shakertown produces cedar shingles, plus a cedar shingle-strip product that goes up easily and a great deal faster than cedar shingles or shakes. The 8' panels also come with fancy cuts, and in a variety of designs and exposures (some patterns available are: diagonal, half cove, arrow, fishscale, octagon, square, diamond and hexagon). Decorative cedar shingles can from time to time be useful in projects, so if you need information on such products, here's a good place to go. Drop them a card or give a call and ask for their free brochures.

TURNINGS

CRAFTER'S MART
P.O. Box 2342
Greeley, CO 80632

Musical wooden Ferris wheels parts and plans are included in Crafter's Mart's one dollar catalog. The seventy-two-page catalog is full of projects, parts and supplies. There are over 350 varieties of varied music box fittings, over 300 project plans, and bulk pricing on wood turnings, such as wheels, spindles, knobs, plugs, pegs and so on. Many of the plans are said to be proven sales designs at crafts fairs. Crafter's Mart takes MasterCard, Visa and Discover.

RAINBOW WOODS
20 Andrews Street
Newnan, GA 30263
(800) 423-2762
(404) 251-2761 FAX

Rainbow Woods offers hardwood turnings. That's a short description: Getting more detailed, we find, in the free Rainbow Woods catalog, jewelry shapes, jewelry findings (hardware to other woodworkers), hardwood dowels, dowel caps, wheels in many sizes, axle pegs, smokestacks, all-purpose and tie-rack pegs, barrels listed as cargo, along with oil drums and milk cans, blocks from ½" to 1½" square, peg people, round balls to 3" diameter, candle cups, shaker and mug pegs, furniture plugs and buttons, dowel pins, fruits and vegetables, spools, pull knobs, gallery rail spindles, larger birch spindles, salt and pepper sets, and on. There may not be every turned-wood part available, but there are plenty for most purposes, including wooden nickels, pill boxes, beads, buckets and stamp boxes. The catalog is fun; the prices are reasonable. Rainbow Woods accepts both MasterCard and Visa.

TATRO, INC.
7011 Marcelle Street
Paramount, CA
(800) 748-5827
(310) 630-6668 FAX

Tatro's free catalog shows many, many wood turnings and shapes, from the old standards, such as Shaker pegs in birch and oak, on to checkers, snowmen, eggs, egg cups, wood scoops, napkin rings, beads—in colors, as well as plain wood—wheels, cargo pieces (barrels, milk cans, milk bottles, drums), stamp boxes, needle boxes, vanity boxes, necklace kits, spindles, finials, fruits, and much else. The turnings are American made. Tatro accepts Discover, MasterCard and Visa.

WOODWORKS
4521 Anderson
Ft. Worth, TX 76117
(817) 281-4447

If you need small hardware, or wood parts, the one buck, fifty-six-page catalog contains a sizable listing of each, including eggs, axles, rabbit and other pattern cutouts, candlesticks, spoked wheels, buttons, dowels, spindles and many more. All turnings are American made. Woodworks has been in business more than fifteen years and prices items based on volume. All items are bulk packed, and case quantities bring discounted prices. Woodworks accepts Discover, MasterCard and Visa.

TYPES OF WOOD

B&B RARE WOODS
10946 West Texas Avenue
Lakewood, CO 80232
(303) 986-2585

B&B Rare Woods offers mail-order veneers in some truly unusual woods, as well as in a reasonably wide array of more standard woods. Their current list shows lovoa, Mozambique, rift white oak, white elm, sugarberry, curly French ash and more. The lists and comments alone are worth a phone call. Veneer thicknesses vary from as little as ¹⁄₄₀" to as much as ¹⁄₂₈". They do not accept credit cards.

BADGER HARDWOODS OF WISCONSIN, LTD.
N1517 Highway 14
Walworth, WI 53184
(800) 252-2373

Select or better hardwoods are listed in Badger's free

annual catalog, as are 20-board-foot special packs, for a total of seventeen species of hardwoods, in sizes from 4/4 to 12/4. All lumber is kiln dried from this company that began in 1989. Badger takes Master-Card and Visa.

BEREA HARDWOODS COMPANY

6387 Eastland Road
Brookpark, OH 44142
(216) 234-7949

Berea offers exotic woods and unusual and figured domestic woods, with turning blocks and squares in burls, spalted and other figures. Berea Hardwoods also carries pen barrels and mechanisms. Call or write for prices. Berea Hardwoods takes MasterCard and Visa.

BOB MORGAN WOODWORKING SUPPLIES, INC.

1123 Bardstown Road
Louisville, KY 40204
(502) 456-2545
(502) 456-4752 FAX

Bob Morgan emphasizes veneers in his catalog, but he also sells a good variety of solid hardwoods, both domestic and imported, including spalted maple, bacote, mahogany, basswood, coco bolo, and poplar. Morgan is noted for packaging cutoffs at low prices, and he now sells ebony mill ends among such packages. Check the redwood burl slabs (up to 48″ × 22″), maple burl slabs to the same size, zirocote mill ends, maple and redwood burl bowl blanks, lignum vintae mill ends and other woods. He also sells ¹⁄₁₆″ curly and bird's-eye maple veneers, lacewood in ¾″ thickness, and burled jewelry-box faces, as well as oak raised-panel cabinet doors. Veneers include maple, white and red oak, cherry, mahogany, tiger oak, walnut, curly maple, ribbon sapele, rosewood, pomele, padauk, zebra wood, teak, fiddleback anegre, African satinwood, African makore, Carpathian elm burl, olive ash burl, mahogany crotch, and a number of pressure sensitive and preglued walnut and oak. Small tools and hardware are spotted throughout the digest-sized catalog as well.

BOULTER PLYWOOD CORPORATION

24 Broadway
Somerville, MA 02145
(617) 666-1340

The emphasis at Boulter Plywood is still on plywood. The free catalog shows Baltic birch and Chilean beech, both void-free types (that is, internal plies are laid up so that there are no gaps or holes inside the face and back plies). Boulter provides the specs and has their hardwood plywood made to fit. Various cuts are available, with plain and rotary slicing being the most common, though some of the oaks are rift sliced and one type of teak is quarter sawn. Face plies available include birch, cherry, mahogany, oak, walnut, pine, maple (plus curly and bird's-eye), teak, rosewood, sapelli, okoume, hickory and butternut. Edge banding veneers for all are available. Italian poplar is offered for its great flexibility, and the list of solid lumbers includes all the preceding, plus meranti, bubinga, goncalo alves, mansonia, padauk, purple heart, zebrawood, black limba, tigerwood, wenge, pippy elm and pippy white oak. To round out their list, Boulter offers MDO, composition panels (flakeboard), lauan, aircraft plywood, wackywood (flexible three-ply lauan), and others—well worth a look. No information was provided on credit cards, so assume Boulter Plywood requires check or money order.

BRISTOL VALLEY HARDWOODS

4300 Bristol Valley Road
Canandaigua, NY 14424
(800) 724-0132

Bristol Valley stocks fishtail oak, padauk, wenge, lacewood, zebra, hickory, mahogany, pines, poplar, butternut, walnut, cherry, birch, white and red oak, and a great many others in the twenty-four species of wood they stock. UPS shipping to Eastern addresses is paid; costs to other areas are slightly higher than their price list shows. Information is free for a quick note; the phone number lists as order-only. Bristol Valley takes MasterCard and Visa.

BRUCE HARDWOOD FLOORS

16803 Dall Parkway
Dallas, TX 75248
(800) 722-4647 Dealer referral hotline
(214) 931-3100

Bruce is the largest manufacturer of hardwood flooring in the United States, with six manufacturing facilities producing maple, oak and hickory flooring in plank, strip and parquet styles. Bruce has unfinished flooring as well as factory-finished material. It may seem odd to add a flooring manufacturer to a woodworker's source book, but give it some thought, and you'll realize there are areas where flooring might make an ideal material to finish a project. Bruce's Design Idea Catalog is a buck, and about the only thing it doesn't tell you is how to install the various types. Bruce's Product Information Brochure is free.

Bruce Hardwood Floors come in colors and patterns that may be used to enhance projects as well as homes and offices and shops.

CALIFORNIA REDWOOD ASSOCIATION
405 Enfrente Drive, Suite 200
Novato, CA 94949
(415) 382-0662

For a wide range of literature on types and uses of redwood lumber, the California Redwood Association can't be beat. The emphasis is on outdoor use, as one might expect, though I've found that redwood makes an interesting material for large and small indoor projects as well. (I built two redwood bookshelves some time ago: They continue to stand in my dining room, where their appearance often draws comments because redwood is seldom used for such projects. Most indoor redwood projects are architectural, covering uses such as wall paneling and molding.) The Association's literature list offers everything from a Design-A-Deck plans kit to nail use information. Exterior and interior finishes are covered in large brochures, and there are pamphlets on the industry and its harvesting methods and the environmental impact of using redwood. I'd suggest giving the Association a call, or dropping them a note, to request the literature list, at which time you can ask

them about shipping costs that are added to literature prices on the list.

CERTAINLY WOOD
11753 Big Tree Road
East Aurora, NY 14052
(716) 655-0206
(716) 655-3446 FAX

The free brochure shows fine veneers, in which Certainly Wood specializes, though they also offer lumber in twenty to thirty species. The brochure is well done, shows a number of unusual woods in full color (Bee's Wing Eucalyptus, Eucalyptus burl, Quilted maple, Silkwood, etc.), and gives a short treatise on different figures, such as Bird's-Eye, Fiddleback, Curly, Mottled, Bee's Wing, and onward, each illustrated in full color. Available veneers include Bee's Wing Andiroba, Bubbly maple, Cat's Paw cherry (this is a new one on me, but it is said to have tiny burls that look like cat's paw prints), gnarly white oak, tiger bog oak, quilted moabi, imbuya burl, grafted walnut, redwood burls, olive ash burls, and on, and further on. Lumber is shipped full length, prepaid, with satisfaction guaranteed. Certainly Wood takes MasterCard and Visa.

COLONIAL HARDWOODS, INC.
7953 Cameron Brown Ct.
Springfield, VA 22153
(800) 466-5451
(703) 451-9217
(703) 451-0186 FAX

With over 120 species in stock, Colonial Hardwoods should have what you need, with stock from ¼" to 4" thick. They stock burls and blocks for woodturners, too. Colonial also carries hardware, hand tools (emphatically *no* power tools), Bartley finishes, and books and will cut special knives for profile molding. They carry Baltic Birch in ⅛", ¼", ½", ⅝", and ¾" and have two interesting sounding Wood ID Kits, I and II, with domestic woods such as white oak, cherry, alder, beech, sycamore, osage orange, sassafras and others in Kit I, and exotics such as Koa, Mansonia, lignum vitae, Goncalo alves, and jatoba in Kit II. There is a total of 64 woods in the two kits (32 in each), with each sample about ½"×3"×6". Each kit is $59.95. Call for prices and a list of woods. Colonial takes Discover, MasterCard and Visa.

CONSTANTINE
2050 Eastchester Road
Bronx, NY 10461
(800) 223-8087

Constantine's has been in business since 1812 in one form or another (not always mail order, and today, not totally mail order with two retail outlets). Almost any aspect of woodworking, with an emphasis on veneers, is to be found in the full-color catalog: Send $1 and get on the catalog list for two years. Constantine's carries many books, videos and unusual finishing supplies, including their own line of water-based finishes, Micro-Mesh abrasive cloth, flocking, basswood plates, picture framing materials, hardware, weaving materials, tools, and on. Constantine's takes MasterCard and Visa.

CREATIONS' WORKSHOP COMPANY

310 First Street
Winlock, WA 98596
(206) 864-6229

This may be your best source for Myrtlewood. They also have lapdesk plans and precut kits in Myrtlewood. Brochures are available. Does not take credit cards at this time.

DUNLAP WOODCRAFTS

Wolf Trap Run Road
Vienna, VA 22182
(703) 631-5147

This producer of Appalachian hardwoods offers curly maple and other fine woods, plus a normal run of maple, oaks, walnut and cherry. Call to check prices on what you need.

EISENBRAND, INC., EXOTIC HARDWOODS

400 Spencer Street
Torrance, CA 90503
(310) 542-3576

This may be the place to check if you need exotic hardwoods that are so exotic other places don't carry what you need: Pink ivory, snakewood, pernambuco, and Brazilian (and nine other) rosewood just start the collection. There are 114 collector's samples available, along with a free price list brochure. The Eisenbrands have select lumber, turning and carving squares, and more than one hundred species from six continents, along with burls, spalts and crotches. They take MasterCard and Visa.

FRANK PAXTON LUMBER COMPANY

Distribution Center and Corporate Office
6311 St. John Avenue
Kansas City, MO 64123
(800) 333-7298

Founded in 1914, Frank Paxton Lumber offers a variety of services including providing rough-cut, surfaced, straight-line ripped and gang-ripped lumber and custom moulding. They offer over fifty hardwood species from all over the world. They also specialize in domestic lumber species. There are Paxton Beautiful Woods stores in Albuquerque, Austin (TX), Chicago, Cincinnati, Columbus, Dallas, Denver, Des Moines, Ft. Worth, Kansas City (MO), Louisville (KY), Minneapolis, New Orleans, Oklahoma City, and Tulsa; you can call the 800 number for help locating a distributor near you or deal with the Kansas City store directly. Their sixty-four-page, full-color book, *Beautiful Woods*, is $7.95 and includes photos, descriptions, and ratings of the many exotic and domestic lumber species that they carry. *Beautiful Woods* also includes lumber terms, buying tips, and information on plywood, veneers and other resources. Paxton Lumber does not have a mail-order catalog, but they will ship anything as long as it is small enough for UPS to handle. They accept MasterCard and Visa.

GOBY'S WALNUT WOOD PRODUCTS

5016 Palestine Road NW
Albany, OR 97321
(503) 926-7516
(503) 928-2262 FAX

Oregon walnut is a gorgeous wood, and Gary and Jan have been milling and selling it since 1975. The free Goby's price list covers 4/4 through 16/4 stock in Number 1&2 Commons through FAS (Firsts and Seconds) and on to Clears at reasonable prices. All lumber is 6" or wider, and other shapes and thicknesses are available, including rough-cut gun stocks blanks and turning stock. Current mill run is $2.50 per board foot, the same as it was for our first edition. FAS has gone up a whole $.15 a foot, in 4/4 and 5/4 and held in other thicknesses. Surfacing adds $.20 a board foot. The Gobys maintain a 40,000 board foot per year milling rate, and a log deck of 30,000 board feet, so stocks are almost always ample. In Gary's current notes, he states they have thirteen logs more than 48" in diameter for special milling. Goby's accepts MasterCard and Visa.

GROFF & HEARNE LUMBER

858 Scotland Road
Quarryville, PA 17566
(800) 342-0001
(717) 284-0001
(717) 284-2400 FAX

Groff & Hearne supplies curly cherry and many other fine woods up to 50" wide, with specialization in walnut and cherry. They use a band saw mill, and slowly air dry lumber before sending it to finish out in the kiln. Lumber is sold rough or dressed, as you prefer, there is no minimum order; and orders may be shipped UPS or common carrier (truck). Groff & Hearne features domestic lumber, including walnut, cherry, red oak, white oak, ash, birch and flame birch, poplar, Honduras mahogany, sassafras, hard maple, tiger maple, bird's-eye maple, with a few exotics such as cocobolo, padauk, purpleheart, zebrawood, and back to the more usual English walnut, butternut, Eastern white pine, apple and chestnut. I don't know where they get the chestnut, but will shortly check prices on that. What's around now is all we're ever going to see, so I'd like to make a small box or two. Their brochure-style price list is free on request, and Groff & Hearne takes Discover, MasterCard and Visa.

HANDLOGGERS EXOTIC HARDWOODS
135 East Sir Francis Drake Boulevard
Larkspur, CA 94939
(800) 461-1969 Orders
(415) 461-1180
(415) 461-1187 FAX

Handloggers aims to provide the highest-quality lumber possible, of exotic and domestic hardwoods. If you've never heard of Billy Webb, Black Bull Hoof, Chechen, Tzalam, and a few others on their list, take heart. Neither had I until I got the list, and I recently wrote a book on wood for woodworkers. Billy Webb, according to Handloggers, is Sweetia panamensis, and I still don't know it. The only point of reference I can find is Swietenia, the genus to which mahogany belongs, and probably wrong. Billy Webb is listed as a light tan to golden brown, even-grained wood, which means it sure doesn't look like mahogany. Chechen is a chocolate to reddish tan color. Black Bull Hoof, Black Maya, Tzalam and a couple others may require a phone call to Handloggers for descriptions. They also offer figured mahogany (in short supply, even at $70 a board foot, 4/4 thickness); American walnut at $7.95 for 12/4; cherry at $5 for 4/4; and western figured maple at $8. All wood is FAS, surfaced two sides, shipped UPS or truck, depending on order size. Each order carries a $5 handling charge. Handloggers will send a free catalog on request and takes MasterCard, Visa and Discover.

HARDEL MUTUAL PLYWOOD CORPORATION
P.O. Box 3265
Olympia, WA 98507
(206) 754-6030
(206) 943-9352 FAX

Hardel is a producer of plywood, located in an area where many such producers congregate. The Hardel plywood lines include sanded plywoods, 303 plywood sidings, and marine-grade panels. They also produce $9' \times 10'$ structural sheathing panels. Sanded precision-dimension panels are available from ¼" to ½" thick and in panel sizes 4×8, 4×9, 4×10, 5×8, 5×9 and 5×10. Write or call for a free brochure.

LOUISIANA-PACIFIC CORPORATION (L-P)
111 Southwest Fifth Avenue
Portland, OR 97204
(503) 221-0800

Louisiana-Pacific produces all kinds of plywood and other wood products, both as engineered wood products (plywoods, oriented strand boards and waferboards, among others) and as lumber, including redwood and pressure-treated versions. One of their most interesting new products, though peripherally related to woodworking, is a blow-in insulation that works with studs, as well as joists—that is, it adheres and stays on vertical surfaces, after which excess is shaved off to give a flat surface. This material, made of 100 percent recycled newspaper, is called Nature Guard. Receive a brochure, free of charge upon request. I am getting ready to build a shop, and am now—in the past five minutes—considering trying to locate a source for this insulation when things get to that stage. Louisiana-Pacific also has brochures on their version of Oriented Strand Board, called Waferwood, and also there is a general brochure, more like a catalog, showing the full line of L-P products, including OSB products that cover lap siding, panel siding, flooring and sheathing, interior paneling, Nature Guard insulation, laminated joists, software, windows, patio doors, and lumber. The least emphasis seems to be on straight lumber products, with manufactured products getting the most. This company is responsible for a lot of wood and a lot of literature.

MACBEATH HARDWOOD
930 Ashby Avenue
Berkeley, CA 94710
(510) 843-4390
(510) 843-9378 FAX

MacBeath Hardwood has warehouses in Montebello, Salt Lake City and San Francisco, as well as in Berkeley, and it operates a dry kiln in Edinburgh, Indiana. About 90 percent of their business is wholesale, and the product list includes maple chopping blocks (at 1½" deep × 25" wide and up to 10' long, these are almost certainly breadboard style, not real chopping block—chopping blocks are made from end-grain hard maple—but should make dandy countertops), and goes on to alder, apitong, ash, balsa, basswood, beech, Eastern birch, cedar, cherry, cottonwood, iroko, jelutong, gum, bird's-eye and other maples (including spalted and curly), red and white oak, pecan, hickory, pine, poplar, black walnut and willow. They also carry exotics such as bocote and bubinga, cocobolo and ebony, goncalo alves and kingwood, lacewood and lignum vitae, and on down to snakewood, teach, tulipwood and vinhatico. The product list is surely interesting, and extensive, well worth asking for, as is the free molding catalog. Their tool catalog is $2, refundable on the first order. MacBeath takes MasterCard and Visa.

MARTIN MACARTHUR HARDWOOD CENTER

Cabinet Shop and Office:
1815 Kahai Street
Honolulu, HI 96819
(808) 845-6688
(808) 845-6680 FAX
Showroom:
841 Bishop Street
Honolulu, HI 98613
(808) 524-4434 phone and FAX

This division of a thirty-year-old koa furniture manufacturer presents hardwood lumber and plywood, both wholesale and retail, and a line of wholesale and retail picture-framing supplies. Both solid and Treeline (koa veneered over poplar) are available. The Hardwood Center is located in the same building as the workshop. They have an exceptionally interesting and well-done brochure on koa and some of the products made from it: Koa is primarily found on Hawaii (the Big Island) and has an exceptional color range, from a pale blond to a deep brown and further to a superb red. The wood has become scarce, and great care is now taken in harvesting these trees, which range up to 60' tall, with a diameter over 3'. There are two other showrooms in Honolulu. Write or call for brochure and price lists.

MESQUITES UNLIMITED

Route 4, Box 322
Wichita Falls, TX 76301
(817) 544-2262

Cameron Harrison deals primarily in mesquite lumber, kiln dried, rough or surfaced. He mails out lots usually under 100 board feet and ships to all states. Call or drop him a note for a price list and brochure, plus a free sample. Mesquites Unlimited takes checks or money orders only, no credit cards.

M.L. CONDON COMPANY, INC.

242 Ferris Avenue
White Plains, NY 10603
(914) 946-4111
(914) 946-3779 FAX

Condon's offers domestic and foreign hardwoods, custom millwork, mouldings, veneers and more in afromosia, anigre, ash, avodire, balsa, basswood, beech, birch, cherry, chestnut, cocobolo, cypress, greenheart, hickory, holly, laurel, lignum vitae, imbuya, koa, Bruynzeel mahogany, paldao, pearwood, padauk, ramin, redwood, sapele, sycamore, teak and many others. Their thirty-two-page, color catalog is $2, and they take credit cards.

NIAGARA LUMBER & WOOD PRODUCTS, INC.

47 Elm Street
East Aurora, NY 14052
(800) 274-0397
(716) 655-2142
(716) 655-2138 FAX

Northern Appalachian hardwoods are the primary product supplied by Niagara Lumber. Species include black cherry, tulip poplar, black walnut, basswood, birch, red oak, rock (hard) maple, mahogany (the only listed exotic), curly soft maple, white oak, white ash, butternut and red elm. All lumber is kiln dried to a 6 to 8 percent moisture content, and surfacing is included at no extra cost. Don't forget when requesting surfacing that there is a thickness loss of at least $3/16''$, and more likely $1/4''$, in each dimension surfaced. One-edge jointing is offered at $.12 a linear foot. Niagara also offers red oak and tulip poplar mouldings and red oak tongue-and-groove flooring and paneling. Prices appear in line with other companies in the business. The brochure is free, as is shipping within the continental United States. Niagara Lumber takes MasterCard and Visa.

PETER LANG COMPANY

3115 Porter Creek Road
Santa Rosa, CA 95404
(707) 579-1341

Peter Lang Company specializes in fine quality, bookmatched, sequentially cut claro walnut boards, fancy-figured bowl-turning blanks, and cutting-and-drying specialty woods for high-quality uses. The company also carries lumber in popular sizes, and current stock includes California and English walnut, myrtle, maple, sycamore, madrone and redwood. From time to time, they get other woods in. Peter Lang Company uses its own version of hardwood grading, starting with #1, as an exhibition grade; #2, excellent; #3, very good; #4, better; and #5, standard or mill-run. Currently, mill-run is about average, at $2.50 for most mills. Prices on wood better than mill-run are difficult to evaluate because of differing grading standards within each mill, but these seem about right. Peter Lang Company accepts American Express, MasterCard and Visa.

SANDY POND HARDWOODS

921-A Lancaster Pike
Quarryville, PA 17566
(800) 546-9663
(717) 284-5030
(717) 284-5739 FAX

As do many shipping lumber companies, Sandy Pond Hardwoods specializes, in their case in tiger and bird's-eye maple, curly ash, quartersawn oak, cherry, flame birch and similar premium woods. Additionally, Sandy Pond carries Northern red oak, white oak, hard maple, white hard maple, cherry, hickory and ash in regular hardwoods. Figured woods, as noted, are usually premium-priced woods, but it pays to check the latest costs and availability. Sandy Pond also carries some exotic species, including mahogany, padauk, purple heart, wenge, bubinga, and a few others. Tim Harper informs me that the company supplies lumber to furniture makers, cabinetmakers and guitar makers around the world, but that each order receives good attention, whether large or small. Prices in their most recent list appear consistent with other companies. Call to request the most recent price and species list. Sandy Pond Hardwoods takes MasterCard and Visa.

TALARICO HARDWOODS

RD 3, P.O. Box 3268
Mohnton, PA 19540
(610) 775-0400

This company supplies wide quartersawn oaks and figured lumber. Woods such as quartersawn white oak, in 12″ and wider sections, are available in both regular and slow growth and may be bookmatched. Curly quartersawn white oak is also available, as is red oak, sycamore, cherry, bird's-eye maple, curly maple, ebony, Australian lacewood, osage orange and walnut. Call for species and price quotes; they do not accept credit cards.

TROPICAL EXOTIC HARDWOODS

P.O. Box 1806
Carlsbad, CA 92018
(619) 434-3030
(619) 434-5423 FAX

For this importer of hardwoods, an SASE (#10) brings a list of available woods. Available are (not all tropical, of course) fiddleback ash, bocote, bloodwood, canary wood, cocobolo, African ebony, goncalo alves, granodillo Cristobal, jatoba, Mexican kingwood, lignum vitae, Cuban mahogany, Mansonia, bird's-eye maple, partridgewood, pink ivory, primavera, purple heart, Brazilian rosewood, Ceylon satinwood, snakewood, teak, Brazilian tulipwood, and ziricote. Prices range from less than $5 for Honduras mahogany (4/4, kiln-dried) to $25 a board foot for Macassar ebony in square logs and lumber form. Some is sold by the pound. Wood is available in different sizes but usually in 4/4, 6/4, 8/4, cants (half logs), crotches and other normal forms. Lumber is 3″ or wider and 3′ or longer, air-dried, and unsurfaced unless otherwise specified. For lumber 8″ and wider, Tropical Exotic Hardwoods charges a 15 percent premium. Prices are FOB, Carlsbad, California. Call and check for the latest prices, methods of avoiding COD shipment, and so on.

STEVE H. WALL LUMBER COMPANY

Route 1, Box 287
Mayodan, NC 27027
(800) 633-4062
(919) 427-0637
(919) 427-7588 FAX

For $1 you get a lumber-and-machinery catalog that covers seventeen different woods, including ash, basswood, birch, butternut, cherry, hickory-pecan, real mahogany, hard maple, red and white oak, soft maple, walnut and poplar. Softwoods include red cedar, cypress and white and yellow pine. Listed prices for unsurfaced (rough) lumber seem in line with those I've seen lately. Freight charges make a major difference in cost, with woodworkers in the west getting hit hardest. Currently, it costs $180 more to deliver 500 board feet of lumber to California than it does to most of the South and even up into Pennsylvania (for newcomers to woodworking, you can build a lot of things with 500 board feet of almost any wood). That's a function of mileage that cannot change, so prices must be compared locally after shipping is figured. Steve H. Wall Lumber does offer some UPS specials in 20-board-foot bundles of clear that may be of interest for those with small projects to complete. There are also special deals (log-run cherry surfaced two sides, to ¹³⁄₁₆″, at $99 a hundred is the current deal, but these will vary). You'll also find some Baltic birch ⅛" plywood and veneer core hardwood plywoods at reasonable prices. Hardwood flooring is also available, as are Freud hand tools, and an array of Mini Max stationary power tools, plus RBI's joint machine.

WILLARD BROTHERS WOODCUTTERS

300 Basin Road
Trenton, NJ 08619
(609) 890-1990

Willard Brothers sawmill offers domestic and exotic hardwoods, cabinet plywoods, veneers, finishes, Freud tools, mulch and Christmas trees. The brothers offer kiln- and air-dried walnut, maple, cherry, white and red oak, poplar, ash, pine, birch, and others. The price list adds domestic species that include the above, butternut, aromatic red cedar, both bird's-eye and curly maple and sassafras. Prices appear in line with others carrying domestic woods lines. Exotics include Australian lacewood, bocote, Brazilian kingwood and tulipwood, bubinga, chechen, cocobolo, ebony, mahogany, morado, padauk, purple heart, rosewood, teak, shedua, wenge, zebrawood and others. Prices for domestic woods are difficult to judge, but these appear reasonable. The sawmill charges a premium of $.25 per board foot on widths 10" and greater (8" and greater with black walnut). Flipping the page brings a supplemental list that includes sycamore, cypress, anegre, spalted maple, nogal, clear pine, redwood, and types of cherry, oak, birch and poplar molding, as well as mahogany, oak, cherry and soft maple wainscoting. It's well worth a look. Willard Brothers takes MasterCard and Visa.

WINTER WOODS

Route 1 Box 765G
Munising, MI 49862
(906) 387-4082

Winter Woods specializes in figured woods, such as tiger (soft maple) and bird's-eye (hard) maple, burls and spalted lumber. In addition to the maples, they carry curly aspen, curly cherry and basswood carving blocks. Prices vary depending on figure, wood species, etc., but those listed appear in line with prices charged elsewhere. Call or write for their free brochure.

Woodworking Supplies
and Services

Woodworking Supplies and Services

ABRASIVES

DAYTON ABRASIVE PRODUCTS, INC.
P.O. Box 335
North Dayton Station
Dayton, OH 45404
(800) 243-9641
(513) 224-8294 FAX

Dayton Abrasive Products presents a line of belts, pressure-sensitive adhesive discs with cloth backing, and paper and cloth abrasive sheets in a wide variety of grits. Call and ask for a price list and free catalog. Dayton Abrasive takes MasterCard and Visa.

ECON-ABRASIVES
P.O. Box 865021
Plano, TX 75086
(800) 367-4101
(214) 377-9779

Emphasizing low cost, Econ-Abrasives presents good-to-excellent prices on sanding belts and other tools. They carry a particularly wide line of belts, and offer wet and dry paper to 600-grit, as well as standard-grit cabinet and finished papers. Econ-Abrasives also carries discs, router bits, wood glue, wood clamps, flap wheels and other products. The catalog is free for a call or note. Econ-Abrasives accepts both MasterCard and Visa.

INDUSTRIAL ABRASIVES CO.
642 North 8th Street
Reading, PA 19612
(800) 428-2222
(800) 222-2292 (in Pennsylvania)

Sanding belts and other abrasive tools are featured in this manufacturer's free catalog. Buy a dozen sanding belts, of many popular sizes, and get a dozen free. The company accepts Discover, MasterCard and Visa.

KLINGSPOR ABRASIVES
P.O. Box 2367
Hickory, NC 28603
(800) 645-5555
(704) 322-3030

Klingspor is an abrasives manufacturer that also sells its products by mail, which makes them ideal for our purposes. Send or call for a free color catalog, which varies in size and content according to sales, possible overstock situations and similar requirements. It is called, sensibly enough, "The Sanding Catalogue" and is the largest I know of in the abrasives end of the business. Headquartered in Hickory, North Carolina, Klingspor has recently expanded to Ventura, California, to better serve a wider market. Products include belt and disc abrasives with a wide variety of coat styles (open and closed) using a number of different backing materials. Prices are reasonable to low, especially with quantity and special-offering discounts. The catalog offers some tools — random-orbit sanders pop out, as does the Ryobi oscillating spindle sander, Porter-Cable's abrasive plane, and Dremel's belt/disk sander. There is more to abrasives than sanding materials, and Klingspor also carries steel wool, rottenstone, pumice and paraffin oils, along with tack cloths to get the mess off before finishing. Klingspor takes MasterCard, Visa and Discover.

MICRO-SURFACE FINISHING PRODUCTS
P.O. Box 818
Wilton, IA 52778
(800) 225-3006
(319) 732-3240
(319) 732-3390 FAX

Micro-Surface will send free information on its micro-mesh abrasives: I got a quick demonstration not long ago, and I find them remarkable, within the limits for which they're intended. If you want to produce a truly slick, high-gloss finish, there may be nothing better. If you're polishing out old or new finishes, shining plastics or metals in the course of projects, give these a try. There are kits for a number of purposes, and specialized kits for high-luster paint finishes, hobby and models, woodworking, boats, households. Micro-mesh is available in 1500, 1800, 2400, 3200, 3600, 4000, 6000, 8000 and 12,000 grades, in 6×12 and 12×12 sheets, and $4'' \times 50'$ and other roll sizes. Coarser grades, Micro-mesh MX, are available in 100, 150, 180, 240, 320, 360, 400, 600, 800 and 1200, in the same sheet and roll sizes, plus $5/8''$ to $2''$ wide tapes. Call for the distributor closest to you.

NORTON CONSUMER MARKETING
1 Bond Street
Worcester, MA 01606
(508) 795-5000

I'm not sure of Norton's exact placement in the list of abrasives manufacturers, except that it has to be close to the top in size, and in quality. There are abrasives for almost every purpose one might imagine, and a huge number of them are useful for woodworking chores. I've just received an interesting brochure covering woodworking sanding products that will allow you to choose and specify to your dealer the Norton products you need. The brochure is beautifully done and is available from the Abrasives Marketing Group, as above.

OLDHAM-UNITED STATES SAW

Burt, NY 14028
(716) 778-8588

The Oldham-United States Saw catalog of their saw blades, router bits and abrasive wheels provides some major choices, from ultrathin kerf carbide blades (Roadrunner series), to carbide-tooth nail-cutting blades, on to steel saw blades, then to Wizard and Supreme Wizard premium series (the Wizard series is designed for power mitering and comes in appropriate sizes from 8¼" to 15"; the Supreme Wizard series is for table and radial arm saws; both series are cutoff styles with sixty or eighty teeth), plus three styles of dado blades, plus masonry and metal cutting abrasive wheels, and then to Viper router bits. A comprehensive array comes from the factory of this company founded in 1857. Literature is free, and Oldham sells only to distributors.

RED HILL CORPORATION

P.O. Box 4234
Gettysburg, PA 17325
(800) 822-4003
(717) 337-3936 FAX

Red Hill offers a free, twenty-page finishing and refinishing products catalog featuring major brands of abrasives in a wide range of available forms, including the new triangle style for the Fein and Ryobi triangle pad sanders. For those working up a real polish, Red Hill has 2,000-grit wet and dry paper. They also carry a flex shaft tool, glue guns, tack cloths and other items. My copy of the catalog came with a closeout sale brochure that listed drill bits and all kinds of shop roll abrasive material, sanding belts and calculators, among other items. Their Permasand tungsten carbide discs and sheets often last one hundred times longer than similar styles of abrasive paper. Red Hill takes MasterCard and Visa.

SAND-RITE MANUFACTURING COMPANY

321 North Justine Street
Chicago, IL 60607
(800) 521-2318
(312) 997-2200
(312) 997-2407 FAX

Sand-Rite manufactures and sells a line of pneumatic drum sanding machines, abrasive rolls, belts and sleeves in all grits and sizes. Sand-Rite has been around since 1942, and it offers what they call a woodworking industry sander. It is heavy-duty, and the price shows that, but it's not outrageously priced for quality, so it is suitable for even small pro shops and the occasional heavily equipped amateur. Sand-Rite also makes their own dust-collection system for use with their sanders. The Sand-Rite combination sander is a larger, more costly version of disc/belt sanders all of us have seen and most of us have used. The 3-horse version weighs 395 pounds and has a 6" belt and 12" disc. Sand-Rite takes MasterCard and Visa.

3M DIY DIVISION

Consumer Relations
515-3N-02
St. Paul, MN 55144-1000

This is the 3M division that handles information on Newstroke snap-off paintbrushes, home-care adhesives, surface-prep products (hand- and power-sanding materials), paint removers, and personal-safety products, such as goggles and face masks of both comfort and respirator types. The firm makes a wide variety of masks and respirators to reduce the effects of the sandpaper and similar products it also produces. I particularly like their disposable general dust and sanding respirator: That's the number 8710, and it comes in contractor packs of twenty, as well as in packs of two or three. Catalogs available on request. Specify which product line interests you (listed above).

ADHESIVES

BORDEN

Home & Professional Products Group
180 East Broad Street
Columbus, OH 43215-3799
(800) 848-9400

Borden's line of wood glues, white glues and specialty adhesives can be of great help to woodworkers. One of their most useful products around the shop is Elmer's Carpenter's Wood Glue for Darker Woods.

This glue is great for the person who works a lot with cherry, mahogany, walnut and similar dark woods because the glue line comes closer to matching the color of the wood. As an aliphatic resin adhesive, it resists gum-up from friction (no balling up during sanding). Of course, the Elmer line includes Glue-All, one of the most successful of the white (polyvinyl) resin glues. Borden's Elmer's line includes a multitude of colored glues intended for schoolchildren, contact cements, caulks, silicone seals, Krazy Glue, threadlockers, rubber cement and similar items, some of great use in shops and some of only occasional use.

DAP, INC.

P.O. Box 277
Dayton, OH 45401-0277
(800) 543-3840
(513) 667-4461

The varied Weldwood adhesives work on all sorts of materials and offer some unique properties—such as extreme water-resistance, changing dilution for different uses (in one type), and so on. The materials are truly very handy, so it makes sense to call for further information.

DARWORTH COMPANY

3 Mill Pond Lane
P.O. Box 639
Simsbury, CT 06070
(800) 672-3499
(800) 624-7767
(800) 227-6095 FAX

FI:X Wood Patch and Touch Up Stik are two major products for repair and construction. The color Touch Up Stiks do minor touch-up jobs in a hurry; the wood patch is made in red oak and white pine, plus ash, maple/alder, white, walnut, natural, pine, oak, dark mahogany/redwood, light mahogany and birch fir. The Wood Patch sands well and accepts stains uniformly. Darworth's new heavy-duty Construction Adhesive—PolySeamSeal—works on most woods, drywall, foam boards and paneling. In the past, I've found this type of adhesive excellent for outdoor project reinforcement, which basically means that Adirondack chairs and similar projects seem to last a good deal longer when adhesive and nails, or screws, are used, instead of just nails or screws. Call or write for further information.

FRANKLIN INTERNATIONAL

Consumer Products Division
2020 Bruck Street
Columbus, OH 43207
(800) 877-4583 Tech service
(614) 443-0241 (in Ohio)
(614) 445-1251 FAX

Franklin International is a leading manufacturer of woodworking adhesives (and a leading maker of caulks and construction adhesives, some of which may be handy on some woodworking jobs). Franklin's TiteBond and TiteBond II are the most widely used woodworking adhesives in the United States. TiteBond is a yellow aliphatic resin wood glue that is moderately moisture-resistant. The much newer Tite-Bond II is a weatherproof glue that is the cheapest true weatherproof woodworker's adhesive on the market. (On average, it is only about 15 percent more expensive than original TiteBond: Comparisons might be made with epoxies and resorcinol for cost. Tite-Bond II wins, though both epoxies and resorcinol offer other features to help make up for great expense, though TBII cuts odor, complexity, and harmful vapor problems, as well as expense.) Franklin does not promote TiteBond II as completely waterproof, but it's the next best thing, unless you're building a boat or some other submerged project. The newest Tite-Bond product is a dark line wood glue called, not so weirdly, TiteBond Dark Wood Glue. It's great for hiding wood lines in walnut and similar dark woods. Literature is available directly, including Product Data Sheets, Material Safety Data Sheets, and Gluing Guides. Check at (800) 347-4583, Monday through Saturday, 8 A.M. to 8 P.M., for the name of your nearest dealer.

THE GORILLA GROUP

P.O. Box 42352
Santa Barbara, CA 93140
(800) 966-3458

As we go to press, I've yet to try Gorilla Glue, but I get all-around good reports from others who have. The maker claims it is 100 percent waterproof, solvent-free, and exceptionally strong. It does need humidity in the wood to work—but I don't know if a cabinetmaker's 6 to 8 percent maximum will suffice. It will take stain, spreads itself, and leaves no glue line. It goes on only one side of the wood, and it is easily cleaned up. Currently, 36 fluid ounces goes for $29.95, and 18 ounces, for $19.95, plus a couple bucks shipping and handling. Gorilla Group accepts Discover, MasterCard and Visa.

GOUGEON BROTHERS
P.O. Box 908
Bay City, MI 48707
(517) 684-7286

The West System 1000 Polyurethane Varnish and epoxy adhesives are available from Gougeon Brothers. West System Epoxy is a two-part adhesive and coating for wood, fiberglass and metal. Strong and waterproof, it doesn't shrink and is easily modified with fillers and additives. *EpoxyWorks* is a biannual publication for modern epoxy users, and is free, as is the absolutely superb West System tech manual and product guide. There is also a free brochure on epoxy composite construction, as well as a comprehensive dealer list. If you're unable to find a local dealer, Gougeon Brothers will sell direct, and they take MasterCard and Visa.

MACCO ADHESIVES
925 Euclid
Cleveland, OH 44115
(800) 364-0015
(216) 344-7319 FAX

Macco has been around since 1948, and it manufactures various adhesives of use to woodworkers. Liquid Nails is their product, and there's a new version, Liquid Nails for Furniture, which is a nonrunning white adhesive that dries clear and, Macco says, is more rigid than yellow carpenter's (aliphatic) wood glues. Liquid Nails for Furniture is a polyvinyl acetate, of fair water resistance that does not stain, has a working time up to fifteen minutes, dries in thirty minutes, and is nonflammable. Shelf life is one year, plus. Thirty-minute clamping may be used. The company sells to dealers, so check at your local lumberyard, hardware store or other outlet.

PDI, INC.
P.O. Box 130
Circle Pines, MN 55014
(612) 785-2156
(612) 785-2058 FAX

PDI produces Plasti-Dip coatings and a number of adhesives. Plasti-Dip coats tool handles to provide a more comfortable grip; it may also be used to color-code a workbench. I've used Plasti-Dip to coat wire and metal used on birdhouses and feeders—it keeps the birds' feet from sticking in damp winter weather and also prevents (and stops) rust. I'll be doing so again in an upcoming project book that's for the birds. (Sorry. Couldn't resist.) But I am doing another birdhouse-project book this year, and I am using

Plasti-Dip. PDI will send along a free how-to brochure if you drop them a line. They sometimes sell direct, and they take Visa, but usually they'll line you up with a local dealer.

SPOTLIGHT
P.O. Box 97
Carlisle, PA 17013
(800) 933-7963 Recorded message

Spotlight is a simple product, a glue additive that makes woodworking glues fluoresce under ultraviolet light. While that may not sound like a big job, it makes those glues readily visible before you slap a finish on your favorite project and find that the stain didn't stain quite the same way in every spot. Spotlight doesn't remove glue spots: It helps you remove them. It has no effect on the glue, but it works best with polyvinyl resins—white glues and the yellow aliphatic resins. It has also been formulated to work with cross-linking PVA glues, such as Franklin's TiteBond II. Under an ultraviolet light source, Spotlight shows up as blue coloring in the glue line, and in any glue spots. Once glue spots are located, they can be removed, and your finishes will be better than ever. Give the 800 number a call: It features a three-minute message. Spotlight accepts MasterCard and Visa.

3M DIY DIVISION
Consumer Relations
515-3N-02
St. Paul, MN 55144-1000

This is the 3M division that handles information on Newstroke snap-off paintbrushes, home-care adhesives, surface-prep products (hand- and power-sanding materials), paint removers, and personal-safety products, such as goggles and face masks of both comfort and respirator types. The firm makes a wide variety of masks and respirators to reduce the effects of the sandpaper and similar products it also produces. I particularly like their disposable, general dust and sanding respirator: That's the number 8710, and it comes in contractor packs of twenty, as well as in packs of two or three. Catalogs are available on request. Specify which product line interests you (listed above).

WOODCARE PRODUCTS
P.O. Box 682677
Park City, UT 84068
(800) 676-GLUE
(801) 647-9993
(801) 647-9590

Pro Bond is a wide line of quick-bonding adhesives, made in thin, medium and thick solutions, with bond times varying from two to three seconds for the thin, to as much as two minutes for the thin. The thick, slower-bonding adhesive also is a gap-filling adhesive, but the thinner materials do not fill gaps. Call or write for free information on Pro Bond instant adhesives.

ANCHORS/FASTENERS

RAWLPLUG CO., INC.
200 Petersville Road
New Rochelle, NY 10802
For inquiries write:
Rawl Inquiry Handling Center
P.O. Box 8116
Trenton, NJ 08650

Write and ask for the *Rawl 47M Drilling and Anchoring Handbook*, free from the Trenton, New Jersey, address. This book not only covers the entire Rawlplug line of fasteners, anchors and drill bits, plus their RS5000 RotoHammer, but also shows when and where to use all the products. If you've ever had to anchor a project in drywall or concrete, you'll already understand how valuable this handbook is as a reference as well as a buyer's guide. (With the handbook in your hot little hand, no home center can tell you such-and-such an anchor style is not and never has been made!) For cabinetmakers and other woodworkers, this guide may prove invaluable.

SIMPSON STRONG-TIE COMPANY, INC.
1450 Doolittle Drive
P.O. Box 1568
San Leandro, CA 94577
(800) 227-1562
(510) 562-7946 FAX

Simpson's line of framing anchors includes some items of definite interest to woodworkers: Rigid-Tie corner connectors, for example, work well to ease the assembly of benches and materials holders, and shelf brackets can save much installation time in creating shop storage. Drop a card to Simpson and request information on either do-it-yourself or RTC materials—or both. Simpson's does not sell direct.

WOODWORKERS' STORE
21801 Industrial Boulevard
Rogers, MN 55374-9514
(612) 428-2199
(612) 428-8668 FAX

Another major mail-order source for many items, Woodworkers' Store carries a wide line of small power tools, hand tools, woods, finishes, plans, jigs, kits, and a very wide line of hardware, including many porcelain parts, oak and birch carvings, and even briefcase handles in two quality levels (the cheaper is covered in vinyl, the more costly in leather). Currently unique is their line of workshop knobs in black plastic or aluminum, in five styles and many more sizes. The knobs make building your own shop jigs a great deal easier, as do some other new kits in the most recent catalog. You'll also find a large line of jewelry-box, chest, drawer, and general cabinet locks, as well as plenty of knockdown fasteners. Woodworkers' Store is another company that sends smaller update catalogs with some frequency, so your $3 buys a great deal of information. The Woodworkers' Store operates eleven retail outlets in Boston, Chicago, Cleveland, Columbus, Denver, Detroit, Milwaukee, Minneapolis, San Diego, Seattle and Buffalo. The retail stores do not accept mail order but may speed access to some items if you happen to be nearby.

BITS AND BLADES

AMANA TOOL CORPORATION
120 Carolyn Boulevard
Farmingdale, NY 11375
(800) 445-0077
(516) 752-1300
(516) 752-1674 FAX

Amana manufactures industrial-grade, carbide-tipped wood-cutting tools, including router bits, saw blades, rosette cutters, planer knives, shaper cutters and dado sets. They've recently come out with a new line of saw blades they call the Ditec 2000. Their free, one-hundred-page annual catalog comes with a free tech manual. Sales are made only through a nationwide network of dealers.

CASCADE TOOLS, INC.
P.O. Box 3110
Bellingham, WA 98227
(800) 235-0272
(800) 392-5077 FAX

Cascade Tools imports and distributes the SY line of carbide tools, primarily router bits and shaper cutters. There are many unusual items in both lines, plus some items such as antikickback devices, Magna-Set precision jointer and planer knife setting jigs, rub collars, dust-collection connectors, router bases, roller brackets, and on, including books and videos, Fas-

Tak air nailers (brad models), and staplers. The seventy-three-page annual catalog is free and is supplemented by a sixty-four-page spring sale catalog, also free. The 800 number takes orders twenty-four hours a day, and Cascade accepts Visa, MasterCard and Discover.

CONNECTICUT VALLEY MANUFACTURING
P.O. Box 1957
New Britain, CT 06050
(203) 223-0076

Convalco Forstner bits are among the best of the type available. The company has been around since 1866 and has been making wood-boring tools since 1874, so there's reason for excellence. This is not a wide-line company: If you don't count different sizes, Convalco makes only a dozen different items, three of which are Forstner bits. Connecticut Valley produces Forstner bits in ⅟₁₆″ steps from ¼″ to 3″ (the steps move to ⅛″ at 1½″). They are the only company I know of to make Forstner bits in a brace shank—for a bit brace. There's a compass cutter, a dowel center set, two plug-cutter styles, a counterbore, two countersinks, and two shape scrapers. Write or call for further information: The Convalco catalog is free, and the company does not accept credit cards, so have your checkbook handy or ask for a dealer's name.

FORREST MANUFACTURING COMPANY, INC.
461 River Road
Clifton, NJ 07014
(800) 733-7111
(201) 473-5236 (in New Jersey)
(201) 471-3333 FAX

A manufacturer of high-grade saw blades, Forrest differentiates to the point where they offer separate blade choices for table saws and radial arm saws. (The table saw blade is primarily a rip blade, though it's listed as all-purpose. The radial arm saw blade, with sixty teeth, is virtually a cutoff blade.) As noted, Forrest products are top-of-the-line; thus, they are somewhat pricey. I've seen their eighty-tooth blade in action, though, after a long term of heavy use, and it still made fine cuts. Also in the Forrest line are blade stiffeners and dado sets. The dado head cuts in all directions and leaves flat-bottomed grooves, with sizes from ¼″ to ²⁹⁄₃₂″ (a set of plastic adjusting shims is included). This is one dado set that will cut oak plywood without splintering. The woodworkers' brochures are free on request, and Forrest also offers a superior carbide-blade-sharpening service that also handles router bits, knives and similar items. They offer related services to restore a blade to like new, or

better, condition. Forrest accepts Visa, MasterCard, American Express and Discover.

FREUD, INC.
218 Feld Avenue
High Point, NC 27264
(800) 472-7307

Jim Brewer at Freud supplied so much detailed information that, adding it to their three catalogs, I ended up spinning, trying to figure what to include and what to leave out. Their current new router bit catalog offers many pages of top-grade bits—call for a copy of that catalog, or a copy of their saw blade catalog, or a copy of their shaper cutter catalog, or copies of all three. Catalogs are free to readers of this book, so mention it. Some company detail, for those who have never heard of Freud (if any such woodworkers exist) includes the fact the company has been in the U.S. market for upward of 20 years. They use a special titanium-bonded carbide in their router bits, make their own carbide for best quality control, and provide special computer-controlled grinding to reduce vibration, burn and chatter. I've used Freud bits and blades and a Freud router and found they live up to company claims. Freud blades and bits are a bit pricey but are also durable and well made, which reduces problems with cost. Freud tools remain good value for the money; however, like all costly tools and accessories, they are definitely items to be thought about before purchase. You can find reduced prices if you search through other listings in this book to find a good discount retailer.

INTEGRA TOOLING & ACCESSORIES
3-1 Park Plaza #106
Old Brookville, NY 11545
(800) 633-6312
(516) 767-2340

Integra sells a line of carbide-cutting tools at wholesale prices to end users. Tools are all manufactured in the United States, Germany and Israel. No Taiwanese tools are sold. The annual catalog is free, and Integra takes MasterCard and Visa.

MAGNATE BUSINESS INTERNATIONAL
1930 South Brea Canyon Road, #170
Diamond Bar, CA 91765
(800) 827-2316, Ext. 128
(800) 733-9076 FAX
(909) 861-1185
(909) 861-2766 FAX

Magnate offers a very wide line of router bits, accessories, and now, Porter-Cable routers, sanders, abrasives and accessories. The company's specialty is high-quality carbide cutting tools with an aim toward marketing at very competitive prices. They also carry circular saw blades, rosette cutters (for use in drill presses), Forstner bits, tenon cutters, bard-point drill bits, lathe knives, molder knives, planer knives, the Woodchuck multiaxis milling machine, and shaper cutters. Call or drop a note for a free copy of the twice-yearly catalog. Magnate takes MasterCard and Visa.

MLCS, LTD.

P.O. Box 4053 C13
Rydal, PA 19046
(800) 533-9298
(215) 938-5070 FAX

The free MLCS catalog features router bits but also offers quite a few other items. The router bits are reputed to be top quality—I've never used any of this brand—and come in a wide variety of profiles, including raised panel, stile-and-rail, multiform moulding makers, French provincial, double ogee and double flute raised panel bits, an ogee raised panel bit with an undercutter, crown moulding bits, and a slew of other moulding bits, plus standard cove and bead, chamfer, Roman ogee, round over, beading, drawer and finger pull, ogee fillet, and thumbnail bits. There are round nose bits, core box bits, keyhole cutting bits, dish cutters, spiral downcut bits, door lip bits, hinge mortising bits, straight bits, bottom cleaning bits, lock miter bits, finger joint bits, tongue-and-groove bits, flush trimming bits, and others. Other products include Forstner drill bits, from $1/4''$ to $3 1/8''$ in size, shaper cutters, their own router table, an adjustable corner clamp and other items. The catalog is definitely worth looking at, inventory is large, and there are experienced woodworkers on staff to help with questions. Check out the showroom shared with Penn State at 2381 Philmont Avenue, Huntington Valley, PA. MLCS takes Discover, MasterCard and Visa.

MOON'S SAW & TOOL, INC.

2531-39 Ashland Avenue
Chicago, IL 60614
(800) 447-7371
(312) 549-7924
(312) 549-7695 FAX

This Chicago company presents a quarterly sale brochure, a small general-lines catalog, plus a catalog of Byrom router bits, free and on request. The catalog is slender but presents many edge-forming and other router bits, under Moon's own brand name, plus a full line of saw blades under Moon's name. Moon also carries Wizard Elite and Roadrunner blades, Freud Forstner bits, planer and jointer knives, Freud saw blades, and Morse band saw blades. The spring sales days brochure shows the Freud $3 1/4$-horse router for a very good price and the Fein triangular sander, also for a good price. There are many clamps in the brochure, as well as all sorts of saw blades. The catalog is well worth looking at, as is the sales brochure. Moon's Saw & Tool takes Discover, MasterCard and Visa.

OLDHAM-UNITED STATES SAW

Burt, NY 14028
(716) 778-8588

The Oldham-United States Saw catalog of their saw blades, router bits and abrasive wheels provides some major choices, from ultrathin kerf carbide blades (Roadrunner series), to carbide tooth nail-cutting blades, on to steel saw blades, then to Wizard and Supreme Wizard premium series (the Wizard series is designed for power mitering and comes in appropriate sizes from $8 1/4''$ to $15''$, while the Supreme Wizard series is for table and radial arm saws: Both series are cutoff styles with sixty or eighty teeth), plus three styles of dado blades, plus masonry and metal-cutting abrasive wheels, and then to Viper router bits. A comprehensive array comes from the factory of this company founded in 1857. Literature is free, and Oldham sells only to distributors.

OCS

Route 6
Bethel, CT 06801
(800) 634-4047
(203) 792-8622

Give OCS a call for a free catalog of saw blades listing a complete selection of scroll saw blades: skip tooth, double tooth, reverse tooth, spiral, metal cutting and pinned; band saw blades: flex back, hard back, furniture band and bimetal; sandpaper in sheets, discs, and belts; books and accessories for scrollsaw and band saw users. OCS accepts MasterCard and Visa.

RAWLPLUG COMPANY, INC.

200 Petersville Road
New Rochelle, NY 10802
For inquiries write:
Rawl Inquiry Handling Center
P.O. Box 8116
Trenton, NJ 08650

Write and ask for the *Rawl 47M Drilling and Anchor-*

ing Handbook, free from the above Trenton, New Jersey, address. This book not only covers the entire Rawlplug line of fasteners, anchors and drill bits, plus their RS5000 RotoHammer, but also shows when and where to use all the products. If you've ever had to anchor a project in drywall or concrete, you'll already understand how valuable this handbook is as a reference as well as a buyer's guide. (With the handbook in your hot little hand, no home center can tell you such-and-such an anchor style is not and never has been made!) For cabinetmakers and other woodworkers, this guide may prove invaluable.

RIDGE CARBIDE TOOL CORPORATION

P.O. Box 497
595 York Avenue
Lyndhurst, NJ 07071
(800) 443-0992
(201) 438-8792 FAX

Ridge Carbide Tool makes custom router bits and shaper cutters from drawings, or to fit wood samples. They also make shaper knives, sand-free woodworking saw blades, and special dado sets, and they have a complete sharpening and repair service. RCT emphasizes that they are not just a phone-mail company with stock tools and stock answers. They manufacture tools to custom specifications and to fit special needs. There is a free catalog of standard stock items, and information is available on custom services and sharpening. RCT accepts MasterCard and Visa.

SUFFOLK MACHINERY CORPORATION

12 Waverly Avenue
Patchogue, NY 11772
(800) 234-SAWS
(516) 289-7153
(516) 289-7156 FAX

In business since 1976, Suffolk Machinery has produced band saw blades in Sweden to their design. They feel the blades are the best available. They do not make standard hook-and-skip blades, but they aim for high-performance models using Swedish silicone steels meant to be run with about 30 percent lower tension than standard blades. They guarantee a 30 percent to 60 percent extension of blade life on their low-tension blades. They offer five different designs, two of which are primarily useful to small-shop woodworkers (a third, the AS54 could be useful, but only if you have a band saw that will use a ¾" blade). The standard PC comes in widths from ³⁄₁₆" to 1", and woodturners like the AS for cutting large burls. Prices for the PC series seem to be in line with other top-of-the-line band saw blades. The catalog is free, and Suf-

folk Machinery takes MasterCard and Visa.

VERMONT-AMERICAN TOOL COMPANY

P.O. Box 340
Lincolnton, NC 28093-0340
(704) 735-7464

Vermont-American is a full-line, tool-accessory company that manufactures circular saw blades from 3⅜" diameter to 16" diameter, jig and bayonet saw blades, reciprocating saw blades, band saw blades, drill bits, counter sinks, router bits, abrasive accessories, tool belts, pliers, cutters, wrenches, nail sets, mallets, cold chisels, punches, blade bushings, dado blades, many specialty tools (driver bits, chisels, wire wheels, tap-and-die sets, screwdrivers, hole saws, hand saws, taper jigs [for table saws]) and many other items. Call or write for free information in the form of product brochures.

WOODCRAFT BANDS, INC.

Route 2, Box 22-18
Vilas, NC 28692
(704) 297-6081

Woodcraft Bands manufactures band saw blades for popular band saw models (Sears, Delta, etc.), and it sells to people who make crafts, furniture and cabinets. Currently, their version of blades for Sears's Craftsman band saws costs about half the Sears version. They also make industrial band saw blades, so that there are dual listings, for hobbyist and professional blades. Request a price list. Woodcraft Bands takes no credit cards.

WOODHAVEN

5323 West Kimberly Road
Davenport, IA 52806
(800) 344-6657
(319) 391-2386
(319) 391-1275 FAX

Woodhaven is a fairly old (now well past a decade) mail-order house for router bits, tables and general router supplies. The newest catalog is more colorful than the one Brad Witt sent a couple years ago, and it shows a wider line of router tables and tabletops. The claim is now that they offer the widest line of router tables and accessories, and I see no reason to dispute the claim. And Woodhaven now offers a plate-inlay template for use with Woodhaven base plates: The plate template is inexpensive and will accept either size of Woodhaven plate, with plate levelers (or you can sand down edges to size another brand of plate). Hinge, lockset, and strike-plate mortise jigs are also offered, as are fences, angle brackets, and a slew of interesting items for the router-using woodworker. I want to get hold of their "Frame & Panel Secrets" video, and the catalog is available on video, though it costs $14.99 that way. For circle-cutting jigs, vacuum-clamp kits, Keller dovetailing jigs, Beall wood threaders, and an array of other items, this catalog offers much of interest to the woodworker. One such item is the Know-Bit. This is not much more than a pointed metal dowel, with the point set to the top when inserted in a router. It then serves as an exact centering device for router, drill press, lathe. It is machined perfectly straight and round, so it also makes a good run-out check when used with a dial indicator. Chuck it into your drill press or router or lathe, and quickly and simply measure the run-out (wobble). The catalog is free by bulk mail, $3 first class. Woodhaven takes Discover, MasterCard and Visa.

YORK SAW & KNIFE COMPANY, INC.
Luxite Division
P.O. Box 733
York, PA 17405
(800) 233-1969
(717) 654-7297
(717) 764-2768 FAX

Luxite saw blades are manufactured in-house, using laser cutting, computerized flattening and heat treating. Robotic grinding and brazing assure sharpness and strength, as does strong quality control. The company manufactures dado sets, crosscut and rip blades, glue line rip blades, combination blades, miter saw blades and other types. York has been in business for more than eighty-five years now, and provides carbide-tipped saw blades to the secondary wood market. Call or write for information on their Luxite carbide saw blades: Extensive sizes and types along with quality make York saw blades of interest to many woodworkers. Their current catalog shows saw blades ranging from 4" (100mm) to 20" (radial arm saw blades that are listed as 1') to 20", with all the favorite sizes of stops. Other blades go to 24" diameter, and dado sets are available in 2" steps from 6" to 14".

CLEANERS

PMS-PRODUCTS, INC.
285 James Street
Holland, MI 49424
(800) 962-1732
(616) 786-9922
(616) 786-9130 FAX

This manufacturer of Boeshield T-9 will provide further information on its spray coating for metal surfaces. The Boeshield T-9 product is a solvent-and-wax formula that goes on thin and dries to a light film said to give months of protection. The spray contains no silicons or Teflon, so it doesn't harm wood, paint or plastics, and it is easily removed with any solvent-based cleaner. PMS-Products also makes Rust Off, a heavy-duty rust and stain remover that is a wide-spectrum cleaner (removes lime as well as rust). Call for further information.

COATINGS

PDI, INC.
P.O. Box 130
Circle Pines, MN 55014
(612) 785-2156
(612) 785-2058 FAX

PDI produces Plasti-Dip coatings and a number of adhesives. Plasti-Dip coats tool handles to provide a more comfortable grip; it may also be used to color-code a workbench. I've used Plasti-Dip to coat wire and metal used on birdhouses and feeders—it keeps the birds' feet from sticking in damp winter weather and also prevents (and stops) rust. I'll be doing so again in an upcoming project book that's for the birds. (Sorry. Couldn't resist.) But I am doing another birdhouse-project book this year, and I am using Plasti-Dip. PDI will send a free how-to brochure if you drop them a line. They sometimes sell direct, and they take Visa, but usually they'll line you up with a local dealer.

PMS-PRODUCTS, INC.
285 James Street
Holland, MI 49424
(800) 962-1732
(616) 786-9922
(616) 786-9130 FAX

This manufacturer of Boeshield T-9 will provide further information on its spray coating for metal surfaces. The Boeshield T-9 product is a solvent-and-wax formula that goes on thin and dries to a light film said to give months of protection. The spray contains no silicons or Teflon, so it doesn't harm wood, paint or plastics, and it is easily removed with any solvent-based cleaner. PMS-Products also makes Rust Off, a heavy-duty rust and stain remover that is a wide-spectrum cleaner (removes lime as well as rust). Call for further information.

CUTTERS

CASCADE TOOLS, INC.

P.O. Box 3110
Bellingham, WA 98227
(800) 235-0272
(800) 392-5077 FAX

Cascade Tools imports and distributes the SY line of carbide tools, primarily router bits and shaper cutters. There are many unusual items in both lines, plus some items such as antikickback devices, Magna-Set precision jointer and planer knife setting jigs, rub collars, dust-collection connectors, router bases, roller brackets and on, including books and videos, Fas-Tak air nailers (brad models), and staplers. The seventy-three page annual catalog is free and is supplemented by a sixty-four-page spring sale catalog, also free. The 800 number takes orders twenty-four hours a day, and Cascade accepts Visa, MasterCard and Discover.

FREEBORN TOOL COMPANY, INC.

6202 North Freya
P.O. Box 6246
Spokane, WA 99207-0904
(800) 523-8988
(509) 484-9932 FAX

Panel cutters are Freeborn's forte—that's all they make and all they want to make. The line is wide, and interesting, if you use a shaper. Cutters are tipped with Tantung, a name that brought a fast "Whaaa?" from me, too. Essentially, Tantung is an alloy of cobalt, chromium, tungsten, columbium and carbon. Heat resistance is far higher than that of high-speed steel, and the resistance to shock is higher than that of carbide—though Tantung will not take as much heat as carbide. Tantung is not intended for use on man-made fiber and plywood materials. Freeborn's range of cutters includes all the usual, such as lock miter and single tongue-and-groove lock miter sets, drawer lock cutters, drop leaf table cutters, and on. It's really not worth going on, for a simple reason: Freeborn also makes custom cutters, so if there's a shaper profile you need and can't find, this company will work with you. Check their catalog and brochures first because there is a plethora of stock shapes. Freeborn does not accept credit cards.

L.R.H. ENTERPRISES, INC.

CO-ST Cutter Bits
7101 Valjean Avenue
Van Nuys, CA 91406
(800) 423-2544
(818) 782-0226
(818) 909-7602 FAX

L.R.H. shaper cutters are available in about 900 profiles.

Shaper cutters from L.R.H.'s in-stock patterns appear to cover about any profile any woodworker is apt to want, but additionally, the twenty-year-old company does custom cutter production. The newest line is the CO-ST Cutters designed to fit ½" and ¾" spindle shapers (sizes more likely to be in the small shop than the larger units). L.R.H. also produces industrial-size cutters and cutters with interchangeable components. Give them a call to request their free catalog of quality cutters. They also make a low-cost stack dado set called the Hogger. L.R.H. does not sell retail: Get the catalog, check out the nearly nine hundred profiles, look over the retail price list, and ask your local dealer to order what you need.

RIDGE CARBIDE TOOL CORPORATION

P.O. Box 497
595 York Avenue
Lyndhurst, NJ 07071
(800) 443-0992
(201) 438-8792 FAX

Ridge Carbide Tool makes custom router bits and shaper cutters from drawings, or to fit wood samples. They also make shaper knives, sand-free woodworking saw blades and special dado sets, and they have a complete sharpening and repair service. RCT emphasizes that they are not just a phone-mail company with stock tools and stock answers. They manufacture tools to custom specifications and to fit special needs. There is a free catalog of standard stock items, and information is available on custom services and sharpening. RCT accepts MasterCard and Visa.

CHARLES G.G. SCHMIDT & COMPANY, INC.
301 West Grand Avenue
Montvale, NJ 07645
(201) 391-5300
(201) 391-3565 FAX

Charles G.G. Schmidt manufactures and distributes industrial woodworking knives and cutters for all types of molders, shapers, planers, tenoners and routers. Their products include wing cutters, window-sash cutters, shaper collars, thin knives, cutter heads and custom tooling. Started in 1926, the company produces standard and custom tools of top materials. Their main catalog, number 300, is sent at no charge, as is "Knives," their list of standard molding and flooring profiles. Charles G.G. Schmidt & Company accepts Discover, MasterCard and Visa.

FRAMING

FRAMEWEALTH
RD 2, Box 261-7
Otego, NY 13825
(800) 524-8582

For those whose interest is in framing pictures or other items, FrameWealth presents a goodly number of framers' moldings, both as ready-mades and as parts. Framers' tools and hardware, from a miter vise to picture wire, are listed. The catalog is free. FrameWealth accepts American Express, Discover, MasterCard and Visa.

MARTIN & MACARTHUR HARDWOOD CENTER
Cabinet Shop and Office:
1815 Kahai Street
Honolulu, HI 96819
(808) 845-6688
(808) 845-6680 FAX
Showroom:
841 Bishop Street
Honolulu, HI 98613
(808) 524-4434 phone and FAX

This division of a thirty-year-old koa furniture manufacturer presents hardwood lumber and plywood, both wholesale and retail, as well as a line of wholesale and retail picture-framing supplies. Both solid and Treeline (koa veneered over poplar) are available. The Hardwood Center is located in the same building as the workshop. They have an exceptionally interesting and well-done brochure on koa and some of the products made from it: Koa is primarily found on Hawaii (the Big Island) and has an exceptional color range, from a pale blond to a deep brown, and further to a superb red. The wood has become scarce, and great care is now taken in harvesting these trees that range up to 60' tall, with a diameter of more than 3'. There are two other showrooms in Honolulu. Write or call for a brochure and price lists.

GUARDS

HTC PRODUCTS, INC.
120 East Hudson
P.O. Box 839
Royal Oak, MI 48608
(800) 624-2027

HTC is the top name in mobile bases for stationary power tools, with 200 standard models (a number that grows each year) and upward of 1,000 models in all. The new Brett Guards for table saws appear to be among the easiest-to-use protectors available—most woodworkers that I know have a pile of unused guards stuffed on back shelves. Even the industrial outfits and workers tend to pull them off, keeping them around for OSHA inspections and not using them otherwise. The reasons are simple: Almost all guards are difficult to use or to set up, often both. Difficulty in use makes for shortcuts that reduce guard effectiveness—or total removal. Thus, if the Brett Guard does as claimed, acceptance will be phenomenal. The catalog is free, a full-color, sixteen-pager, and HTC does not take credit cards (many of their retail accounts do, so ask for a dealer's name if you wish to charge).

HARDWARE

ADDKISON HARDWARE COMPANY, INC.
126 East Amite Street
P.O. Box 102
Jackson, MS 39205
(800) 821-2750
(601) 354-3756
(601) 354-1916 FAX

Addkison Hardware has been around since 1925, and it offers a very large stock of professional-grade, portable, electric power tools and light woodworking machinery (this isn't the place to come for a 25" planer, but you may want to check out contractor's tablesaw pricing). They also have a large stock of router bits, cutters and related accessories, and they carry door and cabinet hardware from more than thirty makers. They don't have their own catalog, but they can send brochures and catalogs where manufacturers make them available. Give them a call to check prices, or get further information on products from such companies as Amerock, Acorn Forged Iron, Allied Brass, Belwith Hardware, Colonial Bronze, Franklin Brass, Grass Hinges, Master Locks, Stanley Hardware and others. Addkison Hardware accepts both MasterCard and Visa.

ANTIQUE HARDWARE STORE

RD 2 Box A
Kintnersville, PA 18930
(800) 422-9982
(215) 847-2447

The Antique Hardware Store features cast iron, brass hardware reproductions for cabinets, ice boxes, bathrooms, kitchens, general household doors, and other rooms. Of greatest interest to woodworkers, cabinet hardware includes some hard-to-find items of reproduction Victoriana, plus some more standard items including different kinds of Chippendale pulls, bail pulls, porcelain knobs, escutcheons, knobs and drop pulls. You want a juke box? Well, Antique Hardware Store carries one: The model for 45s is $6,749, and the CD model is a grand more. Tim Judge says his catalog is free to readers, and it's well worth looking through, both for woodworking-related items and for curiosities, such as the pillbox toilet. Tim accepts Discover, MasterCard and Visa.

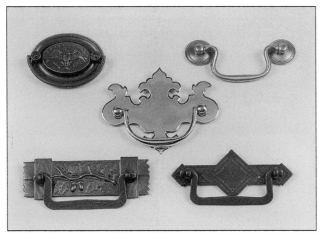

Horton Brasses produces a wide line of classic styles and finishes.

HORTON BRASSES, INC.

Nooks Hill Road
Cromwell, CT 06416
(203) 635-4400
(203) 635-6473 FAX

The Horton catalog of reproduction furniture hardware is a biannual publication of forty-eight pages, specifically designed to show the Horton Brasses and their special finishes. All photos are scaled so the brasses and other hardware are exactly half life-size, and complete dimensions are presented. The reproduction hardware made by Horton Brasses includes brass, wood, porcelain, and hand-forged iron items. All the brasses are exact copies of old brasses, made with attention to the tiniest detail. Many periods are represented: William & Mary, Queen Anne, American Chippendale, Sheraton, Hepplewhite, Empire, Victorian and Mission (arts and crafts). All work is done in the Horton Brasses factory in Cromwell. Furniture hardware is all Horton Brasses makes, but that includes hinges, knobs, drawer pulls, casters, catches, bed bolts, bed irons and covers for bolts. They specialize in drawer pulls and cabinet hardware, bed hardware, table hardware and chest hardware, while also offering the Goddard Company lines of polishes, waxes and cleaners. All hardware comes in the special Horton antique finish, satin finish and a bright finish. Horton Brasses takes MasterCard and Visa.

JAMESTOWN DISTRIBUTORS

28 Narragansett Avenue
P.O. Box 348
Jamestown, RI 02835
(800) 423-0030
(401) 423-2520
(800) 423-0542 FAX

If you're looking for a wide range of fasteners and other boatbuilding and woodworking supplies, the Jamestown catalog's 204 pages (free on request) cover those needs. The fastener section starts with 18-8 stainless steel wood screws; goes on through machine screws, nuts and bolts, cotter pins, cap screws and washers; then swings into silicon bronze fasteners; moves on to hot-dipped galvanized; and punches over to rivets of stainless steel, aluminum and carbon steel. Nails are copper, brass, stainless steel, silicon bronze and galvanized. Jamestown also carries general cleanup, caulk, adhesive and similar items, with a strong emphasis on the West System epoxies (probably the most complete woodworking epoxy line whether for marine or other purposes), and goes on to complete materials for fiberglass lay-up and laminating. There's a strong section on marine finishes and another on accessories such as saw blades, drill bits and hammers. This is an interesting catalog, with supplies not easily found elsewhere. Jamestown operates a store in Beaufort, South Carolina, as well as its Jamestown, Rhode Island, base. While a boatbuilder's catalog may seem a little off-the-wall for woodworkers, it pays to check the odd corners for adhesives and stainless steel and other noncorroding fasteners. (Even when you're not working on outdoor projects, it pays to remember that oak, for example, draws water to it, and thus can screw up plain steel fasteners in a hurry in any kind of a damp environment.) Jamestown takes MasterCard and Visa, and they've been around since 1977.

LARRY & FAYE BRUSSO COMPANY
3812 Cass-Elizabeth
Waterford, MI 48328
(810) 674-8458
(810) 674-4962 FAX

The Brussos produce exceptionally fine, solid-brass hardware for custom cabinetry and fine boxes. All hardware is machined from solid-brass stock, hand fitted, and finished nicely, to produce show-quality hinges. A short while ago, I built a walnut hope chest using their hinges, and I find them truly exceptional. The brass work is fine enough for you to plan a whole project around. I'd suggest checking prices directly because brass stock is fluctuating as usual. Brusso hinges are sold by many woodworkers' mail-order firms, and they are available directly, in quantities of ten and up. Call or write for a retail price schedule. The Brussos don't take credit cards.

LEICHTUNG WORKSHOPS
4944 Commerce Parkway
Cleveland, OH 44128
(800) 321-6840
(216) 464-6764 FAX

Leichtung offers a variety of unusual tools, plus many plans and woodworking supplies in their free catalog. The catalog is digest-sized, but sometimes runs more than ninety pages, and it presents seasonal plans, some kits (varying with the seasons, but often small boxes and clocks, ships, dollhouses), and parts to help in building some of the plan items. The catalog has many styles of clamps and numerous doweling and jointing jigs. It's the only tool catalog I've seen where you're as apt to find wildflower seeds by the small sack, rain gauges, barbecue cleaner, rocks and cowhide gloves as you are Forstner drill bits. I've used a lot of Leichtung's gloves, and I always keep several pair on hand. For the price, they're the best I've seen for light chores, up to and including feeding a planer. The company also has a goodly array of parts bins and jars and hangers for perforated board, both ¼" and ⅛". They also offer a Woodworker's Guild for a $15 annual membership fee. Leichtung Workshops takes American Express, MasterCard, Visa and Discover.

PAXTON HARDWARE
7818 Bradshaw Road
P.O. Box 256
Upper Falls, MD 21156
(410) 592-8505
(410) 592-2224 FAX

Paxton Hardware presents a wide line of period furniture hardware, from classic, solid-brass knobs to escutcheons, on to desk hardware, ice box hardware, label holders, and back to all sorts of hinges. Period hinges, latches and hooks are available in Federal, Chippendale, Queen Anne, Rococo, Arts & Crafts, Mission, Victorian, Campaign, and other styles in brass and iron, as well as in other finishes. Paxton also carries a line of lamp fittings, shades, and complete period lamps. Paxton gets $4 for its color catalog and accepts MasterCard and Visa.

PRECISION MOVEMENTS
4283 Chestnut Street
Emmaus, PA 18049
(215) 967-3156

Precision Movements specializes in clock movements and clock-making supplies. Their fifty-two-page catalog is free, and it describes many movements of many kinds, including quartz movement "Six Packs," which include six movements, six brass second hands, six pairs of brass 3" hands, and six pairs of brass 2¼" hands. Shaft lengths available for the six packs include ⁵⁄₁₆", ⁷⁄₁₆", ¹¹⁄₁₆" and 15", allowing the use of many face materials. The company takes MasterCard and Visa.

RENOVATOR'S SUPPLY
Millers Falls, MA 01349
(800) 659-3211 Customer services
(800) 659-2211 Orders 7 A.M. to midnight, EST
(413) 659-2241 Corporate offices

You're thinking that this is another nut entry, that a renovation-supply place specializing in Victoriana isn't of much help to woodworkers. Well, I'd suggest you check a copy of their free catalog, especially if you need cabinet hardware that is a bit out of the ordinary. There are other items that are fascinating, but the cabinet hardware is most likely to be useful. Renovator's Supply takes MasterCard and Visa.

STANLEY HARDWARE
480 Myrtle Street
New Britain, CT 06053
(203) 225-5111
(203) 827-5729

Call or write for information on Stanley Hardware items. You may want, to save time, to check the full-line catalog at your hardware store, for Stanley makes a line of solid brass, called Classic Brassware—hardware that's great for woodworking projects. There are also plenty of hinges—for cabinets, regular doors and barn doors—for all projects and for shop construction, as well as an array of different flat steel products, including mending plates and corner braces and . . . well, check the catalog.

TURNCRAFT CLOCKS

P.O. Box 100
Mound, MN 55364-0100
(800) 544-1711

Turncraft Clocks is fairly new, specializing in different and unusual, as well as traditional, clock parts and clock plans. The catalog displays a variety of quartz movements, with and without pendulums and chimes, and an even wider variety of clock faces in sizes from 3¾″ up to 12⅜″. Drop a line and request the catalog if you're at all interested in making reasonably simple clocks. Turncraft accepts Discover, MasterCard and Visa.

UNICORN STUDIOS

P.O. Box 370
Seymour, TN 37865

The full-line Unicorn catalog, for $1, features musical movements in one of the largest selections of tunes anywhere, many of which are hard to find—even a few that are unique to Unicorn.

UNITED STEEL PRODUCTS

703 Rogers Drive
Montgomery, MN 56069
(612) 364-7333
(612) 364-8762 FAX

United Steel makes Kant Sag joist and other lumber-connecting hardware for building, which is handy if you're constructing shops and similar projects. They will send a booklet, *Building Decks with Deck Hardware*, which shows the use of lumber connectors, including deck clips, fence brackets and deck brackets, to construct a deck. Their *Lumber Connector Product Guide* is also available; it shows quite nicely the uses of most joist hangers, rafter-and-truss ties, and post beam caps.

VAN DYKE'S RESTORERS

Woonsocket, SD 57385
(800) 843-3320
(605) 796-4425
(605) 796-4085

This company, selling mostly upholstery, refinishers' and restorers' supplies, offers their wholesale catalog for $1. I must admit to interest, though I thought there wouldn't be much: The first point that piqued that interest, though, was the cutline on the letter that came with my first copy: "The World's Largest Supplier & Manufacturer of Glass Eyes." That is simply intriguing, so I had to dive right into the catalog to see what else went on. And plenty does. For any woodworker doing cabinetry, this catalog is a help to find wooden knobs, trunk hardware, table hardware, leather trunk handles, carvings, spindles, hardware in general, including a huge line of solid, cast brass, and reproduction hardware from many areas. There are toy maker's supplies, dollhouse shingles, wheels, pegs and turning squares in walnut and other woods, carving wood, tea cart wheels, oak doorstops, lumber, veneer, deer photographs, wooden-duck carving kits, oil- and electric-lamp kits, marble knobs, embossed seats, artificial fur, and vinyl and glass eyes. Oh yes, there are glass eyes: There are faceted glass-jewel eyes; carousel-horse eyes; doll eyes; pinpoint pupil eyes (available in all colors, which include hazel, straw, yellow, red, black, blue and green); owl eyes; novelty carnival eyes; true-profile veined eyes; and . . . send for the catalog; it's a ball. It has a lot of useful stuff, including much of the above, plus caning materials, books, and so on. Van Dyke's takes MasterCard and Visa.

WAYNE'S WOODS, INC.

39 North Plains Industrial Road
Wallingford, CT 06492
(800) 793-6208
(203) 949-0546
(203) 949-0769 FAX

Wayne's Woods is a hardware manufacturer and sales outlet, with a free catalog. Wayne Malicki specializes in reproduction hardware using brass, glass, porcelain and wood; he also carries a complete line of finishing and refinishing supplies by Behlen, Kwik Kleen and others. The current catalog lists everything from bed rail fasteners to washstand brackets. There are pine cupboard turn catches and wooden wheel casters, solid cast brass drawer pulls, and drop-leaf table brackets. Wayne also has Morris chair hardware, and rolltop desk locks and keys. There's plenty of Victoriana for those who like that, and less ornate patterns, too. Wayne also has hand-carved oak gingerbread and a line of intriguing look hooks, including an English swivel hook and a couple of hall tree hooks that are as ornate as anything you're ever apt to see. Wayne's Woods can custom produce products to your specs, but orders must be of large size, and half must be paid up front. Wayne's Woods takes American Express, MasterCard and Visa.

WILLIAMSBURG BLACKSMITHS
Route 9
P.O. Box 1776
Williamsburg, MA 01096
(800) 248-1776
(413) 268-9317

Williamsburg Blacksmiths makes reproduction colonial wrought-iron hardware: Enough modernity has been added to keep hinges from squealing or groaning, and thumb latches don't rattle. Catches and fasteners all operate smoothly. Much—probably most—of the line is door and window hardware, but some is adaptable to other projects. Also offered is a line of cabinet and close/cupboard items, along with an extensive line of knobs and pulls and various wrought cut nails. New products include rifle hooks, an herb hook, shelf brackets, pivot hooks, switch plates and outlet plates. This is a third-generation family business, working in wrought-iron, tin, copper, brass and pewter. Check the current cost of the deluxe and lavishly done catalog. Williamsburg Blacksmiths takes American Express, Discover, MasterCard and Visa.

WOODWORKER'S HARDWARE
P.O. Box 784
St. Cloud, MN 56302
(800) 383-0130
(612) 255-1102

This free catalog of cabinet and furniture hardware is huge, running past 190 pages, and more than 4,000 listings! As with the first one I saw, there seems to be something for everything and everyone here, from Hafele oak drawer pulls to wrought-iron reproduction Colonial hardware; wire bail pulls; Amerock epoxy-coated drawer slides; wall standards and brackets; pivot door slides; pocket door slides from Blum; lazy Susan setups for cabinetry of many kinds; and organizer rails for compact discs, videotapes, and audiocassettes. There are casters, cable-hole covers, glass-door hinges, halogen lights, oak wood moldings, gallery rails and spindles, Shaker pegs, mug pegs, desktop fasteners, and so on. It's essential that you check to see what's available, for we don't have the space to

even name it all. Woodworker's Hardware takes MasterCard, Visa and Discover.

WOODWORKERS' STORE
21801 Industrial Boulevard
Rogers, MN 55374-9514
(612) 428-2199
(612) 428-8668 FAX

Another major mail-order source for many items, Woodworkers' Store carries a wide line of small power tools, hand tools, woods, finishes, plans, jigs, kits, and a very wide line of hardware, including many porcelain parts, oak and birch carvings, and even briefcase handles in two quality levels (the cheaper is covered in vinyl, the more costly in leather). Currently unique is their line of workshop knobs in black plastic, or aluminum, in five styles, and many more sizes. The knobs make building your own shop jigs a great deal easier, as do some other new kits in the most recent catalog. You'll also find a large line of jewelry-box, chest, drawer, and general cabinet locks, as well as plenty of knockdown fasteners. This company sends smaller update catalogs with some frequency, so your $3 buys a great deal of information. Woodworkers' Store operates eleven retail outlets in Boston, Chicago, Cleveland, Columbus, Denver, Detroit, Milwaukee, Minneapolis, San Diego, Seattle and Buffalo. The retail stores do not accept mail order, but may speed access to some items if you happen to be nearby.

WOODWORKS
4521 Anderson
Ft. Worth, TX 76117
(817) 281-4447

If you need small hardware or wood parts, the one-buck, fifty-six-page catalog contains a sizable listing of each, including eggs, axles, rabbit and other pattern cutouts, candlesticks, spoked wheels, buttons, dowels, spindles and many more. All turnings are American made. Woodworks has been in business for more than fifteen years, and they price items based on volume. All items are bulk packed, and case quantities bring discounted prices. Woodworks accepts Discover, MasterCard and Visa.

LIFTS

AUTON COMPANY
Box 1129
Sun Valley, CA 91353
(818) 367-4340
(818) 362-9215 FAX

Auton pop-up TV lifts are great for hiding television sets in good-looking cabinets. The TV sets then rise slowly to a viewing position and may be retracted after use. Write or call for information.

GIL-LIFT
1605 North River
Independence, MO 64050
(816) 833-0611

For those of us who from time to time build wall-mounted cabinets, this lift-and-hold device for cabinet installation seems to be an excellent solution to a pernicious problem (getting the cabinet to stay in place, without a helper and without a massive framework of jigs and aids—usually of 2 × 4s and 2 × 2s that may or may not be stable and strong enough for the job, while attaching it to the wall). Gil Wyand makes only this one tool, and he will send free information on request.

RAILS

LAVI INDUSTRIES
27810 Avenue Hopkins
Valencia, CA 91355
(805) 257-7800
(800) 624-6225

Founded in 1979, Lavi produces brass rail components for stairways, plie bars and similar uses. While that may not seem an ideal component for woodworkers, I'd suggest thinking a bit about what sort of accents short bars and some accessories might make on projects. (These bars are 1½″ and 2″ in diameter, and the accessories—ball ends, elbows, etc.—sized to scale, so they are obviously not for miniatures and small projects.) Some of the balusters combining wood and brass are very attractive and might serve other uses. Call and ask for brochures on the Lido railings. Lavi doesn't take credit cards.

REPAIRS

BOB SKOGMAN
4112 Elliot Avenue S
Minneapolis, MN 55407
(612) 824-5028

Bob repairs and refurbishes old levels: He is equipped to work on most brands. Give him a call or drop him a note to get details of the process and probable cost.

NEMY ELECTRIC TOOL COMPANY
7635-A Auburn Boulevard
Citrus Heights, CA 95610
(916) 723-1088
(916) 969-1088
(916) 723-1091 FAX

Bill Nemy runs a business that was founded in 1945 and is in its ninth year in its current location. Nemy Electric Tool Company is one of the larger woodworking machinery dealers in northern California. As such, it serves the professional community, the hobbyist, wood-carvers and the cottage-industry woodworker. They also do job-shop work for restoration and antique dealers, and they repair tools. Nemy offers classes in woodworking, wood carving, production techniques, stair building and other skills, while also being a local sponsor of *The New Yankee Workshop* on PBS. Bill has a video out, "Woodworks, Volume I: Arched Raised Panels," projected as the first of a series of thirteen. The video is eighty-three minutes long, and it details building raised panels with a router and router table. Nemy's catalog is $2.50, and their newsletter, "Woodworker's Bulletin," is free. Nemy Electric Tools accepts Discover, MasterCard and Visa.

RESTORATION

CHARLOTTE FORD TRUNKS
P.O. Box 536
Spearman, TX 79081
(806) 659-3027

Charlotte Ford is the only supplier I know of who emphasizes the restoration of old trunks. The company began in 1977, and today it offers a trunk-parts catalog for $2.50 and a five-volume, full-color, step-by-step set of restoration instructions. Each section is twenty-four pages long; it sells for $7.50 per section, or $35 for the package of five. *The Charlotte Ford Trunk I.D. Guide* is $4.50. Not only does Charlotte Ford Trunks mail-order trunk parts and hardware, but it also restores trunks shipped to it. Charlotte Ford accepts Discover, MasterCard and Visa.

NEMY ELECTRIC TOOL COMPANY
7635-A Auburn Boulevard
Citrus Heights, CA 95610
(916) 723-1088
(916) 969-1088
(916) 723-1091 FAX

Bill Nemy runs a business that was founded in 1945

and that is in its ninth year in its current location. Nemy Electric Tool Company is one of the larger woodworking machinery dealers in northern California. As such it serves the professional community, the hobbyist, wood-carvers, and the cottage-industry woodworker. They also do job-shop work for restoration and antique dealers, and they repair tools. Nemy offers classes in woodworking, wood-carving, production techniques, stair building and other skills, while also being a local sponsor of *The New Yankee Workshop* on PBS. Bill has a video out, "Woodworks, Volume I: Arched Raised Panels," projected as the first of a series of thirteen. The video is eighty-three minutes long, and it details building raised panels with a router and router table. Nemy's catalog is $2.50 and their newsletter, "Woodworker's Bulletin," is free. Nemy Electric Tools accepts Discover, MasterCard and Visa.

3M DIY DIVISION
Consumer Relations
515-3N-02
St. Paul, MN 55144-1000

This is the 3M division that handles information on Newstroke snap-off paintbrushes, home-care adhesives, surface-prep products (hand- and power-sanding materials), paint removers, and personal-safety products, such as goggles and face masks of both comfort and respirator types. This firm makes a wide variety of masks and respirators to reduce the effects of the sandpaper and similar products it also produces. I particularly like their disposable, general dust and sanding respirator: That's the number 8710, and it comes in contractor packs of twenty, as well as in packs of two or three. Catalogs are available on request. Specify which product line interests you (listed above).

VAN DYKE'S RESTORERS
Woonsocket, SD 57385
(800) 843-3320
(605) 796-4425
(605) 796-4085

This company, selling mostly upholstery, refinishers' and restorers' supplies, offers their wholesale catalog for $1. I must admit to interest, though I thought there wouldn't be much: The first point that piqued that interest, though, was the cutline on the letter that came with my first copy: "The World's Largest Supplier & Manufacturer of Glass Eyes." That is simply intriguing, so I had to dive right into the catalog to see what else went on. And plenty does. For any woodworker doing cabinetry, this catalog is a help to find wooden knobs, trunk hardware, table hardware, leather trunk handles, carvings, spindles, hardware in general, including a huge line of solid, cast brass and reproduction hardware from many areas. There are toy maker's supplies, dollhouse shingles, wheels, pegs and turning squares in walnut and other woods, carving wood, tea cart wheels, oak doorstops, lumber, veneer, deer photographs, wooden-duck carving kits, oil- and electric-lamp kits, marble knobs, embossed seats, artificial fur, and vinyl and glass eyes. Oh yes, there are glass eyes: There are faceted glass-jewel eyes; carousel-horse eyes; doll eyes; pinpoint pupil eyes (available in all colors, which include hazel, straw, yellow, red, black, blue and green); owl eyes; novelty carnival eyes; true-profile veined eyes; and . . . send for the catalog; it's a ball. It has a lot of useful stuff, including much of the above, plus caning materials, books, and so on. Van Dyke's takes MasterCard and Visa.

DMT's bench whetstone comes in grits from extra fine to extra coarse.

SHARPENING STONES

DIAMOND MACHINING TECHNOLOGY, INC.
85 Hayes Memorial Drive
Marlborough, MA 01752
(800) 666-4368
(508) 481-5944
(508) 485-3924 FAX

Diamond Machining Technology manufactures a wide, and unique, line of sharpening stones in shapes to fit just about any tool. DMT has Diamond Whetstones, Diamond Sanding Disks, Diamond Honing Cones and others, in grits ranging from a rough (extra-coarse) 220 for fast stock removal to 1,200 for giving a tool that final hone and polish. Ask for their free product-user brochure, and check on catalog availability. Most of their product line is sold by top mail-order suppliers, but DMT also sells direct. Call for their catalog. DMT takes American Express, MasterCard and Visa.

TEMPLATES

KELLER & COMPANY
1327 I Street
Petaluma, CA 94952
(800) 995-2456
(707) 763-9336

The Keller dovetail system consists of three different-sized dovetail template sets. It differs from most others in its price range in that it's nonadjustable: Although the lack of adjustability would seem to be a disadvantage of the system, it actually allows very rapid setup and quick production of dovetails, reducing overall problems that on other systems may come close to driving you back to handcut dovetails. Each Keller dovetail set (models 1601, 2401 and 3601) has two templates, one for the dovetails and one for the pins; two carbide-tipped router bits, one dovetail and one straight; and a really simple and good instruction manual. You add only supports for the templates, after which the units are clamped onto the pieces to be cut, the cuts are made, and your project is assembled. It takes about ten minutes to finish detailed template setup, after mounting. I've set up and used two of the Keller sets, and I find them as advertised — easy to use and of fine quality. If you want to machine-cut dovetails and nothing else, then the Keller sets are for you. Give Dave a call if you have any questions on availability or price or if you want a brochure or the new video (currently $8.95 plus $2 shipping).

TRANSFER PAPER

SARAL PAPER COMPANY
436-D Central Avenue
Bohema, NY 11716

Saral makes a wax-free transfer paper, Sally's Artists' Graphite Paper, for getting plans from your drawings to your wood. It's much easier to finish a project when there is no wax on the wood, and it is erasable, so you can move lines and change patterns without problems. Transfer lines can be sponged, washed out or brushed off (try the latter first when working with wood). Drop the company a note for further details.

Index

A

A&I Supply, 108
Aardvark Tool Company, 90
Accent Southwest, 60
Accents in Pine, 60
AccuSpray, 34
Adams Wood Products L.P., 127
Addkison Hardware Company, Inc., 150
Adjustable Clamp Company, 45
Advanced Machinery Imports, 90
Adventures in Crafts, 124
Agrell & Thorpe, Ltd., 124
Airstream Dust Helmets, 102
Akro-Mils, 101
Amana Tool Corporation, 144
Amazon Lumber & Trading Corp., Ltd., 36
American Association for Vocational Instructional Materials, 16
American Association of Woodturners (AAW), 14
American Clamping Corporation, 45
American Coaster, The, 60
American Forest & Paper Association (AFPA), 14
American Machine & Tool Company, 108
American Plywood Association (APA), 14, 60
American Tool Companies, Inc., 45
American Woodworker, 17
American Workshop Series, 60
Americana Designs, 61
AmeriGlas, 56
Anne's Calico Cat Originals, 61
Antique Hardware Store, 151
Arch Davis Design, 17
A.R.E. Manufacturing, Inc., 90
Armor, 24, 61
Artisans School, The, 28
Ashland Barns, 61
Ashman Technical Ltd., 105
Atlas Copco Electric Tools, Inc., 108
Auton Company, 154

B

Badger Hardwoods of Wisconsin, Ltd., 130
B&B Rare Woods, 130
Basic Living Products, 105
Beall Tool Company, 82
Bear Woods Supply Company, 129
Berea College Crafts, 28
Berea Hardwoods Company, 131
Berry Basket, The, 62
Better Built Corporation, 89
Better Homes & Gardens Book Clubs, 17
Betterway Books, 17
Biesemeyer Manufacturing, 91
Bill Bartz Manufacturing Company, 50
Black & Decker (U.S.), Inc., 108
Blue Ridge Machinery & Tools, Inc., 109
Blume Supply, Inc., 109
Bob Morgan Woodworking Supplies, Inc., 131
Book-of-the-Month Club, Inc., 17
Borden, 141
Boulter Plywood Corporation, 131
BrandMark by F&K Concepts, 44
Brenda's Shop, 62
Bridge City Tool Works, 48
Bristol Valley Hardwoods, 131
Brookstone, 24
Bruce Hardwood Floors, 127, 131

C

Calculated Industries, 44
California Redwood Association, 14, 62, 132
Campbell-Hausfeld, 76, 81
Cape Forge, 47
Carter Products Company, Inc., 91
Cascade Tools, Inc., 82, 144, 149
Catskill Mountain Lumber Company, 127
Cedar Shake & Shingle Bureau, 14
Certainly Wood, 132
Channellock, Inc., 51
Charles G.G. Schmidt & Co., Inc., 48, 150

Charlotte Ford Trunks, 155
Cherry Tree Toys, Inc., 63
Clapham's Beeswax Products, Ltd., 36
Clark Craft, 63
Clayton Enterprises, 87
CMT, 83
College of the Redwoods, 28
Colonial Hardwoods, Inc., 132
Colt Clamp Company, Inc., 46
Connecticut Valley Manufacturing, 145
Conover, 79
Constantine, 132
Cooper Industries, 109
Country Accents, 57
Craft Patterns, 63
Crafter's Mart, 130, 64
Creations' Workshop Company, 133
Cupboard Distributing, 64, 124
Cuprinol Products, 34
Custom Wood Cut-Outs Unlimited, 126

D

DAP, Inc., 142
Darworth Company, 34, 41, 142
David Orth Architectural Furniture, 28
Dayton Abrasive Products, Inc., 140
D.C. Precision Tools, Inc., 91
Decorative Woodcrafts, 17
Delmhorst Instrument Company, 48
Delta International Machinery Corporation, 109
Delta Technical Coatings, Inc., 36
DeRose & Company, 79
Designer Furniture Plans, 64
De-Sta-Co., 46
DeVilbiss Air Power Company, 76
DeWalt Industrial Tool Company, 110
Diamond Machining Technology, Inc., 156
Diansupply/Laborsaber Company, 91
Disstim Corporation, 110
DonJer Products, 56

Dover Publications, Inc., 18
Dovetail Joint, 28
Doyel Enterprises, 91
Dremel, 80, 92
Duluth Trading Company, 98, 101
Dunlap Woodcrafts, 133
Duo-Fast Corp., 81, 90
Dynamat, 103

E

Eagle America Corporation, 83
Eagle Woodworking, Inc., 126
Eastern Art Glass, 56
Eastwood Company, 111
Ebac Lumber Dryers, 76
Echo, Inc., 89
Econ-Abrasives, 87, 140
Edmund Scientific, 24
Edward J. Bennett Company, 92
Eisenbrand, Inc., Exotic Hardwoods, 133
Electrophysics, 48
Emmanuelli, Rick, 68
Emperor Clock Company, 64
Enviro-Safety Products, 103
Excalibur, 83, 92
Excalibur Machine Corporation, 87, 92

F

Family Handyman Plan Service, 64
Farris Machinery Company, Inc., 80
Fein Power Tools, Inc., 87
Fine Paints of Europe, 37
Fine Tool Journal, 18
Fine Woodworking, 18
Floral Glass Mirror, Inc., 56
Flecto Company, Inc., The, 36
Foredom Electric Co., 10
Forest Street Designs, 64
Formby's Workshop, 37
Forrest Manufacturing Company, Inc., 145
FrameWealth, 150
Frank Paxton Lumber Company, 133
Franklin International, 142
Freeborn Tool Company, Inc., 149
Freud, Inc., 83, 145
Furniture Designs, Inc., 64

G

G & W Tool Company, Inc., 92
Garrett Wade Company, 44
Gatto Plan Supply, 65
Generac Corporation, 77
General Manufacturing Company, Ltd., 93
Geoff Brown, 50, 77, 105
Georgia-Pacific(G-P), 125
Gil-Lift, 155
Gilliom Manufacturing, Inc., 65
Glass Art, 18
Glass Patterns Quarterly Magazine, 18
Goby's Walnut Wood Products, 133
Gorilla Group, The, 142
Gougeon Brothers, 37, 143
Granberg International, 89
Great Lakes Leather Products Company, 100
Grizzly Imports, Inc., 111
Groff & Hearne Lumber, 133
Guild of American Luthiers, 15

H

Hand Tools Institute, 15
Handloggers Exotic Hardwoods, 134
Harbor Freight Tools, 111
Hardel Mutual Plywood Corporation, 134
Hartville Tool and Supply, 111
Haywood Community College, 29
Heritage Building Specialties, 65
Hickson Corporation, 125
Hida Tool & Hardware, Inc., 47, 51
Hirsh Company, 101
Hitachi, 112
Homeowners' Do-It-Yourself Book Club, 18
Horton Brasses, Inc., 151
HTC Products, Inc., 150
Hyde Tools, 53, 40
Hydrocote, 37
Hymiller School of Fine Finishing & Hand Joinery, 29

I

Industrial Abrasives Co., 87, 140
Infodex Services, 19
In-Line Industries, 93
InstaFloor, 127
Integra Tooling & Accessories, 145

Intellectron, 100
Intermatic, 101
International Tool Corporation, 112

J

James L. Cox School of Woodworking, 29
Jamestown Distributors, 151
Japan Woodworker, 24, 47
J.B. Dawn Products, Inc., 56
JDS Company, 50
Jennings Decoy Company, 65
Jet Equipment & Tools, 112
Jiffy Foam, Inc., 10

K

Kasco, 89
Kaune, Bob, 24
Keller & Company, 157
Kimball Sign Company, 96
Klein Design, Inc., 25, 78, 79
Klingspor Abrasives, 87, 140
Klockit, 65
KnotWhole Publishing, 19
Kreg Tool Company, 78

L

Laguna Tools, 81
Lamp Shop, The, 101
Lampi, 101
Larry & Faye Brusso Company, 152
Lavi Industries, 155
Leichtung Workshops, 46, 66, 78, 112, 152
Leigh Industries, Ltd., 79
Lie-Nielsen Toolworks, 51, 113
Lignomat USA Ltd., 49
Linden Publishing, Inc., 19
Louisiana-Pacific Corporation (L-P), 57, 134
L.R.H. Enterprises, Inc., 149

M

MacBeath Hardwood, 134
Macco Adhesives, 143
MAG Engineering & Manufacturing Company, Inc., 103
Magnate Business International, 145
Makita U.S.A., Inc., 113
Manny's Woodworker's Place, 25
MapleTek Engineering, Inc., 46
Martin & MacArthur Hardwood Center, 135, 150
Martin Senour Paints, 37
Mason & Sullivan, 66

Matthew Burak, Furniture, 128
McFeely's, 113
Meisel Hardware Specialties, 66
Mercury Vacuum Presses, 82
Mesquites Unlimited, 135
Meyer, Bob, 62
Micro-Fence, 84
Micro-Mark, 93, 129
Micro-Surface Finishing Products, 140
Milwaukee Electric Tool Corporation, 113
Mindy's Puzzles, 66
Minwax Company Inc., 38
Miracle Point, 103
M.L. Condon Company, Inc., 135
MLCS, Ltd., 84, 146
Moon's Saw & Tool Inc., 84, 146
Mule Cabinetmaker Machine, Inc., 90
Musicmaker's Kits, Inc., 67
National Hardwood Lumber Association (NHLA), 15
Nelson Designs, 25, 67

N

Nelson & Jacobson, Inc., 93
Nemy Electric Tool Co., 25, 114, 155
Niagara Lumber & Wood Products, Inc., 135
North Bay Forge, 10, 48
North Bennet Street School, 29
Northern Hydraulics, 114
Northwest School of Wooden Boatbuilding, 30
Norton Consumer Marketing, 140
Nova Tool Company, 44
Nyle Corporation, 76

O

OCS, 146
Oldham-United States Saw, 85, 141, 146
Oregon School of Arts & Crafts, 30
Ornamental Mouldings, 128
Osmose Wood Preserving, Inc., 35, 67

P

Parks Corporation, 38
Paxton Hardware, 152
PDI, Inc., 143, 148
Peco Sales, Inc., 49
Penn State Industries, 114
Performance Coatings, Inc., 38

Performax Products, Inc., 38, 88
Peter Lang Company, 135
Peters Valley Craft Center, 30
Phantom Engineering, Inc., 85
Pinecraft Patterns, 67
Pleasure Crafts, 68
PMS-Products, Inc., 148
Pootatuck Corp., 50
Popular Woodworking, 19
Portable Products, Inc., 101, 104
Porta-Nails, Inc., 85
Porter-Cable, 114
Powermatic, 115
Practical Products Company, 116
Prairie Woodworking, 57
Precision Movements, 152
Procorp, Inc., 10
Professional Boatbuilder Magazine, 19
Purdue University, 31

Q

Quaker State Woodworking Supply, 66, 88, 116

R

Rainbow Woods, 130
Rawlplug Co., Inc., 144, 146
RBIndustries, Inc., 94
Record Tools, Inc., 80, 116
Red Hill Corporation, 141
Renovator's Supply, 152
Ridge Carbide Tool Corporation, 85, 147, 149
RJS Custom Woodworking, 26, 68
Robert Larson Company, Inc., 116
Rocking Horse Shop, The, 26, 68
Rockingham Community College (RCC), 31
Rodale Press, Inc., 20
RotoZip Tool Corporation, 86
Royal Sawdust Company, 69
Royalwood, Ltd., 56
Rubbermaid, Inc., 98, 99
Rust-Oleum, 39
Ryobi American Corporation, 117

S

Safety Speed Cut Manufacturing Company, 94
Sand-Rite Manfacturing Company, 88, 141
Sandvik Consumer Tools Division, 45, 46, 52, 117

Sandy Pond Hardwoods, 136
Sansher Corporation, 40
Saral Paper Company, 157
Savogran, 100
SawTrax Manufacturing Company, 94
S-B Power Tool Company, 117
Scherr's Cabinets, 126
School of Classical Woodcarving, 31
Scrollsaw Patterns, 69
Sears Roebuck & Company, 117
Seco Investments Company, 118
Seyco, 26, 69, 94, 118
Shakertown 1992, Inc., 129
Shopcarts, 98
ShopNotes, 20
Shopsmith, Inc., 81
Shop-Vac Corporation, 105
Show Business, 20
Silver Metal Products, 105
Silverton Victorian Millwork, 129
Simpson Strong-Tie Company, Inc., 144
Singley Specialty Company, Inc., 88
Skogman, Bob, 155
Smith, Roger K., 51
Solo-Saw, 94
Sonin, Inc., 48, 49
Southern Forest Products Association, 15
Specialty Furniture Designs of Michigan, 69
Spotlight, 143
Stanley Door Systems, 100
Stanley Hardware, 152
Stanley Tools, 118
Stanley-Bostitch Fastening Systems, 82
Star Bronze Company, 35, 39, 40
Steussy Creations, 95

Steve H. Wall Lumber Company, 136
Stewart-MacDonald, 69
Stihl, Inc., 89
Stone Mountain Power Tool Corporation, 118
Suffolk Machinery Corporation, 147
Sun Designs, 26, 70
Sunhill NIC Company, Inc., 119

T
Talarico Hardwoods, 136
Tashiro's, 47, 52
Tatro, Inc., 125, 130
Taunton Press, 27
Taylor Design Group, 79
Terrco, Inc., 10
Thompson & Formby, Inc., 39
3M DIY Division, 44, 103, 141, 143, 156
TiP Sandblast Equipment, 35
Titan, Inc., 35
Today's Woodworker, 20
Tomorrow's Heirlooms, 70
Tool Crib of the North, 119
Tool Merchant, The, 21
Tools On Sale Division, 46, 119
Tormek U.S.A., 77
Toys and Joys, 70
Trend-Lines, 27, 70, 119
Trojan Manufacturing, Inc., 95
Tropical Exotic Hardwoods, 136
Turncraft Clocks, 70, 153

U
UGL (United Gilsonite Laboratories), 39
Unicorn Studios, 153
United Steel Products, 153
University of Rio Grande, 31
U.S. Safety, 104

V
Van Dyke's Restorers, 153, 156
Vaughan & Bushnell Manufacturing Company, 52
Velvit Products Company, 41
Veritas Tools, 119
Vermont-American Tool Company, 147

W
Wagner Electronic Products, 49
Wagner FineCoat, 36
Warren Tool Company, 11
Wayne's Woods, Inc., 153
Weekend Woodcrafts, 21, 70
Weekend Woodworking Projects, 21, 71
Wells Lamont, 100
Western Wood Products Association, 15, 71
Whiteside Machine Company, 86
Whole Earth Access, 120
Wholesale Glass Brokers, 56
Wilke Machinery Company, 95, 120
Willard Brothers Woodcutters, 137
William Zinsser & Co., 39, 40
Williams & Hussey Machine Co., Inc., 80, 96
Williamsburg Blacksmiths, 154
Wilson, John, 29, 65, 124
Windmill Publishing, 21
Windsor Forge, 120, 125
Winfield Collection, 71
Winter Woods, 137
Wood, 22, 71
Wood Moulding & Millwork Producers, Association (WMMPA), 16, 72
Wood Strokes, 22

Wood Turning Center, 16
Woodartist, 72
Woodcare Products, 143
Woodcraft, 120
Woodcraft Bands, Inc., 147
Woodcrafts by Oscar Hubbert, 72, 126
Wooden Memories, 72
WoodenBoat Magazine, 22
WoodenBoat School, 31
WoodenBoat Store, 72, 125
Woodhaven, 27, 86, 147
Wood-Met Services, 72
Wood-Mizer Products, Inc., 77, 89
Wood-N-Crafts, Inc., 129
Woodpeckers, Inc., 79, 86
Woods Wire Products, 104
Woodshop News, 22
Woodsmith, 22
Woodwork, 23
Woodworker, 23
Woodworkers Alliance for Rainforest Protection (WARP), 16
Woodworker's Book Club, 23
Woodworker's Business News, 23
Woodworker's Hardware, 154
Woodworker's Journal, 23
Woodworkers' Store, 27, 73, 86, 121, 144, 154
Woodworker's Supply, 121
Woodworking Machinery Distributors Association, 16
Woodworks, 126, 130, 154
Worcester Center for Crafts, 32
Workbench, 24
Workshoppe Originals, 73
Yestermorrow, Inc., 32

Y
York Saw & Knife Company, Inc., 148